A SHORT LIFE
OF
SHAKESPEARE
WITH
THE SOURCES

♠

Abridged by
CHARLES WILLIAMS from
Sir EDMUND CHAMBERS'S
*William Shakespeare: A Study of
Facts and Problems*

♠

Copyright © 2018 Read Books Ltd.
This book is copyright and may not be
reproduced or copied in any way without
the express permission of the publisher in writing

British Library Cataloguing-in-Publication Data
A catalogue record for this book is available from
the British Library

CHARLES WILLIAMS

Charles Walter Stansby Williams was born in London in 1886. He dropped out of University College London in 1904, and was hired by Oxford University Press as a proof-reader, quickly rising to the position of editor. While there, arguably his greatest editorial achievement was the publication of the first major English-language edition of the works of the Danish philosopher Søren Kierkegaard.

Williams began writing in the twenties and went on to publish seven novels. Of these, the best-known are probably *War in Heaven* (1930), *Descent into Hell* (1937), and *All Hallows' Eve* (1945) – all fantasies set in the contemporary world. He also published a vast body of well-received scholarship, including a study of Dante entitled *The Figure of Beatrice* (1944) which remains a standard reference text for academics today, and a highly unconventional history of the church, *Descent of the Dove* (1939). Williams garnered a number of well-known admirers, including T. S. Eliot, W. H. Auden and C. S. Lewis. Towards the end of his life, he gave lectures at Oxford University on John Milton, and received an honorary MA degree. Williams died almost exactly at the close of World War II, aged 58.

SHAKESPEARE'S MONUMENT

Note

THIS book is an abridgement of *William Shakespeare: a Study of Facts and Problems*, by Sir Edmund Chambers, published in 1930 in two volumes. It has been made for the convenience of those who cannot possess and perhaps do not find it easy to consult the major work, but have nevertheless a vivid interest in all that can be known of Shakespeare. The antagonistic economic and cultural circumstances of our time tend to increase the number of such readers. Being one of them, I have wanted to make for them the kind of book that I should myself desire. I have therefore retained as much as possible concerning Shakespeare's life, even at the cost of omitting important critical and bibliographical matter.

The reference is in all cases to the two-volume work; that is a sufficient bibliographical entry. The authorities, the evidence, the discussions, the delicate controversies are there, and nothing is here which is not fully justified by those volumes. But this book is not meant for the controversialist; it is meant for the man who reads the plays and who desires to know something of the Stratford playwright. Many of us have heard of the Grant of Arms, the Mountjoy depositions, or the Will who have never had an opportunity to see them; many of us vaguely know the stories of the poaching affray, the holding of horses, the acting of Adam, who have not the smallest idea of the sources and dates of such stories or of their credibility. The documents and the original anecdotes are here. The only omissions are the many pages of legal and sometimes Latin phraseology which were the results of Shakespeare's acquirements of property and could be of interest only to lawyers or building societies.

NOTE

Sir Edmund Chambers has been good enough to permit this 'base use' of his work and to give assistance in a few places. But he has no responsibility for the process of abridgement. If his bright thing seems here to have come to confusion, it is he more than any other critic who has a right to complain. But on the whole I hope that such complaint will not be necessary, and that this book may play a part in clearing away the confusion which exists in ordinary unspecialized minds about what is and what is not known of Shakespeare.

C. W.

Contents

PRINCIPAL DATES	vi
PEDIGREE OF SHAKESPEARE AND ARDEN	viii
I. SHAKESPEARE'S ORIGIN	1
II. SHAKESPEARE AND HIS COMPANY	25
III. THE PLAYS: PUBLICATION	67
IV. THE PLAYS: AUTHENTICITY AND CHRONOLOGY	83
V. THE SONNETS	122
APPENDIX I. RECORDS	133
APPENDIX II. CONTEMPORARY ALLUSIONS (TO THE FIRST FOLIO, 1623)	187
APPENDIX III. TRADITION (FROM 1625)	222
INDEX	253

List of Plates

SHAKESPEARE'S MONUMENT	frontispiece
SHAKESPEARE'S SIGNATURES: (a) DEPOSITION, (b) CONVEYANCE, (c) MORTGAGE	facing page 150
SHAKESPEARE'S SIGNATURES: (d) WILL 1, (e) WILL 2, (f) WILL 3	facing page 166
DROESHOUT ENGRAVING	,, ,, 202

PRINCIPAL DATES

1556, November 24.   Will of Robert Arden.
1558, November 17.   Accession of Queen Elizabeth.
1561, February 10.   Administration of Richard Shakespeare.
1564, April 26.   Christening of Shakespeare.
1568, September 4.   Election of John Shakespeare as Bailiff.
1582, November 27.   Licence for Marriage of Shakespeare.
1583, May 26.   Christening of Susanna Shakespeare.
1585, February 2.   Christening of Hamnet and Judith Shakespeare.
1592, March 3.   Production of 1 *Henry VI*.
1592, September 3.   Death of Robert Greene.
1593, April 18.   Registration of *Venus and Adonis*.
1593, May 30.   Death of Christopher Marlowe.
1593, September 25.   Succession of Ferdinando Lord Strange as Earl of Derby.
1594, April 16.   Death of Earl of Derby.
1594, May 9.   Registration of *Lucrece*.
1596, July 22.   Death of Henry Lord Hunsdon.
1596, August 11.   Burial of Hamnet Shakespeare.
1596, October 20.   Grant of Arms to John Shakespeare.
1596, November 9.   Burial of George Peele.
1597, March 17.   Appointment of George Lord Hunsdon as Lord Chamberlain.
1597, May 4.   Fine on Purchase of New Place.
1598, September 7.   Registration of *Palladis Tamia*.
1599.   Opening of Globe Theatre.
1601, February 8.   Revolt of Robert, Earl of Essex.
1601, September 8.   Burial of John Shakespeare.
1602, May 1.   Conveyance of Land in Old Stratford.
1602, September 28.   Copy for Cottage in Chapel Lane.
1603, March 24.   Death of Queen Elizabeth.
1603, May 19.   Patent for King's men.
1605, July 24.   Conveyance of Tithes in Stratford.
1607, June 5.   Marriage of Susanna Shakespeare to John Hall.
1608, February 21.   Christening of Elizabeth Hall.
1608, September 9.   Burial of Mary Shakespeare.

PRINCIPAL DATES

1608–9.	Acquisition of Blackfriars Theatre by King's men.
1609, May 20.	Registration of *Sonnets*.
1610.	Probable Migration of Shakespeare to Stratford.
1613, February 14.	Marriage of Princess Elizabeth to Frederick Elector Palatine.
1613, March 10.	Conveyance of Blackfriars Gate-House.
1613, June 29.	Fire at Globe Theatre.
1616, February 10.	Marriage of Judith Shakespeare to Thomas Quiney.
1616, March 6.	Death of Francis Beaumont.
1616, March 25.	Will of Shakespeare.
1616, April 23.	Death of Shakespeare.
1619.	Printing of Jaggard's Quartos.
1623, August 6.	Death of Anne Shakespeare.
1623, November 8.	Registration of First Folio.
1626, April 22.	Marriage of Elizabeth Hall to Thomas Nash.
1635, November 25.	Death of John Hall.
1647, April 4.	Death of Thomas Nash.
1649, June 5.	Marriage of Elizabeth Nash to John Bernard.
1649, July 11.	Death of Susanna Hall.
1662, February 9.	Burial of Judith Quiney.
1670, February 17.	Burial of Elizabeth Bernard.

PEDIGREE OF SHAKESPEARE AND ARDEN

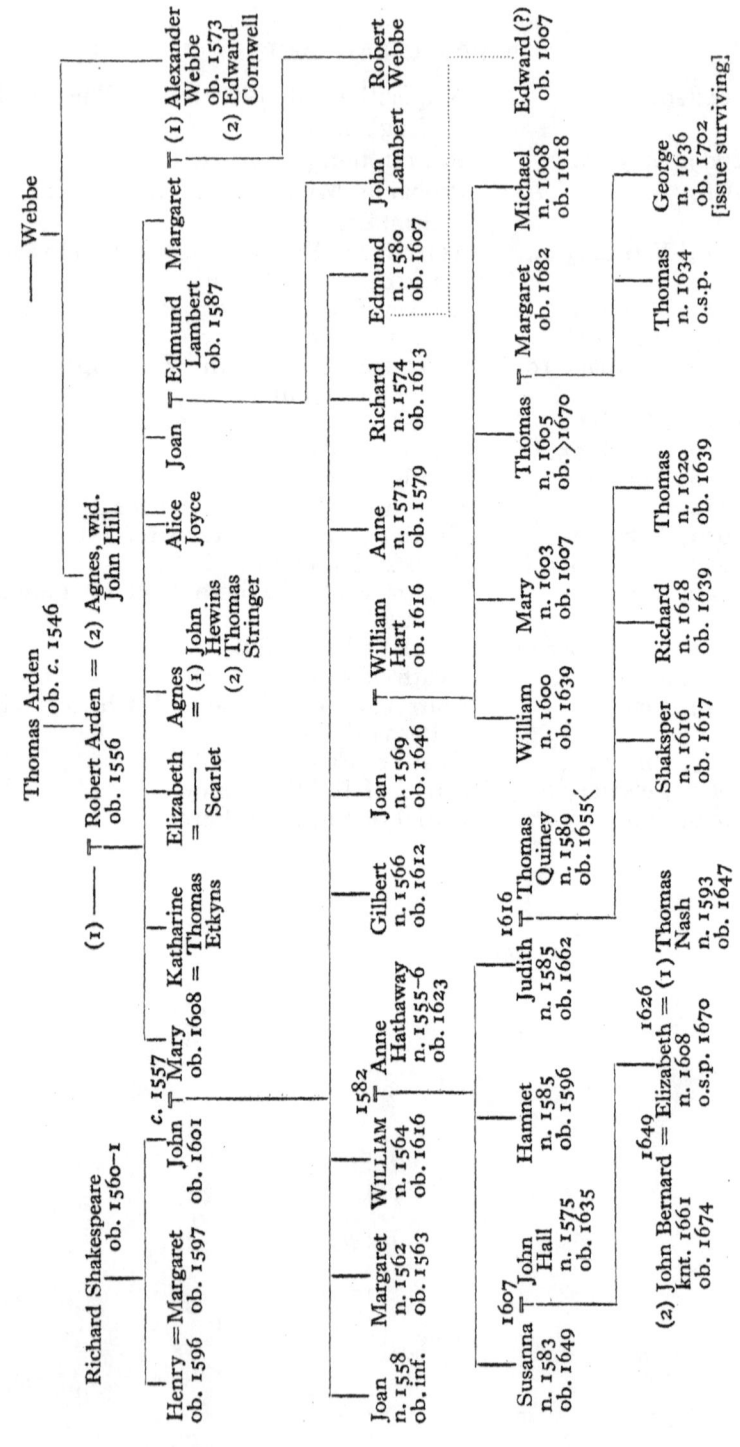

I
SHAKESPEARE'S ORIGIN

WILLIAM SHAKESPEARE was born of burgess folk, not unlike those in *The Merry Wives of Windsor*. Stratford-on-Avon was a provincial market town, and counted with Henley-in-Arden after the city of Coventry and the borough of Warwick among the business centres of Warwickshire. It stood on the north bank of the Avon, where a ford had once been traversed by a minor Roman thoroughfare. A medieval wooden bridge had been replaced at the end of the fifteenth century by the stone one which still survives. The great western highway, following the line of Watling Street to Shrewsbury and Chester, passed well to the north through Coventry. But at Stratford bridge met two lesser roads from London, one by Oxford and under the Cotswolds, the other by Banbury and Edgehill; and beyond it ways radiated through Stratford itself to Warwick, Birmingham, Alcester, and Evesham. 'Emporiolum non inelegans' is the description of the place in Camden's *Britannia* (1586), and Leland, who visited it about 1540, records that it was 'reasonably well buyldyd of tymbar', with 'two or three very lardge stretes, besyde bake lanes'. Topographers give the name of Arden to Warwickshire north of the Avon and distinguish it as the Woodland from the cultivated champaign of the Feldon to the south. But even on the north bank of the river there were open cornfields, as well as many enclosed pastures, and frequent hamlets tell of early clearings on the fringe of Arden. The lord had his *boscus* at Stratford in the thirteenth century and later a park, but Leland says that little woodland was visible there in his time.

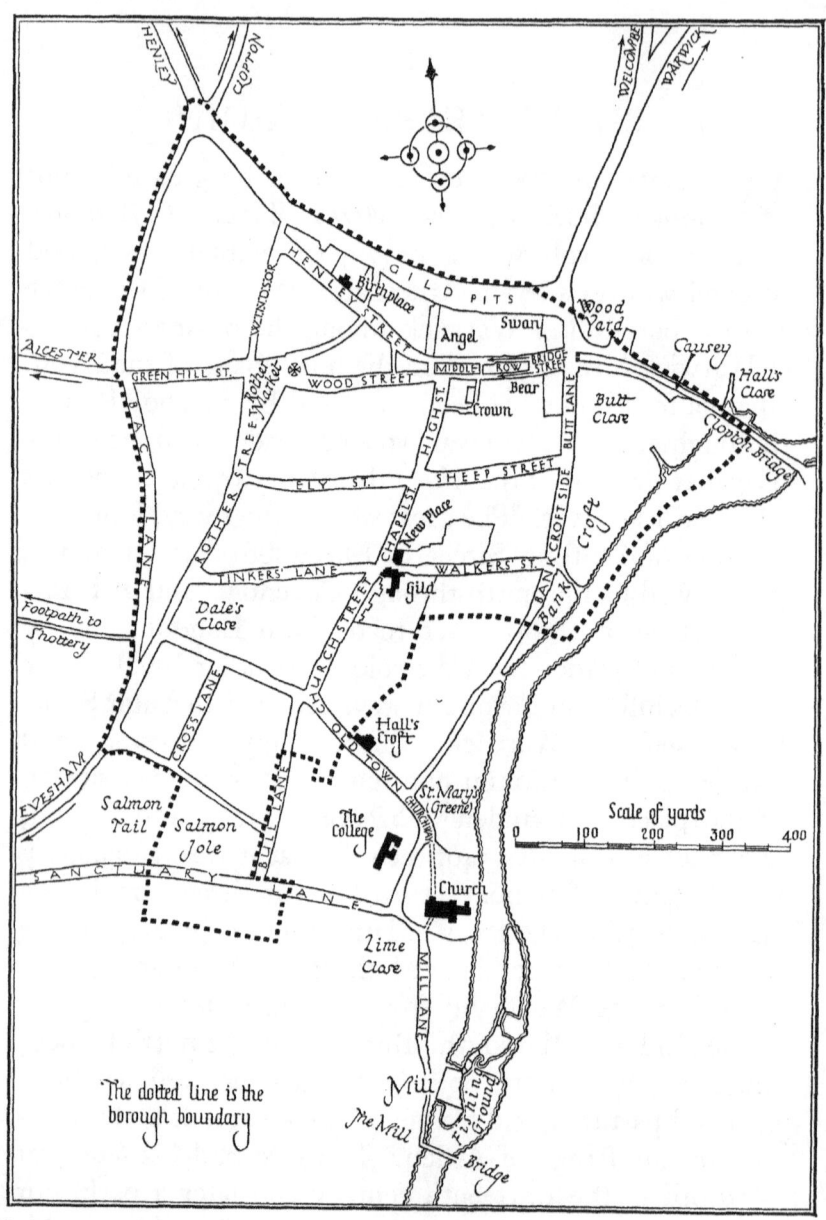

TOWN OF STRATFORD-ON-AVON
based upon the Ordnance Survey Map with the sanction of the Controller of H.M. Stationery Office.

SHAKESPEARE'S ORIGIN

The town of Stratford only occupied a small part of a large parish which bore the same name. This was ten miles in circuit and had 1,500 houseling people in 1546. Mercian kings had made wide grants to the bishops of Worcester, with a 'hundredal' jurisdiction independent of the sheriff over the liberty of Pathlow, for which they held wayside courts at Pathlow itself and at Gilleputs in Stratford. There was a monastery, afterwards discontinued, for the bishop and his household. Much of the dominion, even in Saxon times, had passed from the bishops by devolution to thanes and in other ways, and in the sixteenth-century parish there were several manors. The hamlet of Clopton was held by the family of that name; Luddington by the Conways of Arrow; Drayton by the Petos of Chesterton; Bishopston by the Catesbys of Lapworth and afterwards by the Archers of Tanworth; part of Shottery by the Smiths of Wootton Wawen. But the principal manor still remained with the bishop up to 1549. In this lay the borough itself, the 'Old Town' which divided it from the parish church of Holy Trinity on the southern outskirts, and a considerable stretch of agricultural land in the fields of Old Stratford, Welcombe, and Shottery. The bishop had also the distinct township of Bishop's Hampton, to the east of Stratford. On the south side of the river were the Lucy manor of Charlecote, the Greville manor of Milcote, and the Rainsford manor of Clifford Chambers in Gloucestershire. The hamlet of Bridgetown beyond the bridge was partly in the borough and partly in Alveston. To the north-east and north-west of Stratford were the villages of Snitterfield and Aston Cantlow. They had been 'Warwickslands', lordships of the dominant families of Beauchamp and Neville, and had reverted to the Crown on attainder. For all these places Stratford was the natural urban centre.

The borough had come into existence under Bishop John de Coutances (1195–8), who had laid out part of his demesne in quarter-acre plots of uniform frontage and depth. These were held as burgages, practically on a freehold tenure, subject to shilling chief rents, and with rights of division and disposition by sale or will. A separate manor court was presided over by the bishop's steward, but the burgesses probably chose their own bailiff and sub-bailiffs as executive officers. The court sat twice in the year, for 'leets' or 'law days' near Easter and Michaelmas. At these officers were appointed, transfers of burgages were recorded, small civil actions for debt and the like were heard, by-laws for good order were made, and breaches of these, with frays and infringements of the 'assizes' of food and drink and other standards for the quality of saleable articles, were punished. Side by side with the manorial jurisdiction had grown up the organization of the Gild of Holy Cross, which ministered in many ways to the well-being of the town. It dated from the thirteenth century. Early in the fifteenth it absorbed smaller gilds, and thereafter an almost continuous register preserves the admissions of brothers and sisters, and the payments for the souls of the dead, whose masses were sung by the priests of its chapel. The members of the gild were bound to fraternal relations and to attendance at each other's funerals in their Augustinian hoods. Periodical love-feasts encouraged more mundane intercourse. The gild had accumulated much property, in and about Stratford, from pious gifts and legacies. It helped its poorer members and maintained an almshouse. A school, which had existed in some form as far back as 1295, was one of its activities. This had an endowment from Thomas Joliffe for the gratuitous teaching of grammar by one of the priests. The gild buildings, which stood just within the borough, owed their latest form to Sir Hugh Clopton, Lord Mayor of London in 1492. He, too, had built the bridge. The gild was at the height of its reputation in the middle of the fifteenth century, and attracted members of distinction from far beyond the limits of Stratford. Later it suffered a decline, perhaps due in part to the rise of trade gilds, in which the craftsmen of the town were linked for business purposes. Probably the gild chapel counted for more in the religious life of the borough than the comparatively distant church. This belonged to a college of priests under a warden, which also had acquired much landed property, in addition to the ample tithes of the large parish.

The reign of Edward VI was a period of considerable change for Stratford. The gild and the college were both dissolved under the Chantries Act of 1547, and their revenues went to the Crown. Provisional direction was given for the continuance of the school. In 1549 Bishop Nicholas Heath was driven, apparently for inadequate compensation, to transfer his manor, with that of Bishop's Hampton, to John Dudley, Earl of Warwick and afterwards Duke of Northumberland, who aspired to restore the old domination of the Beauchamps and Nevilles in the county. On his attainder in 1553 Mary granted it to the duchess, and after her death in 1555 to the hospital of the Savoy. But this grant was almost immediately vacated, and the manor remained with the Crown until 1562, when Elizabeth gave it to Northumberland's son Ambrose Dudley, now in his turn created Earl of Warwick. On his death in 1590 it again reverted to the Crown, but was sold and acquired by Sir Edward Greville of Milcote. Another event of 1553 had, however, reduced the importance of the manor and its court in local affairs. The inhabitants, perturbed by the loss of valuable elements in their civic life, petitioned for incorporation as a royal borough; and this, presumably through the influence of Northumberland, then in power, was accorded by a charter of 28 June 1553. The government of the borough was entrusted to a Bailiff and a Council of fourteen Aldermen and fourteen Capital Burgesses, with powers to provide for good order and the management of corporate property, to fill vacancies in their number, and to make annual election of the bailiff, serjeants at the mace, constables, and such other officers as might prove necessary. The Council was to have the return to royal writs within the borough, to the exclusion of the sheriff, and the bailiff to hold Crown office as escheator, coroner, almoner, and clerk of the market. With a chosen alderman, he was to act as justice of peace. Authority was given for a weekly market and for two annual fairs, with a court of pie-powder. There was also to be a court of record under the bailiff, with jurisdiction in civil causes, where the amount in dispute was not more than £30. To meet the municipal expenses, the charter granted the property of the late gild, worth about £46, and the reversion of a lease of the parish tithes granted by the college, with the reserved rent of £34. The rest of the college property remained with the Crown. The funds granted were charged with the maintenance of the almshouse, and with salaries for the schoolmaster, the vicar, and his curate. A general reservation, which afterwards led to trouble, was made for the rights of the lord of the manor, and in particular the election of the bailiff was to be subject to his approval, and he was to have the appointment of the schoolmaster and vicar. For some years from 1553 the records leave it rather difficult to disentangle the activities of the bailiff and his brethren from those of the court leet. But soon after a recognition of the charter by Elizabeth in 1560, the Council was regularly at work,

SHAKESPEARE'S ORIGIN

holding its meetings at 'halls' every month or so in the buildings of the old gild, making its by-laws, surveying its property, approving leases, ordering the market, the fairs, and the almshouse, and raising small levies for public or charitable purposes to supplement its regular funds.

It had at first a town clerk and afterwards a steward, who assisted the bailiff at the court of record. This, in addition to its jurisdiction between civil litigants, chiefly in cases of debt, took over the imposition of penalties for breaches of by-laws or of the assize. Frays may be assumed to have fallen to the justices of peace. The leet, although shorn of many of its functions, continued to be held. It presumably dealt with matters peculiar to the manor, such as the transfer of burgages. The constables, although chosen by the Council with other officers at Michaelmas, were sworn in at a leet. Disputes arose with the lords of the manor, about toll-corn, about commoners' rights, about the approval of bailiffs. Internal discipline also gave trouble. The aldermen and principal burgesses did not always attend halls regularly, and some of them were inclined to shun the responsibilities of office when their turns came. Towards the end of the century the Council was much occupied with affairs in London.[1] The industries of Stratford were decaying and there had been disastrous fires. Suits were made to the Crown for exemption from subsidies, and for an enlarged charter. One was in fact granted by James in 1610, which extended the boundary of the borough to include the Old Town.

Stratford has been represented as a dirty and ignorant town, an unmeet cradle for poetry. There is some want of historical perspective here. No doubt sanitary science was in its infancy. But, after all, penalties for the breach of by-laws, if they are evidence that the by-laws were

[1] Cf. pp. 156–8.

sometimes broken, are also evidence that they were enforced. Nor was contemporary London, with the puppy dogs in its Fleet and its unscoured Moorditch, in much better case. Stratford had its paved streets and much garden ground about its houses. It was embosomed in elms, of which a survey of 1582 records a vast number in closes and on the backsides of the burgages. And all around was fair and open land with parks and dingles and a shining river. There was much give and take between town and country-side. The urban industries, weaving, dyeing, tanning, shoe-making, glove-making, smithing, rope-making, carpentry, were such as subserve or are fed by agriculture. Many of the burgesses were also landholders in the parish or in neighbouring villages. There was much buying of barley, for the making and sale of malt, which was a subsidiary occupation of many households. Sheep, cattle, ducks, and ringed swine ran on the common pasture called the Bank Croft. Although remote, the town was not out of touch with a larger civilization. Access to Oxford was easy, and to London itself, by roads on which carriers came and went regularly. Nor was it entirely bookless. Leading townsmen could quote Latin and write a Latin letter if need be. The Grammar School was probably of good standing. The schoolmaster's salary, which Joliffe fixed at £10, was increased to £20 by the charter. This was much more than the £12 5s. paid at Warwick or than the amounts usual in Elizabethan grammar schools, outside Westminster, Eton, Winchester, and Shrewsbury. It was better than the emoluments of an Oxford or Cambridge fellowship. The actual curriculum of the school is unknown; it was probably based on those planned by Colet for St. Paul's in 1518 and Wolsey for Ipswich in 1529. Colet required an entrant to be able to 'rede and write Latyn and Englisshe sufficiently, soo that he be able to rede and wryte his owne lessons'. But London had its sufficiency of elementary schools, and the easier standard of Stratford was content if a child was 'fet for the gramer scoll or at the least wyez entred or reddy to enter into ther accydence & princypalles of gramer'. Even the preparation seems at first to have been given by an usher attached to the grammar school, whom the chamberlains paid 'for techyng ye chylder'. But by 1604 an independent teacher had for some time taught reading and his wife needlework, 'whereby our young youth is well furthered in reading and the Free School greatly eased of that tedious trouble'. In the grammar school itself there would be little but Latin; the grammar of Colet himself and William Lilly, revised and appointed for use in schools under successive sovereigns; some easy book of phrases, such as the *Sententiae Pueriles* of Leonhard Culmann or the *Pueriles Confabulatiunculae* of Evaldus Gallus; Aesop's *Fables* and the *Moral Distichs* of Cato; Cicero, Sallust, or Caesar, Ovid in abundance, Virgil, perhaps Horace or Terence; probably some Renaissance writing, the *Bucolica* of Baptista Spagnolo Mantuanus or the *Zodiacus Vitae* of Marcellus Palingenius. There is not likely to have been any Greek. About sixteen a boy was ripe for the University. Sir Hugh Clopton had left six exhibitions to Oxford and Cambridge; it is not known whether the Corporation continued them.

Such was the environment of the youthful Shakespeare. His father, John Shakespeare, was not of native Stratford stock; there are no Shakespeares in the gild register. John makes his first appearance in Stratford at a leet of 29 April 1552, when he was fined one shilling for having an unauthorized dunghill in Henley St. He may reasonably be identified with a John Shakespeare of Snitterfield, who administered the estate of his father Richard in 1561. Richard had held land on two manors at Snitterfield, in part as tenant to Robert Arden of Wilmcote in Aston Cantlow. He is traceable there from 1528–9, and may possibly have come from Hampton Corley in Budbrooke. But his ultimate origin has eluded research. When grants of arms to John Shakespeare were applied for, the heralds recited ancestral service to Henry VII and a reward of lands in Warwickshire. No confirming record has been found. Shakespeares were thick on the ground in sixteenth-century Warwickshire, particularly in the Woodland about Wroxall and Rowington to the north of Stratford. John Shakespeare, as administrator to his father, is called *agricola* or husbandman. Later his brother Henry is found holding land at Snitterfield, where he died, much indebted, in 1596. Other documents call John a yeoman. Technically a yeoman was a freeholder of land to the annual value of fifty shillings, but the description was often applied to any well-to-do man short of a gentleman. A more precise designation is that of 'glover' or 'whittawer'. A whittawer cured and whitened the soft skins which were the material of the glover's craft. There can be little doubt that John Shakespeare combined these occupations, and was a freeman of the Mystery of the Glovers, Whittawers and Collarmakers, which was one of the Stratford trade gilds. It does not weigh for much against the contemporary use of these terms that John Aubrey called him a butcher in 1681, and that Nicholas Rowe, who made the first attempt at a systematic biography of the poet in 1709, called him a wool-dealer. Likely enough, he had subordinate activities; he is mentioned as selling both barley and timber. It is possible that he is the John Shakespeare who was tenant of Ingon meadow in Bishop's Hampton about 1570. He is clearly distinct from a John Shakespeare of Clifford Chambers, traceable there from 1560 to his death in 1610, and from a second John Shakespeare of Stratford, a corvizer who dwelt in the town from 1586 to about 1595, and whose progeny early biographers confused with his. The poet's father married Mary Arden, daughter of that Robert from whom the grandfather had held land. He was of the ancient house of the Ardens of Park Hall, although the precise degree of relationship is uncertain. Mary was a co-heiress in a small way. Robert left her some land in Wilmcote called Asbies by his will of 1556, and had probably already settled other property there upon her. She was also entitled to a share in a reversionary interest of his Snitterfield estate. The marriage must have taken place between the date of the will and 15 September 1558, when a daughter Joan was christened at Stratford. She must have died early. The actual day of William's birth is unknown.[1] A belief that it was April 23, on which day he died in 1616, seems to rest on an eighteenth-century blunder. In 1556 John Shakespeare bought two houses, one in Henley St. and one in Greenhill St. In 1575 he bought two other houses, the locality of which is not specified. In 1590 he owned two contiguous houses in Henley St. Of these the westernmost is now called the 'Birthplace' and the easternmost the 'Woolshop'. But this tradition does not go back beyond the middle of the eighteenth century. Certainly the 'Woolshop' was the purchase of 1556. But whether John was living in the 'Birthplace' in 1552, or whether he was then living as a tenant in the 'Woolshop', and bought the 'Birthplace' in 1575, has not been established.

However this may be, the purchases suggest that John Shakespeare prospered in business. And he became prominent in municipal life. Between 1557 and 1561 he appears as juror, constable, and 'affeeror' or assessor of

[1] Cf. p. 133.

fines at the court leet, and was himself again fined for leaving his gutter dirty and for not making presentments as ale-taster before the court of record. In 1561 and 1562 he was chosen as one of the chamberlains, and it is perhaps evidence of his financial capacity that he acted, quite exceptionally, as deputy to the chamberlains of the next two years. Probably he was already a capital burgess by 1561, although his name first appears in a list of 1564. His subscriptions to the relief of the poor during that year of plague-time are liberal. In 1565 he was chosen an alderman, and in 1568 reached the top of civic ambition as bailiff. In view of contemporary habits, it is no proof of inability to write that he was accustomed to authenticate documents by a mark, which was sometimes a cross and sometimes a pair of glover's dividers. But it is unfortunate, because it leaves us ignorant as to how he spelt his name. The town-clerk, a constant scribe, makes it 'Shakspeyr' with great regularity; but some twenty variants are found in Stratford documents. After a customary interval John was again justice of the peace as chief alderman in 1571. A few years later there are indications of a decline in his fortunes. Throughout his career there had been suits by and against him for small sums in the court of record. These, however, appear to have been part of the ordinary routine of business transactions as conducted in Stratford. An occasional appearance in the High Courts involved larger sums. In 1571 John proceeded against Richard Quiney, the son of an old colleague Adrian Quiney, for £50. In 1573 he had himself to meet the claim of Henry Higford, a former steward of Stratford, for £30. He failed to appear and a warrant for his arrest, and if not found, outlawry, was issued. He was still in a position to spend £40 on house property in 1575. But at the beginning of 1577 he suddenly discontinued attendance at the 'halls' of the Corporation, and never again appeared, except on one or two special occasions. In the following year he was excused from a levy for the relief of the poor, and rated at an exceptionally low amount for the expenses of the musters, which still remained unpaid in 1579. His wife's inheritance was disposed of. The small reversion in Snitterfield was sold for £4. Asbies was let at a nominal rent, probably in consideration of a sum down. The other Wilmcote holding was mortgaged to Mary's brother-in-law Edmund Lambert for £40, to be repaid at Michaelmas 1580. It was not repaid. John Shakespeare afterwards claimed that he had tendered payment, and that it was refused because he still owed other sums to Lambert. This he does not seem to have established. He also maintained that Lambert's son John, to whom possession passed in 1587, agreed to buy the property outright from the Shakespeares and their son William, and failed to keep his agreement. This John Lambert denied. There was litigation in 1589 and again in 1597, but the property proved irrecoverable. A singular incident of 1580 still lacks an explanation. John Shakespeare and one John Audley, a hat-maker of Nottingham, were bound over in the Court of Queen's Bench to give security against a breach of the peace. They failed to answer to their recognizances and incurred substantial fines. That of Shakespeare amounted to £20 for his own default and £20 more as surety for Audley. In 1587 an entanglement with the affairs of his brother Henry seems to have added to his embarrassment. And in the same year the patience of the Corporation was exhausted, and a new alderman was appointed in his place, 'for that Mr Shaxspere dothe not come to the halles when they be warned nor hathe not done of longe tyme'. Further court of record suits suggest that he was still engaged in business. On 25 September 1592

he was included in a list of persons at Stratford 'heareto-
fore presented for not comminge monethlie to the churche
accordinge to hir Majesties lawes'; and to his name and
those of eight others is appended the note, 'It is sayd that
these laste nine coom not to churche for feare of process
for debtte'. As arrest for debt could be made on Sundays
in the sixteenth century, the explanation seems, in the light
of John Shakespeare's career since 1577, extremely probable. But the notion of a religious romance in the drab
life of a town councillor has proved too much for his
biographers, and much ingenuity has been spent in inter-
preting what little is known of John's personal and official
life on the theory that he was in fact a recusant. The
theorists differ, however, as to whether he was a Catholic
or a nonconforming Puritan, and there is little evidence to
support either contention. So far as the recusancy returns
of 1592 are concerned, the position is clear. They had
nothing to do, as has been suggested by a confusion of
dates, with the anti-Puritan legislation of 1593. In 1591
England was expecting a renewed Spanish attempt at
invasion, and county commissions were issued and
announced by proclamations of October 18. The instructions to the commissioners are known. They were to
collect the names of those who did not attend church,
not to 'press any persons to answer to any questions of
their conscience for matters of religion', but if they found
wilful recusants, to examine them as to their allegiance to
the Queen, their devotion to the Pope or the King of
Spain, and any maintenance of Jesuits or seminary priests.
Clearly Catholics alone, and not Puritans, were in danger.
Beyond the return itself, the only document which may
bear upon John Shakespeare's religion is the devotional
will or *testamentum animae* found in the roof of one of his
Henley St. houses in the eighteenth century. It is not

likely that this is a forgery, but if the John Shakespeare who made it was the poet's father, it probably dates from his early life, and carries little evidence as to his religious position under Elizabeth. Of his personality there may be some genuine reminiscence in a seventeenth-century report of how a visitor, as to whose identity there must be some blunder, found in his shop 'a merry cheeked old man that said "Will was a good honest fellow, but he durst have cracked a jest with him at any time"'.[1] Although no longer a member of the Corporation, John was called upon to advise them on some difficulties with the lord of the manor in 1601. And on September 8 of that year he was buried. No will or administration is known, but of all the property which passed through his hands, only the Henley St. houses are found in those of the poet.

Of William Shakespeare's own early days there is but little on record. We are told by Rowe, presumably on the authority of inquiries made by Thomas Betterton at Stratford, that his father bred him at a free school, but withdrew him owing to 'the narrowness of his circumstances, and the want of his assistance at home'. There is no reason to reject this, which agrees with what we know of John's financial history, or to look for a free school other than that of Stratford itself. It is unfortunate that no early lists of pupils are preserved there. Rowe's words suggest a somewhat premature withdrawal. From Stratford also comes the earlier report of one Dowdall (1693) that the poet had run away from apprenticeship to a butcher. He does not say that his master was also his father. But the story shows that Aubrey was not alone in his belief as to John Shakespeare's occupation, which he confirms by saying that William followed his father's trade and 'when he kill'd a calfe, he would doe it in a high

[1] p. 227.

style, and make a speech'. Perhaps this really points to some early exercise of mimic talent. 'Killing a calf' seems to have been an item in the repertory of wandering entertainers.[1] Rowe also learnt of Shakespeare's early marriage and departure from Stratford as a result of deer-stealing. The documents concerning the marriage involve a puzzle.[2] It took place towards the end of 1582, not in the parish church of Stratford, or in any of the numerous likely churches whose registers have been searched; possibly in the chapel at Luddington, where an entry is said to have been seen before the register was destroyed. A licence for it was issued from the episcopal registry at Worcester on November 27, and a bond to hold the bishop harmless was given by two sureties on the following day. The procedure was regular enough, and carries no suggestion of family disapproval. But the register of licences gives the bride's name as Anne Whateley of Temple Grafton and the bond as Anne Hathwey of Stratford. Once more, romantic biography has scented a mystery. The probable solution is that the bond, as an original document, is correct, and that the clerk who made up the register blundered. Rowe, who certainly never heard of the bond, knew the name as Hathaway. There were several Hathaways in the parish of Stratford, and Anne's parentage is not quite clear. She may have been of Luddington, but more likely of Shottery, where one Richard Hathaway, of a family which bore the *alias* of Gardner, occupied the tenement of Hewland, now known as Anne Hathaway's cottage, and in 1581 left money to a daughter Agnes, then unmarried. That Agnes

---

[1] *Account* of Princess Mary for Christmas 1521, 'Itm pd. to a man at Wyndesore, for kylling of a calffe before my ladys grace behynde a clothe'. J. Raine, *Priory of Finchale* (Surtees Soc.), ccccxli, cites a 'droll performance' called 'killing the calf' by an eighteenth-century entertainer.

[2] p. 140.

and Anne, in common usage although not in strict law, were regarded as forms of the same name is unquestionable. If there was any element of haste or secrecy in the affair, it may have been due to the fact that Anne was already with child. A kindly sentiment has pleaded the possible existence of a pre-contract amounting to a civil marriage. A daughter Susanna was baptized on 26 May 1583, and followed by twins, Hamnet and Judith, on 2 February 1585. Guesses at godparents are idle where common names, such as Shakespeare's own, are concerned. But those of the twins, which are unusual, point to Hamnet or Hamlet Sadler, a baker of Stratford, and his wife Judith.

The story of deer-stealing has been the subject of much controversy. Rowe's account has the independent confirmation of some earlier jottings by Richard Davies who became rector of Sapperton in Gloucestershire in 1695.[1] Probably, like Rowe, he drew upon local gossip. Rowe says that the exploit was in the park of Sir Thomas Lucy of Charlecote, that in revenge for prosecution by Lucy Shakespeare made a ballad upon him, and that as a result of further prosecution he was obliged to leave Stratford. Davies says that he was whipped and imprisoned by Lucy, and that in revenge he depicted Lucy as a justice with 'three lowses rampant for his arms'. There is an obvious reference here to *Merry Wives of Windsor*, i. 1, in which Justice Shallow complains that Falstaff has beaten his men, killed his deer, and broken open his lodge, and threatens to make a Star Chamber matter of it as a riot. He is said to bear a 'dozen white luces' in his coat, and Sir Hugh Evans makes the jest on louses. The Lucy family had held Charlecote since the twelfth century, and bore the arms *Vair, three luces hauriant argent*. The Sir

[1] p. 232.

Thomas of Shakespeare's day was a prominent justice of peace, and represented Warwickshire in the parliaments in 1571 and 1584–5. It has been held that the whole story is nothing but a myth which has grown up about the passage in the *Merry Wives of Windsor* itself. But so far as the essential feature is concerned, we are not called upon to reject it. Deer-stealing was a common practice enough, and was regarded as a venial frolic, even for young men of higher standing than Shakespeare's. Details are another matter. Lucy cannot have whipped Shakespeare, if he proceeded under the ruling game law of 1563, in which the only penalty prescribed was imprisonment. Possibly, if the affair could be regarded as a riot, it might bear a more serious complexion. Nor does Lucy appear to have had a 'park', in the legal sense, at Charlecote. At his death in 1600 he had only a free-warren. It is true that the learned lawyer Sir Edward Coke included roe-deer, but not fallow deer, among beasts of warren, and although other authorities appear to dissent, it was certainly so decided in 1339. It is also true that the Act of 1563 appears to give protection to deer in any enclosure then existing, whether it was a legally enclosed park or not, and the free-warren at Charlecote may well have come under this provision. If the deer was not in an enclosure protected by the game law, any foray upon it would have been no more than a trespass, to be remedied by civil action, and neither whipping nor imprisonment would have been possible. Rowe, however, only speaks of prosecution, and of a ballad, which may have amounted to a criminal libel. A single stanza, claimed as the opening of this ballad and containing the jest on lousiness, came into the hands both of William Oldys and of Edward Capell in the eighteenth century, with a history ascribing it to information derived from inhabitants of Stratford by a Mr. Jones who died in 1703.[1] If so, it represents a third tradition as old as those of Davies and Rowe. A complete version produced in 1790 by John Jordan, an out-at-elbows poet and guide for strangers in Stratford, was probably not beyond his own capacities for fabrication. There is, however, yet another alleged fragment of the ballad, in a different metre, said on very poor authority to have been picked up at Stratford about 1690 by the Cambridge professor Joshua Barnes. Its jest on deer horns carries the familiar Elizabethan insinuation of cuckoldry against Lucy, whose monument to his wife at Charlecote lauds her domestic virtues. Obviously the fragments are inconsistent, and neither is likely to be genuine. But some weight must be attached to the fourfold testimony through Davies, Rowe, Jones, and Barnes to a tradition of the deer-stealing as alive at Stratford about the end of the seventeenth century. There is later embroidery which need not be taken seriously. A writer in the *Biographia Britannica* (1763) ascribes Shakespeare's release from imprisonment to the intervention of Elizabeth; another in 1862, professedly on the authority of records at Charlecote, to the Earl of Leicester, who died in 1588, but to a pique of whom against Lucy the inspiration of the *Merry Wives of Windsor* is none the less attributed. Towards the end of the eighteenth century, perhaps owing to the discovery that there was no park at Charlecote, the story was transferred to the neighbouring park of Fulbrook. This, however, had been disparked by 1557, was not in the hands of the Lucy family during Shakespeare's boyhood, but was bought by them in 1615 and subsequently re-emparked. Some hit at Sir Thomas is probably involved in the *Merry Wives of Windsor* passage. But it would not be a justifiable inference that the presentment

[1] p. 246.

of Justice Shallow as a whole, especially in *Henry IV*, is in any way meant to be a 'portrait' of the worthy justice. Such portraiture seems quite alien from the method of Shakespeare's art. A belief, once established, that a distinguished citizen of Stratford had enjoyed a wildish youth, may have encouraged later tales of Shakespeare's drinking exploits, for which no origin other than the inventiveness of innkeepers need be sought.

We cannot give any precise date to the *Hegira*. A story current at Stratford in 1818 that the venison was stolen to grace the marriage feast is obviously part of the embroidery. Children can be baptized but not begotten without a father, and it is reasonable to suppose that Shakespeare was still in Stratford during 1584. We do not know whether his wife was at any time the companion of his absence. There is no record of her in London, and none in Stratford until after the purchase of New Place. But the boy Hamnet was buried at Stratford on 11 August 1596. On the other hand it is no proof of Shakespeare's continuance in Stratford that according to his father's allegation he concurred in the offer to sell the Wilmcote property to John Lambert about 1587. This seems to have been only an oral transaction, and wherever William was, there is no reason to suppose that he was beyond communication with his family. The words of Rowe's deer-stealing narrative and of Dowdall's parallel story of an escape from apprenticeship imply a migration direct to London. But these can hardly be pressed. We have no certainty of Shakespeare's presence in London before 1592, when a scoffing notice by Robert Greene shows that he was already an actor and had already begun to write plays.[1] This is no doubt consistent with some earlier sojourn, which may have been of no long duration. A

[1] p. 187.

SHAKESPEARE'S ORIGIN

supposed earlier allusion to him as 'Willy' in Spenser's *Tears of the Muses* (1591) is now almost universally rejected. We have therefore a very considerable hiatus in his history, extending over a maximum of eight years from 1584 to 1592, to take into account; and it is obvious that many things may have occupied this interval, of which we are ignorant. Tradition, apart from some statements as to his introduction into theatrical life, has done little to fill the gap. It was the actor William Beeston who told Aubrey that he had been a schoolmaster in the country.[1] Beeston's memory might well go back to Shakespeare's own lifetime, and the statement is not in itself incredible. The course at Stratford, even if not curtailed, would hardly have qualified him to take charge of a grammar school; but his post may have been no more than that of an usher or an *abecedarius*. Nor need we suppose that his studies, even in the classics, terminated with his schooldays. The most direct contemporary evidence is that of Ben Jonson, who ascribed to him but 'small Latin, and less Greek', writing naturally enough from the standpoint of his own considerable scholarship. There has been much argument on this subject from the time of Richard Farmer's *Essay on the Learning of Shakespeare* (1767), and much enumeration of the books, ancient and modern, erudite and popular, which may, directly or indirectly, have contributed material to his plays. The inferences have not always been discreet. One may reasonably assume that at all times Shakespeare read whatever books, original or translated, came in his way. We do not know what library he had of his own. Many volumes bear his signatures, and they are mostly forgeries. Some claim has been made for an Aldine *Metamorphoses* of 1502, for a translated Montaigne of 1603, and for a translated Plutarch

[1] pp. 229, 231.

of 1612. Sceptics point out that he named no books in his will; there was no reason why he should, unless he wished to dispose of them apart from his other chattels. As with Shakespeare's general learning, so with his law. His writing abounds in legal terminology, closely woven into the structure of his metaphor. Here, again, the knowledge is extensive rather than exact. It is shared by other dramatists. Our litigious ancestors had a familiarity with legal processes, from which we are happily exempt. But many have thought that Shakespeare must have had some professional experience of a lawyer's office, although this was not the final opinion of the much-quoted Lord Campbell; and there are those who will tell you by which Stratford attorney he was employed. This is only one instance of the willingness of conjecture to step in where no record has trod. On similar grounds Shakespeare has been represented as an apothecary and a student of medicine. That he was a soldier rests on a confusion with one of many William Shakespeares at Rowington; and that he was a printer on the fact that Richard Field, who issued his poems, came from Stratford. In a sense, these conflicting theories refute each other. However acquired, a ready touch over a wide space of human experience was characteristic of Shakespeare. For some of this experience we need look no farther than Stratford itself; the early acquaintance with hunting and angling and fowling; the keenly noted observation of rural life, mingling oddly with the fabulous natural history which contemporary literature inherited from the medieval bestiaries. For the rest, we cannot tell where it was garnered. But we are entitled to assume a roving and apperceptive mind, conversant in some way with many men and manners, and gifted with that felicity in the selection and application of varied knowledge, which is one of the secrets of genius. What has perhaps puzzled readers most is the courtesy of Shakespeare; his easy movement in the give and take of social intercourse among persons of good breeding. We have not, indeed, to think of the well-to-do inhabitants of Stratford as boors; but the courtesy of a provincial town is not quite the courtesy of a Portia. Probably the true explanation is that, once more, it is a matter of apperceptiveness, of a temper alive, not only to facts, but to human values.

A sprinkling of Shakespeares in the southern Cotswolds and a 'tradition' cited in 1848 of a residence by the poet at Dursley have led to the supposition that he may there have found a temporary refuge. Justice Shallow is asked to countenance William Visor of Woncote against Clement Perkes of the hill; and it is pointed out that a Vizard was bailiff at Dursley in 1612, and that neighbouring families of Vizard of Woncot or Woodmancote and Perkes of Stinchcombe Hill long survived. The conjunction of names might be more than a coincidence. But Perkes itself was a common name in Warwickshire and Worcestershire as well as in Gloucestershire, and in fact a Clement Perkes was born at Fladbury, Worcestershire, in 1568. Many Shakespearean names occur in Stratford documents. On most little stress can be laid. It is intriguing to find a Fluellen and a Bardolfe in the same list of recusants as Shakespeare's father, although Shakespeare knew Bardolfe as the title of a nobleman, and a Stephen Sly of Stratford to match the Christopher and Stephen Sly of *The Taming of the Shrew*, although 'Slie' and 'Don Christo Vary' were already given by the source-play of *A Shrew*. Christopher Sly, however, calls himself of Burton Heath, presumably Barton-on-the-Heath, where the Lamberts dwelt; and Marian Hacket, the fat ale-wife of Wincot, must belong to the Wincot which lies partly in Clifford

Chambers and partly in Quinton, where a Sara Hacket was baptized in 1591. It is perhaps only a fancy that Clement Swallow, who sued John Shakespeare for debt in 1559, may have contributed with Sir Thomas Lucy to the making of Justice Shallow of Clement's Inn. Possibly the drowning of a Katherine Hamlet at Tiddington on the Avon in 1579 may have given a hint for Ophelia's end. All this amounts to very little. Whatever imprint Shakespeare's Warwickshire contemporaries may have left upon his imagination inevitably eludes us. The main fact in his earlier career is still that unexplored hiatus, and who shall say what adventures, material and spiritual, six or eight crowded Elizabethan years may have brought him? It is no use guessing. As in so many other historical investigations, after all the careful scrutiny of clues and all the patient balancing of possibilities, the last word for a self-respecting scholarship can only be that of nescience.

>   Ah, what a dusty answer gets the soul,
>   When hot for certainties in this our life!

II
SHAKESPEARE AND HIS COMPANY

Any intelligible study of the life and work of the playwright Shakespeare must have its prelude in a retrospect of the state of theatrical affairs, as they stood at the opening of the last Elizabethan decade, when that playwright made his first appearance. The story may begin with the year 1583, which was something of a turning-point in the history of the playing companies. In that year Edmund Tilney, the Master of the Revels, was called upon by Sir Francis Walsingham, the Secretary of State, to select a body of players for the direct service of the Queen. The Queen's men were taken from the most important of the existing companies, those of the Earl of Sussex, of the Earls of Leicester and Oxford, possibly of the Earl of Derby and Henry Lord Hunsdon. All these had made recent appearances at court. They received the rank of Grooms of the Royal Chamber, probably without fee, and were entitled to wear the royal livery and badge. The reasons for the appointment must be matter for conjecture. It was not the practice of the economical Elizabeth to multiply household officers merely as appanages. And it may be suspected that the departure of 1583 was an incident in the endeavour of the government to assert a direct control of the London stage against the claims of the City corporation. If so, it was not the only such incident. A power to regulate public entertainments within their area belonged to the traditional privileges of the City, as of other incorporated towns. Moreover, a proclamation issued early in Elizabeth's own reign, on 16 May 1559, had specifically imposed upon mayors of towns, as upon justices of peace elsewhere, the duty of licensing plays, and had instructed them to disallow such as handled 'matters of religion or of the gouernaunce of the estate of the common weale'. Obviously many of the circumstances of plays were proper matter for local control. A local authority was best qualified to fix suitable times and places, and to take precautions against disorder, structural dangers, and infection. The plan would work well enough, so long as the authority was reasonable. The City of London had not, from the point of view of Elizabeth's government, proved altogether reasonable. The Queen required plays for her Christmas 'solace' at court; and, in order that these might be economically provided, it was desirable that the players should have an opportunity of making their living through public performances. The Corporation was composed of heads of households and employers of labour, who found that plays distracted their servants and apprentices from business and occasionally led to disorder. Moreover they were not uninfluenced by a growing puritan sentiment. There had been friction for some years before 1583. The Privy Council had made more than one attempt to persuade the City to delegate the licensing to independent persons, no doubt such as would be acceptable to the Privy Council itself. This had been refused, and a hint of the royal prerogative had been given in a patent to the Earl of Leicester's men in 1574, which gave them authority to perform, in London and elsewhere, such plays as had been allowed by the Master of the Revels. The City responded in the same year with a complete code of play-regulations for their area. These need not have been oppressive, if not applied oppressively. But the players probably had their misgivings; and they contributed perhaps more than the Privy Council itself to the defeat of the City, by setting up theatres just outside its boundaries, where they came under the control of county justices, less active and interfering than the mayor and his brethren. It was not a complete remedy. In summer the apprentices flocked to the plays even farther from their masters' doors, but in winter the comparative inaccessibility of the new houses made recourse to the City inn-yards still inevitable. Meanwhile the puritan sentiment grew, and a spate of controversial sermons and treatises lifted the City into an attitude of complete opposition to the stage. Short epidemics of plague, during which the Privy Council and the City were agreed that plays must be inhibited, brought a complication. It proved easier to get restraints established than to get them withdrawn when the plague was over. In 1581 the patience of the Privy Council was exhausted, and the precedent of 1574 was followed and extended in a new commission to the Master of the Revels, giving him a general power over the whole country, not merely to license individual plays, but to 'order and reforme, auctorise and put down' all plays, players, and playmakers 'together with their playing places'. The powers of justices and mayors under the proclamation of 1559, as well as the ancient privileges of the Corporations, could thus, where necessary, be overruled. Perhaps, in exasperation, the City now committed a tactical blunder. An order was sent to the gilds, requiring all freemen to forbid the attendance of their 'sarvants, apprentices, journemen, or children' at plays, whether within or without London. It was a *brutum fulmen*, which could not possibly be made effective, particularly beyond the liberties. But the City would not accept defeat, and it was probably during 1582 that, in defiance of the Master of the Revels and his commission, an ordinance was passed, replacing the regulations of 1574 by a simple prohibition of plays within the area. The establishment of a company with the status and dignity of royal servants may reasonably be regarded as a counter-move on the side of the government. The City was overawed to the extent of appointing two inn-yards for the Queen's men in the winter of 1583. In the following year they again proved recalcitrant. The players brought their case before the Privy Council, and there was an elaborate exchange of arguments and proposals; no formal decision is upon record. But it is clear from events that the City were defeated. They had obtained a small concession in a standing prohibition of plays on Sundays. But on the main issue they had to submit to the power of the royal prerogative, and to content themselves with showing cause for restraints of plays as often as possible, and pressing for the extension of such restraints to the Middlesex and Surrey suburbs.

The Queen's men remained the dominant London company for several years after 1583. They did regular service at court during each Christmas season, according to an old routine, in plays carefully chosen by the Revels officers and rehearsed before the Master. Seventeen plays are credited to them for the five winters from 1583-4 to 1587-8. It may have been a subsidiary object of their formation to reduce the number of companies which the City was called upon to tolerate. If so, it was partly counteracted by the fact that the Queen's men proved strong enough to occupy more than one playhouse. There was a protest against this in the negotiations of 1584, and it may explain an arrangement by which the Curtain was taken for a term of seven years from Michaelmas 1585 as an 'easer' to the Theatre. But the relations between companies and playhouses during this period are very obscure. Certainly the Queen's made some use of the Theatre, and some use of various inn-yards during the winter. And in the hot days of summer a section of them, or perhaps the whole company if plague was sporadic, travelled the provinces, where their livery generally secured them exceptionally liberal rewards. The older companies, robbed of their best men, became insignificant. Derby's disappear from the records; Leicester's, Sussex's, Oxford's, and Hunsdon's survived in the provinces. The chief rivals of the Queen's men at court were, however, the boy players. They were to some extent a survival. In the earlier Tudor dramatic annals the great choirs of St. Paul's and the Chapel Royal had been at least as conspicuous as the professional companies. In 1576 a playhouse had been constructed in an old building of the Dominican priory at Blackfriars, and this seems to have been occupied about 1583 by boys drawn from both these choirs, together with others from the private chapel of the Earl of Oxford. The boys followed the classic and literary tradition which humanism had brought into the drama, and their Masters employed academic scholars, such as George Peele and John Lyly. No doubt this served them better at court than with the general London public. Lyly seems to have been the moving spirit of the Blackfriars combination, and soon after it broke down in 1585, he began a new series of plays for Paul's. The Queen's men, on the other hand, probably contented themselves with pieces of more old-fashioned and popular types. One of their members was Richard Tarlton, of part of whose *Seven Deadly Sins* a 'plot' or tiring-house outline is preserved. It shows an attempt at utilizing classical themes. But Tarlton's considerable reputation was evidently in the main that of a joyous jester and buffoon.

The death of Tarlton in September 1588 probably shattered the fortunes of the Queen's men; and with it begins a very difficult phase of company history. Matters were complicated through the controversy aroused in 1589 by the anti-ecclesiastical tracts published under the name of Martin Marprelate. In this both the Queen's men and the Paul's boys took part, possibly at the instigation of Richard Bancroft, afterwards Bishop of London. If so, Bancroft's action was officially disapproved, and the players suffered. The Paul's company was suppressed. The Queen's was not, but was probably required to leave London for a time. '*Vetus Comedia* hath been long in the country', says a pamphlet of October 20. From the records of their journeys it is clear that, from the death of Tarlton onwards, the Queen's men were gradually losing their hold of London. Their court performances only number eleven for 1588–94 against the seventeen for 1583–8. In the country their livery served them better. But they had to split their forces, to join up with stray companions of the road, and to diversify their entertainments with acrobatic tricks. They were reverting to the hand-to-mouth existence of the medieval minstrels. It is perhaps significant that in 1592 the City took advantage of the situation to suggest that public plays were no longer necessary, and that the Queen's service might be adequately provided for by 'the privat exercise of hir Maiesties own players in convenient place'. They approached Archbishop Whitgift, and the cynical ecclesiastic advised them to bribe the Master of the Revels. But the money was not forthcoming, and other players took the place of the Queen's. The disorganization of the hitherto dominant company was, indeed, an obvious opportunity for new men. Two companies come to the front. One is the Lord Admiral's; the other Lord Strange's.

On 5 November 1589, both companies were playing in the City. Perhaps one or both of them had failed to take warning from the fate of the Queen's and to keep their tongues off Martin Marprelate, for the Lord Mayor made an attempt to suppress plays, on the ground that Tilney 'did utterly mislike the same'. The Admiral's submitted, but Strange's showed contempt and performed at the Cross Keys, with the result that some of them found themselves in prison. 'Admiral's' are named as at court during the following winter, giving a play on 28 December 1589 and 'activities' on 3 March 1590. 'Strange's' are not, nor are any provincial visits ascribed to them during 1590. 'Admiral's', however, did an autumn tour, perhaps by Ipswich, Maidstone, Winchester, Marlborough (July 25), Gloucester (Sept. 17), Coventry, and Oxford. In the following winter there were plays at James Burbadge's house, the Theatre, and here events occurred about which John Alleyn was afterwards called upon to give evidence in a Chancery case. The dispute was between Burbadge and one Mrs. Brayne, who claimed a share in the profits of the house, and charged Burbadge with contempt of court in disregarding an order which she considered to be in her favour. She paid several visits to the Theatre to demand her rights. One of these was in November 1590, and a deposition by John Alleyn on 6 February 1592 suggests that it was on this occasion that James Burbadge spoke words of contempt, and his youngest son Richard beat one of Mrs. Brayne's supporters about the legs with a broomstick. Alleyn claims that he 'did as a servaunt wishe the said James Burbage to have a conscience in the matter'. Burbadge, however, said that 'yf ther wer xx contempts and as many iniunccions he wold withstand them all'. And then Alleyn goes on to relate that 'when this deponent about viij daies after came to him for certen money which he deteyned from this deponent and his fellowes, of some of the dyvydent money betwene him & them, growinge also by the vse of the said Theater, he denyed to pay the same. He this deponent told him that belike he ment to deale with them, as he did with the poor wydowe, meaning the now complainant, wishing him he wold not do so, for yf he did, they wold compleyne to ther lorde & M^r the lord Admyrall, and then he in a rage, litle reuerencing his honour & estate, sayd by a great othe, that he cared not for iij of the best lordes of them all.' Alleyn was, however, called upon to make a second deposition in reply to interrogatories on behalf of Burbadge, in which he was pressed as to the date of these events, and on 6 May 1592 he said that they took place 'about a yere past'. The words about the Admiral were spoken in the 'attyring house' in the presence of James Tunstall. Presumably we must take this as Alleyn's most considered dating, and treat the tenure of the Theatre by the Admiral's as lasting to at least about May 1591. The court records for the winter of 1590–1 are on the face of them rather odd. The Privy Council Register notes the issue of a warrant for plays and 'activities' on December 27 and February 16 by the 'Admiral's'; the *Chamber Accounts* show payments for these days to 'George Ottewell and his companye the Lord Straunge his players'. It is difficult to resist the inference that the two companies whose names are thus treated in official documents as equivalent had in fact appeared at court together. And if so they had probably been 'exercising' their court plays together in public performances, under an arrangement with James Burbadge which put the Theatre at their disposal. They may also have had the Curtain, since the lawsuit already cited tells us that it still served as an 'easer' for the Theatre. But the relations with Burbadge indicated by John Alleyn's evidence could hardly fail to bring any such arrangement to an end. Provincial notices suggest an autumn tour of 'Admiral's' men in 1591, closely resembling that of 1590, by Southampton, Winchester, Bath, Gloucester, and Oxford. 'Strange's' seem also to have been at Bath. And there is some reason to suppose that by the summer of 1591 a new London head-quarters had already been found at Philip Henslowe's Rose on the Bankside. The Alleyn papers at Dulwich contain an order by the Privy Council withdrawing a previous one which had restrained 'Strange's' men from playing there and had enjoined them to play three days a week at Newington Butts. With it are petitions from the company and from Henslowe and the Thames watermen asking for the concession. Unfortunately neither order is recorded in the Privy Council Register, and the documents themselves are undated. The players' petition, however, was written 'nowe in this longe vacation'. It recites that 'oure companie is greate, and thearbie our chardge intollerable, in travellinge the countrie, and the contynuance thereof wilbe a meane to bringe us to division and seperacion'. Henslowe's petition begs that he may have leave 'to have playinge in his saide howse duringe such tyme as others have'. It does not look, therefore, as if there had been any general inhibition of plays. This seems to point to 1591 rather than to 1592, the only other possible year. In 1592 there was such a general inhibition on June 23, and it was to last to Michaelmas, and therefore through the 'longe vacation'. No less than six court plays are credited to 'Strange's' during the winter of 1591–2, on December 27 and 28, January 1 and 9, and February 6 and 8; none to the 'Admiral's'. The Queen's and Sussex's also appeared, once each, and a little-known company of the Earl of Hertford's men. On February 19 Henslowe begins a daily record for 'Strange's' which lasts to June 23. Then came the inhibition provoked by some recent disorders, probably arising from an agitation against alien artisans in London; and before its termination at Michaelmas plague had broken out. 'Strange's' were at Canterbury by July 13, and are also traceable at Gloucester, Coventry, Cambridge, and Oxford (Oct. 6). Notices of 'Admiral's' men during this year are scanty. There is a possible one at Aldeburgh and a certain one at Ipswich on August 7. But here the Admiral's were not alone. The payment is apparently a joint one to the Earl of Derby's and to the Lord Admiral's players. By Derby's I think we must assume Strange's to be here meant. The Earl does not seem to have had a company after 1583. Strange's men would naturally have worn the Stanley badge, and a mistake is intelligible. Late in the year, on December 19, 'Admiral's' men were at Leicester. The plague, however, lulled a little about Christmas, and plays at court became possible. Two were given by a company which at this juncture makes a rather surprising first appearance in dramatic annals, that of the Earl of Pembroke, and three by 'Strange's'. These men also got another month's season with Henslowe. But fresh plague led to a fresh inhibition on 28 January 1593, and on January 31 or February 1 the season ended. 'Admiral's' men were already on the road as far afield as Shrewsbury on February 3. 'Strange's' seem to have remained idle for a time, perhaps hoping for the plague to subside. Edward Alleyn was at Chelmsford with companions on May 2, and a record of 'Strange's' at Sudbury in 1592–3 may perhaps identify them. On May 6 a special travelling warrant was issued by the Privy Council in favour of 'the bearers hereof, Edward Allen, servaunt to the right honorable the Lord Highe Admiral, William Kempe, Thomas Pope, John Heminges, Augustine Phillipes and Georg Brian, being al one companie, servauntes to our verie good Lord the Lord Strainge'. It is a little uncertain whether or not the 'being al one companie' is meant to cover Alleyn; in any case he was maintaining some personal relation to the Admiral. For a tour which followed, and in which Alleyn took part, the route was by Maidstone, Southampton, Bath, Bristol (Aug. 1), Shrewsbury, Leicester, and Coventry (Dec. 2). Alleyn, writing from Bristol, contemplated visits to Chester and York, and a return to London about All Saints' Day. Possibly the prolonged plague caused a change of purpose. The letters show that the company was travelling as 'Strange's'. It is Derby's at Leicester and Coventry, but on September 25 Strange had succeeded to the earldom. At Shrewsbury the payment was to 'my l. Stranges and my l. Admyralls players'. Probably the two tours crossed here. The 'Admiral's' appear to have gone on to Bath. Two other companies of interest to us were also on the road in 1593. One was Sussex's, who like 'Strange's' obtained on April 29 a special travelling warrant from the Privy Council. They went far afield, to Sudbury, Ipswich, York (August), Newcastle (September), and Winchester (Dec. 7). The other was Pembroke's, the new court aspirants of the preceding Christmas. They made for their Lord's quarters in the Welsh marches, covering Rye, Bath, Ludlow, Bewdley, Shrewsbury, York (June), Coventry, Leicester, Ipswich. At Bath the careful chamberlains record a receipt of two shillings for a bow that Pembroke's men had broken. It is an allegory, for soon Pembroke's were themselves broken. There are no precise dates, and it is possible, although not very likely, that some of the visits may belong to the end of 1592. But that Pembroke's were in the provinces during 1593 we learn from a letter of September 28 in that year from Henslowe to Alleyn. They had by then, he says, been at home for five or six weeks, because they could not save their charges with travel, and had been obliged to pawn their apparel. The only company at court for the Christmas of 1593-4 was the Queen's. But there was a short cessation of plague, and Henslowe's book records a short season from December 26 to February 6 by Sussex's men. This had been purely a provincial company from 1585 up to its appearance at court on 2 January 1592. But it was working with a travelling group of Queen's men in 1591, and after a fresh outbreak of plague and a consequent inhibition on February 3, this relation was now renewed in a second short season with Henslowe from 1 to 9 April 1594. Meanwhile 'Derby's' men were at King's Lynn, Ipswich (May 8), and Southampton (c. May 15). The Earl had in fact died in the north on April 16, and although this does not appear to have been known at Southampton, when the company reached Winchester on May 16 they were described as the Countess of Derby's. 'Admiral's' men were with Henslowe from May 14 to 16. The plague was now really over, and a reorganization of the companies became possible. On June 5 a company of Chamberlain's men is heard of for the first time since 1588-9. It was playing with Admiral's men, probably on alternate days, for Henslowe at Newington Butts. The arrangement seems only to have lasted until June 15. The companies then parted, and to the end of the reign shared the supremacy of the London stage. On October 8 Lord Hunsdon was negotiating with the City for the housing of 'my nowe companie' at the Cross Keys. Most of the men named as 'Strange's' on 6 May 1593, William Kempe, Thomas Pope, John Heminges, Augustine Phillips, and George Bryan, became Chamberlain's men. So did Richard Burbadge and others. Edward Alleyn, on the other hand, continued or resumed his service with Charles Howard, the Lord Admiral. This complicated chronicle raises some problems which are perhaps beyond solution. What was the precise nature of the association between the Admiral's and Strange's men, and what period did it cover? The court documents of 1590–1 suggest that it began not later than 1590, and probably from that year to 1594 it amounted to an amalgamation. It may have begun a little earlier, with the expulsion from the City in November 1589. It is of course only for 1590–1 that the identity at court of the 'Admiral's' and 'Strange's' is demonstrated, but the reputation of Edward Alleyn about 1592 renders it almost incredible that he was never called upon to appear before the Queen between 1590–1 and 1594–5; and if he did so appear, it can only have been as a 'Strange's' man in 1591–2 and 1592–3. In these years 'Strange's' are at least as predominant at court as the Queen's men had been in their day. In 1593 there is the clearest evidence that Alleyn, although retaining a personal status as a servant of the Admiral, was travelling as a 'Strange's' man. Obviously his personal gifts, histrionic and financial, made him the effective manager of the company. We may call it 'the Alleyn company'.

The fragmentary nature of the evidence makes a dramatic history of the period extremely difficult. The work of even the best-known writers is uncertain in extent and chronology, and much of it has come down in mutilated form. Marlowe's authorship of *Tamburlaine* is a matter of inference; it is only by an accident that we know the *Spanish Tragedy* to be Kyd's. Some at least of the anonymous plays are probably due to untraced pens. No satisfactory attribution of so remarkable a piece as *Arden of Faversham* has been arrived at. One may venture the suggestion that the rise of Alleyn was due, not only to his own powers as an actor, but also to his early employment of better dramatists than the Queen's could boast. All of Marlowe's known work, except *Dido* and possibly *Edward II*, seems to have been for companies with which he was associated. The *Spanish Tragedy* may have been written for him; if not, he made use of it later. Peele, Lodge, Greene, Porter, all contributed to his repertory. He carried on the tradition of the literary drama, which Spenser mistakenly believed to have perished with Lyly. Very likely the Queen's, in their post-Tarlton days, attempted to follow suit. It is only an impression that they put their money on Greene as against Marlowe. It need not be assumed that Marlowe, or Greene, or any other writer not himself an actor, was tied to a particular company. We know that Greene's university education did not prevent him from selling *Orlando Furioso* first to the Queen's, and then, when the Queen's were in the country, to the Admiral's.

It is during this period of hasty seasons broken by plague, of the setting up and ruin of ephemeral companies, that Shakespeare first emerges as player and playwright. Robert Greene, from his squalid death-bed, on 3 September 1592, left a literary testament. It foreshadows the end of an epoch, that of the domination of the stage by University pens. Greene's eclipse was shortly to be followed by that of Marlowe on 30 May 1593. But Marlowe and two others, probably Peele and either Nashe or Lodge, were the objects of Greene's address *To those Gentlemen his Quondam Acquaintance, that spend their wits in making plaies*.[1] It is a bitter attack upon the companies, who have been beholden to him for the lines they have spoken and have now deserted him. They will desert his friends likewise, since they have now a writer of their own.

Yes trust them not: for there is an vpstart Crow, beautified with our feathers, that with his *Tygers hart wrapt in a Players hyde*, supposes he is as well able to bombast out a blanke

[1] p. 187.

verse as the best of you: and beeing an absolute *Iohannes fac totum*, is in his owne conceit the onely Shake-scene in a countrey.

The invective was printed in *Greenes Groats-worth of Wit*, shortly after the author's death, and Henry Chettle, who prepared it for the press, made something of an apology for it in his own *Kind-Harts Dreame*, itself registered before the end of 1592.[1] The letter had been 'written to divers play-makers' and was 'offensively by one or two of them taken'.

It is probable that the first play-maker here referred to is Marlowe and the second Shakespeare, although this implies some looseness in Chettle's language, since Greene's letter was obviously not written to Shakespeare. But there is nothing in the letter as we have it which could be offensive to any play-maker except Marlowe, who is spoken of as an atheist and Machiavellian, and Shakespeare, who is openly attacked. The others, presumably Peele and Nashe, 'young Iuuenall, that byting Satyrist, that lastlie with mee together writ a Comedie', are handled in a more friendly spirit. However this may be, Greene's letter in itself is sufficient to show that by September 1592 Shakespeare was both a player and a maker of plays. And it is a fair inference from Greene's tone that he was only just taking rank as a serious rival to the University men. How far back are we to put the beginnings of his dramaturgy? Probably as far as 1591, if he is responsible, as their inclusion the 1623 Folio suggests, for *2, 3 Henry VI*. Greene's letter parodies a line from *3 Henry VI*, which must therefore itself have existed as early as 1592. The relation of these parts to *1 Henry VI*, produced by Alleyn's company on 3 March 1592, is best explained by regarding

[1] p. 188.

them as earlier productions of the same company, and since they were not being played in 1592, they had presumably been laid aside. As, moreover, the supplementary play is likely to have followed after no long interval, we may conjecturally put them in 1591. That, then, is the earliest year to which there is ground for ascribing any dramatic work by Shakespeare that we know of. And even as a player his career may not have begun long before 1592. It is a mere fantasy that he was enlisted by Leicester's men on a visit to Stratford-on-Avon in 1586–7. Tradition tells us, through the mouth of Dowdall (1693), that Shakespeare 'was received into the playhouse as a serviture', and through that of Rowe (1709) that he was 'at first in a very mean rank'.[1] Both imply a direct transference from Stratford, which looks like a foreshortening of history; and both probably mean the same thing, that he was at first a hired man and not a sharer, which is likely enough. Malone (1780, 1790) had heard from the stage that he was originally employed as a prompter's attendant or call-boy, but the statement is dropped from his revised *Life*. A story not given by Rowe, but apparently known to him and originally derived from Sir William Davenant, tells how before Shakespeare became an actor he occupied himself in taking charge of horses at the playhouse door, and showed dexterity in the employment.[2] For what it is worth, the story points to the Theatre or Curtain, as these were the only houses reached by horseback. Both were in the hands of Alleyn's company or its component elements in 1590–1, and this company may well have seen his first beginnings, alike as actor and as writer.

After Greene's outburst of 1592, Shakespeare's position becomes shadowy again, up to the regrouping of the companies in 1594. The only plays that can very well be

[1] pp. 233, 238.   [2] p. 247.

assigned to this period are *Richard III*, *Titus Andronicus*, and *Comedy of Errors*. Of these *Richard III* is certainly a continuation of *2, 3 Henry VI*. It is not in Henslowe's list of performances by the Alleyn company, but it seems clear that *2, 3 Henry VI* must have passed to Pembroke's, and *Richard III* may have been done for them. Perhaps it reappears as the *Buckingham* given by Sussex's men in 1593-4, although the name would also fit a play on Henry the Eighth. The title-page of *Titus Andronicus* suggests that it was played successively by Alleyn's company, Pembroke's, and Sussex's, and any touches put to it by Shakespeare might have been for either, the last most plausibly, of these. *The Comedy of Errors* may have been 'the Gelyous comodey' produced by the Alleyn company on 5 January 1593, but about this one cannot be certain. It is at any rate possible, however, that Shakespeare may have been writing for three companies during 1592-4. Much research has been devoted to a conjecture that he spent part of this period in northern Italy. It is certainly true that when the plague was over he began a series of plays with Italian settings, which were something of a new departure in English drama. But the evidence is inconclusive, in view of what he may have learnt through books and the visits of others, or through converse with some of the many Italians resident in London. Supposed travels, now or at another time, to Ireland or to Denmark, are even more speculative. One is on safer ground in pointing out that the plague years gave opportunity for the development of literary ambitions outside the range of the drama, which took shape in the narrative poems of *Venus and Adonis* (1593) and *Lucrece* (1594). Each was dedicated with an elaborate epistle to Henry Wriothesley, Earl of Southampton, a young nobleman of Catholic antecedents, who was just beginning to make a figure at court. Some critics detect a great advance in the poet's intimacy with his patron between the two addresses. This is perhaps rather super-subtle. In the first Shakespeare offers 'the first heire of my inuention', that is, his first published work, and will 'take aduantage of all idle houres, till I haue honoured you with some grauer labour'. In the second, 'What I haue done is yours, what I haue to doe is yours, being part in all I haue, deuoted yours.' Each is subscribed 'in all dutie'. The phrasing in both cases seems to fall well within the normal scope of dedicatory formulas. Not many idle hours would have been at Shakespeare's disposal had he done all the revisionary work and early drafts or fragments of plays with which some writers credit his pupil pen. If one can trust the apparent testimony of *Willobie his Avisa*, he had at any rate sufficient leisure, in or shortly before 1594, for an unsuccessful love affair.[1]

An Elizabethan patron was expected to put his hand in his pocket. Rowe tells us that Shakespeare met with 'many great and uncommon marks of favour and friendship' from Southampton, and on Davenant's authority that the Earl 'at one time, gave him a thousand pounds, to enable him to go through with a purchase which he heard he had a mind to'.[2] The sum named is quite incredible. The aggregate of Shakespeare's known purchases in real estate and tithes throughout his life does not reach £1,000. Probably a cipher has been added to the figures during the transmission of the story; and some such amount as £100 Shakespeare may have spent on acquiring a share in the Lord Chamberlain's company, when it was formed during 1594. There is no ground for supposing that he was the William Shakespeare who had enough spare cash to lend one John Clayton £7 in May 1592, and had to

---

[1] pp. 131, 190. [2] p. 239.

sue for it in 1600. At any rate Shakespeare comes before us on 15 March 1595 with an assured theatrical status as a payee on behalf of the Chamberlain's men for plays given at court in the winter of 1594, and therefore doubtless a sharer in the company. The Chamberlain's men, as we have seen, established themselves, like the Admiral's men who were destined to become their principal rivals, on the break-up of the Alleyn combination in the spring of 1594. Ferdinando Earl of Derby died on April 16. On May 16 men under the protection of his widow were playing at Winchester, and 'Admiral's' men were playing for Henslowe in London. Very shortly afterwards the patronage of the Lord Chamberlain, Henry Lord Hunsdon, must have been obtained. But the parting with Alleyn may not yet have been quite complete, since on June 5 Henslowe began to record performances by 'my Lord Admeralle men & my Lorde Chamberlen men' at Newington Butts. The plays given included *Titus Andronicus*, *Hamlet*, and *Taming of A Shrew*. It may be that *A Shrew* was already *The Shrew*, but the *Hamlet* was certainly not Shakespeare's. Probably this arrangement terminated on June 15, when Henslowe drew a line across the page of accounts, after which these three plays no longer appear. Thenceforward the two companies may be taken to have been quite distinct. It is best to assume that as a business organization the Chamberlain's company, unable to rely on financial support from Alleyn, made a fresh start, and that its capital was contributed by the sharers. No doubt there was some apportionment of the 'books' belonging to the old combination, and in some way all those for Shakespeare's earlier plays seem to have passed into the hands of the Chamberlain's. The company's history, first under the designation of the Chamberlain's men, and then under that of the King's men, is continuous throughout

Shakespeare's career, and there is nothing to show that he ever wrote for any other company. It became dominant at court, giving thirty-two performances during Elizabeth's reign to twenty by the Admiral's and thirteen by other companies. And during this period its run of prosperity seems to have been substantially unbroken. Plague only threatened once, for a short period in 1596. The players had of course to face the restraint of 28 July 1597, when offence was given by *The Isle of Dogs*, for which they were not responsible, and in August and September they undertook their only prolonged provincial tour between 1594 and the end of the reign. But they stood to gain by the settlement under which only two companies were to be tolerated, and although a Privy Council order of 22 June 1600 limited each company to two performances a week, it is clear that the restriction was not long enforced. On the other hand they had to face fresh competition from the revival of the boy companies in 1599 and 1600, which for a time hit them pretty hard, and from the toleration of a third company of men in 1602. Some ruffles there were from time to time with the censorship. *Richard II* was printed in 1597 without the abdication scene, which had probably been thought unsuitable for an Elizabethan public. Falstaff had to be substituted for Oldcastle in *Henry IV* and Broome for Brooke in *Merry Wives of Windsor*. Brooke was the family name of the Lords Cobham, who also claimed an hereditary interest in Sir John Oldcastle. In 1598 there were complaints in Scotland that 'the comedians of London should scorn the king and the people of this land in their play'. We do not know that these comedians were the Chamberlain's men. The Scots are hardly treated in *Edward III*, printed in 1596, which may be theirs, and it is conceivable that the absence of the Captain Jamy episode (iii. 2. 69–153) from the 1600 quarto of *Henry V* may be due to censorship, although other explanations are also possible. There is no sign, however, that these incidents brought any trouble upon the company. It is even more remarkable that they suffered nothing on account of the performance of *Richard II*, which they gave at the behest of some of the followers of the Earl of Essex, as a prelude to his misguided outbreak of 8 February 1601.[1] Elizabeth grumbled at the popularity of the play, but showed no resentment against the poet or the players. It may be that during 1600–1 they were absent for a short time from London. There are no certain provincial notices of them, but there is a possible one at Oxford, and the title-page of the Q 1 of *Hamlet* records that it had been played at Oxford and Cambridge and elsewhere, as well as in London itself, before it was published in 1603. But it is not clear that the journeying, if it took place, was due to *Richard II*, and the company was at court on 24 February 1601, only a fortnight after the Essex affair, and again as usual during the following Christmas. Perhaps we may credit Elizabeth's leniency, at least in part, to her personal liking for Shakespeare's art. Of this we are informed both by Ben Jonson's lines and by the tradition of her impatience to see Falstaff in love. The alleged interchange of royal courtesies over her dropped glove, when the poet was enacting a king upon the stage, must, one fears, be abandoned.[2] No doubt the Tudor lady had moods in which she was capable of scourging those whom she most favoured. But the Lord Chamberlain was never far from the royal chair. The Hunsdons, father and son, were Elizabeth's nearest cousins and her close personal adherents. Of all the court, they could least be suspected of sympathy with seditious tendencies. It was easy enough to slip in a word to save

[1] pp. 174–7.   [2] p. 250.

honest men from the consequences of their indiscretions. After all, the company had only been a cat's-paw for the conspirators. It is impossible to suppose that Shakespeare, in writing *Richard II*, deliberately intended to suggest the analogy between Richard and the queen. For topics of political controversy there was no room in the Elizabethan theatre, although the position was somewhat altered under the laxer and less popular administration of James. You could beat the patriotic drum against the Spaniards, of course. You could flout the Scots, at least under cover of an historical play. Even here there might be a risk, as the wind of diplomacy veered. But you could not ventilate the grievances of the subject, of which indeed there were few except the monopolies, or touch upon ecclesiastical affairs, or champion the conflicting views of Essex and Burghley as to bringing the war to an end, or above all meddle with the dangerous *arcana* of the succession problem. Least of all could you do this, if you were in a company which, since the Queen's men were never in London, had practically become an official part of the royal household with a privileged and remunerative position, the preservation of which depended entirely on the avoidance of offence. It is hard to see what the topical theorists suppose that the censorship was about. They have a dilemma to face. Either the portraits must have been so veiled as to be unrecognizable, alike to the naked Elizabethan eye and through the microscope of modern research. Or alternatively the playwright would have tasted the Marshalsea and the players would have gone to pad the hoof in the provinces.

Essex had a popularity which failed him lamentably when the critical moment came; and of this there is an echo in a chorus to *Henry V*. The theorists, however, assume that Shakespeare was linked to his fortunes through their common friendship for Southampton, whom Essex led to his ruin. And the disaster is sometimes held to account for the critical attitude to society which becomes apparent in *Hamlet*. How far Shakespeare's relations with Southampton outlasted the early dedications is very uncertain. The only external fact which might connect them is a letter of 1599 from Lady Southampton to her husband in Ireland, in which she jests on the birth of a son to Sir John Falstaff and Dame Pintpot.[1] It is most unlikely that by Sir John Falstaff she meant Shakespeare himself. There are the *Sonnets*, and Southampton has been very generally accepted as the friend to whom, over a long period of years, many of these were written. It is still possible to be sceptical. The identity of the friend may have eluded us. But if we are to find him in a known patron of Shakespeare, some at least of the facts point to William Lord Herbert, afterwards Earl of Pembroke, rather than to Southampton. The earlier supporters of this identification did not get all the evidence.[2] And although Southampton was still alive when the First Folio was published, it was to Pembroke and his brother that Heminges and Condell dedicated it. If Shakespeare was indeed writing for the company of Pembroke's father in 1592-3, he may already have been in touch with the Herberts, and a projected marriage in 1595 between the son and Elizabeth Carey, granddaughter of the first and daughter of the second Lord Hunsdon, would be an adequate explanation for the earliest sonnets. Elizabeth Carey ultimately married Sir Thomas Berkeley, and it is quite possible that *Midsummer-Night's Dream* celebrated the occasion. It is reasonable to assume that the services of players to the lords of their companies were not merely nominal.

[1] p. 194.   [2] See chap. v.

The only fellow-poet to whom Shakespeare directly refers in his plays is Marlowe:[1]

> Dead shepherd, now I find thy saw of might,
> Whoever loved, that loved not at first sight?

Some jesting at Chapman there may be in *Love's Labour's Lost*, and if he was the rival poet of the *Sonnets*, which is not assured, Shakespeare treated him there with a courtesy touched by irony. Rowe (1709) had heard that Shakespeare and Jonson were 'profess'd friends', and that the acquaintance between them began with 'a remarkable piece of humanity and good nature', when Shakespeare commended a play of Jonson's to the consideration of his company.[2] One would gladly think that Shakespeare is the Virgil of Jonson's *Poetaster*.

> That, which he hath writ,
> Is with such judgement, labour'd, and distill'd
> Through all the needful uses of our lives,
> That could a man remember but his lines,
> He should not touch at any serious point,
> But he might breathe his spirit out of him.

It is not in fact likely that Virgil was any one but Virgil, or that Shakespeare was the 'so happy a Genius' who collaborated in the lost first version of *Sejanus*. Jonson's considered judgement of Shakespeare is to be found in his First Folio lines and in his later *Timber*. It shows both admiration for the poet and affection for the man. It does not detract from the genuineness of the admiration that it was not uncritical. Jonson had a critical mind, and Shakespeare's way of writing did not altogether answer to his theory of what dramatic structure should be. Therefore he told Drummond that Shakespeare 'wanted Arte'. He censured a line in *Julius Caesar*, which Shakespeare appa-

---

[1] *As You Like It*, iii. 5. 81.   [2] p. 240.

rently altered. He disliked the solutions of continuity in the action of *Henry V*. He thought that some of the incidents in the *Tempest* and *Winter's Tale* made 'nature afraid', and that *Pericles* was a 'mouldy tale', which in some respects it was. Perhaps he found 'horror' in *Macbeth*. All this is legitimate criticism by one poet of another. And if Jonson smiled at Shakespeare's 'small Latine, and lesse Greeke', his judgement chimes precisely with the reference, so full of admiration and discriminating kindliness, in the recently recovered lines of Francis Beaumont:[1]

> Here I would let slip,
> If I had any in me, scholarship,
> And from all learning keep these lines as clear,
> As Shakespeare's best are, which our heirs shall hear
> Preachers apt to their auditors to show
> How far sometimes a mortal man may go
> By the dim light of Nature.

In private talk Jonson may have adopted a more slighting tone towards his friend's erudition. He is said thus to have incurred the resentment of John Hales. But if he chaffed Shakespeare's assumption of a motto in *Every Man out of his Humour* he became in return, according to repute, the mark for Shakespeare's epigrams. Friends need not spare each other, writing in the same tavern, and over the same quart pot. Is Jonson in Shakespeare's plays? About 1599 he became involved in the *Poetomachia*. This started as a quarrel between him and Marston, and there is no reason to suppose that Shakespeare's was one of the 'petulant stiles' with which Jonson complained that for three years he had been provoked on every stage. But while he was preparing his *Poetaster* (1601) against Marston, he seems to have learnt of the intended production

[1] pp. 215-17.

by the Chamberlain's men of Dekker's *Satiromastix*. Dekker, therefore, as well as Marston, appears in *Poetaster*, together with a company of players, whose personalities are treated in no friendly spirit. If Jonson made any allusion to Shakespeare in this controversy, it can only be in the *Apologetical Dialogue* written after the appearance of *Satiromastix* later in 1601. Here, after defending his 'taxation' of some of the players, he adds:

> Onely amongst them, I am sorry for
> Some better natures, by the rest so drawne,
> To run in that vile line.

A contemporary notice does, however, connect Shakespeare's name with the *Poetomachia*. In *3 Parnassus*, a Cambridge play, probably produced in the winter of 1601-2, William Kempe, talking of academic writers, is made to say,

'Why heres our fellow Shakespeare puts them all downe, ay and Ben Jonson too. O that Ben Jonson is a pestilent fellow, he brought up Horace giving the Poets a pill, but our fellow Shakespeare hath given him a purge that made him betray his credit.'

The 'pill' is in *Poetaster*; the 'purge' has been sought in various plays of Shakespeare. It is often taken to be the description of Ajax in *Troilus and Cressida*, i. 2. 19, which seems unnecessarily elaborate for its place, refers to 'humours', and has not much relation to the character of Ajax as depicted in the play. Other suggestions are Nym in *Henry V* and *Merry Wives of Windsor*, and the censorious and libertine Jaques of *As You Like It*. There may well enough be glances at Jonson in all of these, particularly in Nym, who rarely speaks in *Henry V*, and never in *Merry Wives of Windsor*, without using the word 'humour'. But it is not likely that any one of them was the 'purge'. All the plays concerned, except *Troilus and Cressida*, are too early in date, since the writer of *3 Parnassus* clearly regarded the 'purge' as an answer to the 'pill'. Probably the 'purge' was *Satiromastix* itself. Horace is promised one in i. 2. 294, although there is none of a literal kind in the play. The Cambridge writer may have thought that Shakespeare was responsible for it, since he introduces Kempe as a fellow of Burbadge and Shakespeare, although Kempe had left the Chamberlain's men in 1599, and Danter, who was long dead, as a printer.

Shakespeare's success as a playwright appears to have terminated all other literary ambitions. His free handling of the dramatic form gave him ample scope for a wide variety of poetic expression. The narrative poems, if we may judge by the frequency of allusions to them and the number of reprints, won an early and lasting popularity. But they had no successors. The only occasional verses which bear Shakespeare's signature are the set on *The Turtle and Phoenix*, contributed to a volume in honour of one Sir John Salisbury in 1601. No dirge for Elizabeth or paean for James came from his pen. He stood aloof from the practice of commendatory writing, with which most of his contemporaries vaunted each other's wares. The few pieces ascribed to him in manuscript anthologies, like those in *The Passionate Pilgrim*, carry little authority. The authenticity of *A Lover's Complaint*, printed with the *Sonnets*, is gravely doubted. The *Sonnets* themselves are an exception. They continue the poetic impulse of the early work, and their composition covers a period of three years and more, probably from 1595 to 1599 or 1600. One must suppose that some at least of them were originally intended for publication. How else could the immortality in verse promised to the poet's friend be secured? Shakespeare was known to Meres as a sonneteer in 1598. But unless a volume of 1602 has been lost, the *Sonnets* remained in manuscript to 1609, when they were printed without any token of oversight by the author. To whomsoever written, William Herbert, or Henry Wriothesley, or an unknown, or a group of unknowns, the *Sonnets* give us glimpses of a soul-side of Shakespeare imperfectly revealed by the plays. A perturbed spirit is behind the quiet mask. Here is a record of misplaced and thwarted affections, of imperfections and disabilities, inseparable perhaps from an undesired way of life, which clog a mind conscious enough of its own power. Shakespeare, the myriad-minded, is

> Desiring this man's art and that man's scope.

He is tired of life before his time, conscious of 'tann'd antiquity' in the full tide of years, brooding on the decay of beauty and the passing of friends, letting his imagination play freely around thoughts of death. One must not take too literally a way of writing which has some elements of traditional convention in it, or attempt to construct a complete personality from the transient utterances of individual moods. But when all such allowance is made, there is some disharmony between the tone of the *Sonnets* and that of the vivid comedies, abundant in their rendering of the surface of things, which were contemporary with them. They lead up more naturally to the questionings of *Hamlet* and to the distasted essays in disillusion which followed.

A reasonable measure of worldly prosperity came to Shakespeare. We do not know that he ever let go altogether of Stratford. The boy Hamnet died in 1596. Sentiment would trace a reflection of the event in the sympathetic treatment of Arthur in *King John*, which chronology at least does not forbid. The two daughters, Susanna and Judith, remained. There had been no more children. About 1596 Shakespeare may have begun to pick up the broken threads of family life. His father survived to 1601. No will or administration is known, but it is evident that the Henley St. houses, all that was left of John's property, came into his son's hands, subject no doubt to a life-interest for the widow. Probably it was the poet's money which financed an unsuccessful attempt of 1597 to recover the lost Arden inheritance at Wilmcote, as well as an application to the Herald's Office in 1596 for a grant of family arms, which John had contemplated and dropped when he was bailiff of Stratford in 1568-9. The grant was duly made, and the arms *Or on a bend sable a spear of the first steeled argent*, with a falcon bearing a spear as the crest, adorn the poet's monument.[1] In 1599 there was a second application for leave to impale the arms of Arden, but if this grant too was made, neither Shakespeare nor his descendants appear to have availed themselves of it. The responsible heralds incurred some criticism for assigning arms to a person of base degree, and defended themselves by reciting John's substantial position and civic dignities. In 1597 Shakespeare established himself in his native town through the purchase, for £60 if the sum named in the fine can be trusted, of the substantial freehold house of New Place. This stood opposite the Gild Chapel, at the angle formed by Chapel St. and Chapel Lane, and had a large garden. It had been built at the end of the fifteenth century by Sir Hugh Clopton, and had passed by purchase through other hands. There was a curious hitch in the transaction with Shakespeare. William Underhill, the vendor, was poisoned by his son Fulke, and Shakespeare had to secure warranty through a fresh fine with another son Hercules, to whom the felon's estate had

[1] pp. 138-40.

been granted. About 1540 New Place was described as 'a praty howse of brike and tymbar'. But in 1549 it was out of repair, and that Shakespeare may have had to put it in order is suggested by the sale of a load of stone from him or his father to the Stratford corporation in 1598. In the same year he had in Stratford a store of ten quarters of malt, a commodity in which the well-to-do inhabitants of the town largely dealt, somewhat to the impoverishment of their neighbours in a time of dearth.[1] In 1598 also the correspondence of Richard Quiney of Stratford shows Shakespeare in friendly relations with a fellow-townsman, who applied to him for a loan to meet expenses in London, and at the same time in search of an investment.[2] Oldys has a stage tradition that he drew Falstaff from a landowner who had refused to sell to him.[3] He ultimately, in 1602, bought for £320 from the local family of Combe a freehold property in the open manorial fields of Old Stratford, extending to a hundred and seven acres of arable land, with twenty acres of pasture and rights of common. This he probably let for tillage by the existing tenant occupiers. And in the same year he acquired, for the use of his gardener, one may suppose, a cottage in Chapel Lane, which was copyhold of the manor of Rowington. He cannot as yet have dwelt much at New Place, although he is not known to have leased it. In London he is traceable in 1597 as living in St. Helen's, Bishopsgate, where, like other poets, he neglected to pay his taxes. But by the end of 1599 he had moved to the liberty of the Clink on the Surrey Bankside.[4] In both places he would have been in close proximity to his playhouse, at first the Theatre or Curtain, then the Globe.[5]

So Shakespeare stood, when Elizabeth made way for James. He too, no less than his predecessor, was 'taken',

[1] p. 154. [2] p. 156. [3] p. 245. [4] pp. 146–8. [5] See p. 252.

according to Ben Jonson, with the flights of the 'Swan of Avon'; and there is no reason to doubt that Shakespeare remained a *persona grata* after the change of reign. Several of his older plays were chosen to appear with new ones at the court performances of 1604–5. One need not be so sure as was Sir Sidney Lee that the letter, said to have been once at Wilton, in which Lady Pembroke invited the king to see a representation of *As You Like It* in 1603, is to be put down as mythical. It certainly cannot now be found, but its existence was recorded by a competent historian in 1865.[1] An anonymous writer about 1709 speaks of an 'amicable' letter, already also lost, but once in Sir William Davenant's hands, from James to the poet himself.[2] Commentators have not refrained from guessing that it was in acknowledgement of the honour paid to the new royal house in *Macbeth*.

The *status* of the former Lord Chamberlain's men suffered no diminution under James. On the contrary it was enhanced. They now became King's men and sworn officers of the royal household as Grooms of the Chamber in ordinary without fee. The appointment did not entail any regular household duties, other than those of players. But there was an exception in August 1604, when grooms were needed to attend the Constable of Castile, who came as an ambassador from Spain, and Shakespeare with eleven fellows waited in their red liveries during the peace negotiations. They acted now under the authority of a royal patent, which entitled them to appear both in London and in any city, university, or other town throughout the realm. We have no great certainty as to the playhouses used by the Chamberlain's men at the beginning of their career. They had the Theatre in 1596 and probably from 1594, and they may also have occupied city inns during the

[1] p. 177.   [2] p. 242.

winter until that practice was stopped in 1596. In 1598 they were at the Curtain. The Theatre in fact was in bad repair, and after long disputes between the Burbadges and the ground landlord, its timbers were pulled down and carried to the Bankside. Here in the course of 1599 was opened the Globe. This is the house named in the patent to the King's men, and it remained in their possession throughout. In 1608 they acquired the lease of the Blackfriars, and this they began to occupy in the autumn of 1609. Being a roofed house, it was more convenient for winter performances than the Globe, which it seems to have gradually displaced as the head-quarters of the company. The court performances under James were more frequent than had suited the economical disposition of Elizabeth, and during 1603–16 a hundred and seventy-seven fell to the lot of the King's men. This was far more than half the total number given. But there were difficulties to be faced. The rivalry of the boys was continued by other young aspirants, and there were now generally four and sometimes five companies playing in London. Even the King's men themselves did not steer quite clear of troubles with the censor, and there was a restraint in 1608, for which they were not responsible, but which threatened a permanent suppression, and had to be bought off at considerable expense. More serious, however, was the effect of plague. The epidemic, from which London had been practically free for a decade, broke out again in 1603. The theatres had been closed in March, when Elizabeth's illness became dangerous, and hopes of a season on the arrival of James in May were frustrated. The King's men had to travel. The plague had subsided by the next spring, and the theatres were opened on April 9. The rest of the year was free from infection, but there were recrudescences in each of the next three summers, and a worse visitation

SHAKESPEARE AND HIS COMPANY 57

in that of 1608, which lasted to nearly the end of 1609. It is probable that plays were more or less automatically suspended, at first when the weekly deaths from plague reached thirty, and from 1608 when they reached forty over a rather wider area. On this basis there would have been closures during the greater part of October to December 1605, July to December 1606, July to November 1607, and from the end of July 1608 to the end of November 1609. During all five years the King's men travelled. Theatrical profits must have been badly hit, in spite of special royal subsidies to the company, in 1603-4 for their 'maintenance and relief', and in 1608-9 and 1609-10 to enable them to undertake 'private practice' for the King's service at Christmas. Possibly this did not exclude the admission of spectators to one of the 'private' theatres. The Whitefriars seems to have been available in 1608-9, although we do not know that the King's men occupied it. In 1609-10 they had the Blackfriars. After 1609 there was no serious plague until 1625. But there was generally a little travelling in the summer.

The company, in the strict sense, consisted of 'sharers', who were bound together by some deed of association, and divided the profits, after setting aside the proportion allocated to the owners of the playhouse, and meeting the current expenses. But there were also hired servants, some of whom may have been primarily actors, while others were musicians, and others again stage attendants. We hear of the stage-keeper, the tireman, and the book-keeper or prompter, who was an important personage. Probably all, except the book-keeper, were available upon occasion to take minor parts. There were also boys, who took the female parts. They seem to have been bound, perhaps for three years, to individual sharers, who undertook to give them training.

A distinction must be drawn amongst the sharers themselves. Some of them were also 'housekeepers', having acquired an interest in the ownership of the Globe or the Blackfriars or of both houses. One of these was Shakespeare. When the Globe was built in 1599, Burbadge and his brother Cuthbert, who seem to have had an option on the site from the ground landlord, kept a half-interest for themselves and portioned the other half among Shakespeare, Phillips, Pope, Heminges, and Kempe. The housekeepers were responsible, perhaps for the erection, and certainly for the maintenance, of the fabric, and divided the proportion of takings paid over by the body of sharers as rent. Similarly when a lease of the Blackfriars was surrendered to Burbadge by the Queen's Revels in 1608, he made new ones, under which Shakespeare, Heminges, Condell, and Sly each received an interest. Both at the Globe and the Blackfriars the holdings were redistributed from time to time, as housekeepers went out or it was desired to admit additional ones, and consequently the value of Shakespeare's interests fluctuated. We do not know how long he retained them. The tenancies were 'in common', and therefore alienable to persons who were not members of the company. But they do not seem to have passed under his will, and therefore he may have parted with them before his death; that of the Globe very likely in 1613, when the fire made a heavy expenditure on rebuilding inevitable.

As to Shakespeare's own acting, we have little to go upon, except late and rather conflicting hints through stage tradition. He 'did act exceedingly well' says Aubrey. But Rowe got the impression that he was no 'extraordinary' actor, and that 'the top of his performance was the Ghost in his own *Hamlet*'. A story, dubious in its details, describes him as playing the very minor part of

Adam in *As You Like It*.[1] Chettle, desiring to be courteous, reported him as 'exelent in the qualitie he professes', and 'qualitie' is a term more than once applied to the occupation of an actor. Davies of Hereford speaks of his kingly parts.[2] It is hazardous to infer that he played the king in Peele's *Edward I* from the lines (761–2):

> Shake thy speres in honour of his name,
> Vnder whose roialtie thou wearst the same.

We may gather from *Richard III* and again from *Hamlet* that he was interested in the technique of his profession, and perhaps from the *Sonnets* that he found its practice irksome. He, too, drops out of the actor-lists after *Every Man in his Humour* (1598) and *Sejanus* (1603), and it may be that after a time his plays, together, perhaps, with the oversight of their production, were accepted as a sufficient return for his share in the company. If so, he presumably did not get any special payment for them, although at an earlier date he may, as Oldys apparently learnt, have received £5 for *Hamlet*. It seems clear that Sir Sidney Lee has much over-estimated his theatrical income at more than £700. The evidence is complicated, but it is hardly possible that, as sharer and housekeeper, he can ever have earned more, even in the best years, than about £200. This of course would make him quite well-to-do by Jacobean standards.

We may think, then, of Shakespeare, early in the reign of James, as still making his head-quarters in London, but more free than of old for occasional sojourn in Stratford. Here he brought small actions in the Court of Record against one Phillip Rogers for the value of malt supplied and for a money debt in 1604, and against one John Addenbroke and his surety Thomas Horneby for

[1] p. 247.   [2] p. 208.

a money debt in 1608-9. And here he added to his investments in 1605 by purchasing for £440 the lease of a parcel of local tithes which had once belonged to the Stratford college. Malone thought he had evidence, not now forthcoming, that Shakespeare's London abode was still on the Southwark Bankside in 1608. Professor Wallace, however, discovered a lawsuit which showed that in 1604 he was lodging in the house of Christopher Mountjoy, a Huguenot tire-maker, in Cripplegate ward, and became involved in the family affairs of his landlord.[1] Some information obtained by Aubrey from the actor William Beeston, a son of Christopher, indicates that at some time he also lived in Shoreditch.[2] Aubrey tells also of annual visits to Stratford, of the humour of Dogberry picked up from a constable at Grendon, which was in fact out of the road, and of lodging in Oxford at the house of John Davenant, a vintner who kept a tavern afterwards known as the Crown. This must have been much later than the days of Dogberry. Davenant is not known to have had the tavern before 1613, although he may have had it in 1601. A tavern was not normally a place for the reception of travellers, and if Shakespeare did not really lodge at the adjoining Cross inn, which seems also to have been at one time in Davenant's hands, he must have been a private guest. The house still stands in the Cornmarket St., and we may, if we like, fancy Shakespeare occupying a room in which some interesting mural decoration of the sixteenth century has recently been uncovered. A gloss on the story, over which Aubrey hesitated, made Shakespeare the father of Sir William Davenant, born in 1606. It has not much authority and may owe something to Davenant's willingness to be suspected of more than a literary affiliation to the greater poet.

[1] pp. 149-54.   [2] p. 229.

The temper of *Hamlet* and *Troilus and Cressida* leads up, naturally enough, to the long unrolling of the Jacobean tragedies. These are not without evidence of mental strain and sometimes exhaustion. Shakespeare's spirit must have been nearly submerged in *Lear*, and although the wave passed, and he rose to his height of poetic expression in *Antony and Cleopatra*, he seems to have gone under in the unfinished *Timon of Athens*. The chronology of the plays becomes difficult at this point, and it is therefore frankly a conjecture that an attempt at *Timon of Athens* early in 1608 was followed by a serious illness, which may have been a nervous breakdown, and on the other hand may have been merely the plague. Later in the year Shakespeare came to his part of *Pericles* with a new outlook. In any case the transition from the tragedies to the romances is not an evolution but a revolution. There has been some mental process such as the psychology of religion would call a conversion. Obviously the philosophy of the tragedies is not a Christian philosophy, and in a sense that of the romances is. Richard Davies, a Gloucestershire clergyman of the end of the seventeenth century, stated that Shakespeare 'dyed a papist'.[1] He may or may not have been misinformed, but Sir Sidney Lee was hasty in assuming that we can, without more ado, 'dismiss as idle gossip the irresponsible report', and that it 'admits of no question' that Shakespeare 'was to the last a conforming member of the Church of England'. How did Sir Sidney know that Davies was irresponsible or a gossip? What little is recorded of him suggests that he was a man of scholarly attainments. It was by no means unusual for a seventeenth-century Catholic to be buried in his parish church.

It was perhaps about this time that Shakespeare's thoughts began to turn to New Place as a permanent

[1] p. 232.

habitation. If so, he deferred his purpose for a time, since his cousin Thomas Greene, the town clerk of Stratford, who appears to have been living in the house, noted in connexion with a transaction of 1609 that he had found he could stay there for another year. We may put therefore in 1610 the beginning of Shakespeare's final years at his native Stratford, spent, according to Rowe, 'as all men of good sense will wish theirs may be, in ease, retirement and the conversation of his friends'. Even at Stratford time had brought some changes. His elder daughter Susanna had married John Hall, a local physician of some note, in 1607, and had herself a daughter Elizabeth. His younger daughter Judith was still unmarried. His mother had died in 1608. His brother Edmund had, like himself, become an actor in London, although not, so far as we know, in his company, and his death in 1607 had followed that of a base-born son. Two other brothers, Gilbert and Richard, were still alive in Stratford, and died, apparently unmarried, in 1612 and 1613 respectively. His sister Joan had married William Hart, a hatter, and had three sons. Shakespeare's breach with London was not a complete one. He still wrote his plays for the King's men. But the intervals between them became longer, and in 1613, when the wedding of the Princess Elizabeth meant a period of theatrical pressure, he seems to have fallen back upon some kind of collaboration with the younger pen of John Fletcher. After 1613 he wrote no more. Occasionally he visited his old haunts. He was in London on 11 May 1612, when he made a deposition in Christopher Mountjoy's lawsuit, and showed a rather imperfect memory of events which had taken place eight years before. He was there in March 1613, when he designed an *impresa* for Burbadge to paint, and for Francis Earl of Rutland to parade at the annual Accession tilt.

He was there on 17 November 1614, when Thomas Greene discussed Stratford business with him and his son-in-law Hall. And it was in London property that during 1613 he made his last investment, buying for £140 and immediately mortgaging for nearly half its value an old building in the Blackfriars, which had once been a gate-house to a lodging for the Prior of the Dominicans, and at later dates a head-quarters of Catholic intrigue.

But our imaginative setting for the last days of Shakespeare must be the open fields and cool water-meadows and woodland of Stratford, and the great garden of New Place, where the mulberries he had planted were yet young. He seems to have taken no part in municipal affairs. He made his contribution to the expenses of promoting a Bill for the better repair of highways, and gave hospitality to a preacher of one of the annual sermons founded by pious legacies. Tradition and his will show that he lived upon friendly terms, not only with the leading citizens, but with well-to-do gentry of the town and its neighbourhood. Prominent among these were a family of Combes. Thomas Combe, whose grandfather had been a spoiler of the monasteries and his father apparently a Catholic, occupied the mansion of the dissolved college. He had died in 1609 and left two young sons. Upon his brother John, who was a rich money-lender, Shakespeare is credited by repute with exercising his epigrammatic wit. If so, a legacy which he received under John's will of 1613 shows that kindly relations endured. In 1614 young William Combe, who was a freeholder at Welcombe on the Stratford manor, was drawn into a scheme for enclosing some of the open fields, and a controversy arose, which disturbed the peace of Stratford for some years. Shakespeare had himself no rights of common in the area affected, but both he as a tithe-holder and the Corporation, who owned the reversion of the tithes, might suffer loss, if the enclosure led to the conversion of arable land into pasture. So far as Shakespeare was concerned, an agreement for indemnification was made, and he seems to have taken no further interest in the matter. If he had troubles in these years, they were concerned with his daughters. Susanna Hall in 1613 had to bring an action in the ecclesiastical court for the protection of her character from a slander of incontinence. Judith, on 10 February 1616, married Thomas Quiney, and the ceremony, which took place in a season prohibited by canon law, led to the subsequent excommunication of the pair. By the time the sentence was pronounced, the poet may have been already dead. John Ward tells that 'Shakespear, Drayton, and Ben Jhonson, had a merry meeting, and itt seems drank too hard, for Shakespear died of a feavour there contracted'[1]. There is no reason to reject this report. Ward had been a student of medicine, and became vicar of Stratford in 1662. Drayton is known to have been in the habit of spending his vacations at 'the Muses' quiet port' of Clifford Chambers near Stratford, where dwelt Sir Henry Rainsford, whose wife Anne had been Drayton's Idea. Attempts have been made to determine the precise nature of Shakespeare's medical history, mainly upon the basis of tremors in the signatures to his will. But the diagnoses of doctors are even less reliable when the patient is not before them than when he is. The will itself was probably drafted in January 1616, but interlineated and partly rewritten later, and finally signed, without the formality of a fair copy, on 25 March.[2] There are small bequests to the poor, to various Stratfordians, and to Shakespeare's 'fellows' Burbadge, Heminges, and Condell, who are to buy rings. Thomas Combe, the brother of William, is to

[1] p. 228.   [2] pp. 162-70.

have Shakespeare's sword. The widow, amply provided for by legal dower on the Stratford property, although that on the Blackfriars house had been barred, gets the second best bed by an interlineation. Joan Hart is to occupy her present house, which was one of those in Henley St., for life, and to have £20 and the poet's wearing apparel. Each of her three sons gets £5. Subject to certain contingencies, Judith Quiney is to have a marriage portion of £150, and another £150 later. She is also to have a silver and gilt bowl. The rest of the plate is for Elizabeth Hall; the other chattels and the leases for her parents. The real property in Stratford and London is entailed successively upon Susanna and her heirs male, Elizabeth and her heirs male, Judith and her heirs male, with remainder to the poet's right heirs.

Death took place on April 23. The little that was mortal of Shakespeare lies under the chancel of Stratford church. A doggerel curse on the stone above, locally believed to be from his own pen, has fortunately prevented exhumation. From the chancel wall a bust by Gheerart Janssen watches quietly. Above is the coat of arms; below a laudatory inscription. The face is full and heavy, with a dome-like head; the modelling may have been from a mask. The present colouring dates from the middle of the nineteenth century, and as for some time before that the bust was whitewashed, it cannot be relied upon. The engraving by Martin Droeshout in the First Folio gives no more attractive presentment, and none of the innumerable portraits which pass as Shakespeare's carry any guarantee of authenticity. Aubrey asserts that the poet was 'a handsome well shap't man: very good company, and of a very readie and pleasant smooth witt'. There is no other reference to his personal appearance, but sufficient testimony to his manners. Rowe had gathered that he was held in esteem for his 'exceeding candor and good nature', but may be only echoing Ben Jonson, who wrote in verse of 'my gentle Shakespeare' and in prose described him as 'honest, and of an open, and free nature'. We cannot, indeed, ascribe to Shakespeare that rigid propriety of conduct, the absence of which in more modern poets it has too often been the duty of their family biographers to conceal. The indications of the *Sonnets* and perhaps *Willobie his Avisa*, John Manningham's contemporary talk of a more ephemeral intrigue, the gossip about Mistress Davenant, do not leave an impression of complete fidelity to Anne Hathaway. But as to the normal sobriety of his life we may be content to accept the report of William Beeston to Aubrey that 'he was not a company keeper' and that he 'wouldnt be debauched, & if invited to, writ, he was in paine'.[1] The hope, apparent in Shakespeare's will, of founding a family was not destined to fulfilment. Susanna Hall had no sons. Elizabeth Hall, who married successively Thomas Nash of Stratford and John, afterwards Sir John, Bernard of Abington in Northamptonshire, had no children. Judith Quiney had, but the last died in 1639. Shortly afterwards steps were taken to terminate the entail. Lady Bernard left the Henley St. houses to the Harts in 1670, and the last remnants of Shakespeare's property were sold by a distant kinsman as her residuary legatee after Sir John's death in 1674. There are no existing descendants of Shakespeare.

[1] p. 229.

III
THE PLAYS: PUBLICATION

THE regulation of the London book-trade had been settled before any play of Shakespeare could come in question, by an Order in the Star Chamber of 23 June 1586. This provided for limiting the number of printers and of their presses, and put the licensing of books in the hands of the Archbishop of Canterbury and Bishop of London. It was in fact delegated to correctors, most of whom were episcopal chaplains or prebendaries of St. Paul's. On the business side, the detailed administration was in the hands of the Company of Stationers, who in their turn were subject to the linked supervision of the Privy Council and the ecclesiastical Court of High Commission. All the London booksellers, some 250 in number with their journeymen, and the great majority of the twenty or so printers, many of whom exercised the double trade, were freemen of the Company. Elected officers, a Master, two Wardens, and a Court of Assistants, governed its affairs. Most of our knowledge of the system is due to the well-preserved records of the Company. The most important document is the Register, by the entry of his 'copy' in which a stationer might secure the sole right of selling a book, other than such as were held by the Company itself or by the crown printer, or by individuals, who were not always freemen of the Company, under privileges granted by letters patent. The privileges, however, did not affect plays; small affairs commercially, and generally handled by the less important stationers. The Company imposed severe penalties upon breaches of copyright. A great many plays were never entered in the Register at all, for reasons which remain obscure. In some cases a desire to save the sixpenny fee on entry may have operated; in others the manuscript may have been illegitimately obtained, although it is not clear how far, if at all, the Company concerned itself with such matters. An unentered book presumably carried no copyright. But transfers of books from one stationer to another were also registered, and it seems that such a transfer might secure copyright, even when there had been no original entry. Sometimes stationers went out of business without disposing of their copyrights, and in such cases the books became derelict, and available for reprinting by others. Whether copyright also lapsed, when a book had been entered, but never published, is uncertain. In theory, it must be supposed that the Company were expected not to enter a book without seeing the allowance of the licenser upon the manuscript or a print. Practice did not always follow theory, where insignificant or obviously safe publications were concerned. But in 1599 special instructions were given by the archbishop and bishop 'that noe playes be printed excepte they bee allowed by suche as haue aucthoritye'; and thereafter in making entries, the Company's clerk generally recited the name of the licenser by whom, in addition to a warden, the authority was given, or added a note that printing was not to take place until proper authority was obtained. Presumably such conditional entries gave provisional protection to the copyright. The entries suggest that about 1607 an arrangement was made by which the Master of the Revels normally acted as the official for licensing plays. It is possible that, if the manuscript produced already bore the Master's allowance for acting, no further reference to him was necessary. It must not be assumed that, because a play was not registered for copyright, it had not been licensed.

The publication of Shakespearean plays, in separate

THE PLAYS: PUBLICATION

issues known as the Quartos, was first approached by a group of publishers, among whom shifting business relations seem to have existed, and some of whose proceedings, from a literary and probably also from a commercial point of view, were discreditable. John Danter, a printer, registered and published *Titus Andronicus* in 1594, and entrusted it for sale to Edward White and Thomas Millington. In the same year Millington registered and published *2 Henry VI*, describing it as the first part of *The Contention of York and Lancaster*, and followed it in 1595, apparently on the strength of the same registration, with *3 Henry VI*, as *The True Tragedy of Richard Duke of York*. In 1597 Danter published *Romeo and Juliet* without registration. In 1600 Millington, now conjoined with John Busby, published *Henry V*. This again was unregistered, but copyright was established by a transfer in the same year to Thomas Pavier. In 1602 Busby registered *Merry Wives of Windsor* and transferred it on the same day to Arthur Johnson, who at once published it. Finally, also in 1602, Millington transferred to Pavier, 'saluo iure cuiuscunque', not only *The Contention*, now described as the first and second parts of *Henry VI*, but also *Titus Andronicus*. This had been Danter's, but Danter, who had been more than once in trouble with the Company for infringing privileges, was now dead, and possibly Edward White, who had reissued the play in 1600, and Millington were able to claim it under the arrangement by which they sold it. The 'saluo iure cuiuscunque' must have been a reservation for the interest of White, who reissued it again in 1611. So much for this group. With the exception of *Titus Andronicus*, all their plays appeared in extremely bad texts, the nature of which will presently require examination. Meanwhile, other publishers had got to work with better texts. Cuthbert

Burby published *Love's Labour's Lost* in 1598 and *Romeo and Juliet* in 1599. This, which is described on its title-page as 'newly corrected, augmented, and amended', was evidently meant to replace Danter's text, and as *Love's Labour's Lost* bears a similar description, it is extremely likely that of this too there had been an earlier bad version. Danter, having failed to register, could be ignored; it is not so clear why Burby himself did not register either play. A more substantial contribution than Burby's was that of Andrew Wise, who duly registered and published *Richard II* (1597), *Richard III* (1597), and *1 Henry IV* (1598) by himself, and somewhat later *2 Henry IV* (1600) and *Much Ado About Nothing* (1600) in conjunction with William Aspley. He transferred the first three to Matthew Law in 1603, and is not heard of again. No doubt the other two remained with Aspley. *Midsummer-Night's Dream* was registered and published by Thomas Fisher in 1600. Of him, too, nothing is known after 1601. Probably the book became derelict. In 1598 James Roberts registered *Merchant of Venice*, subject to an unusually worded condition that he should first obtain licence from the Lord Chamberlain. No publication by him is known, but in 1600 he transferred the play to Thomas Heyes, for whom he then printed it. In 1602 he registered *Hamlet*. This was published in the next year by Nicholas Ling and John Trundell. The printer was not Roberts, but Valentine Simmes. The text was a bad one, much like those already noted. A good one, claiming on its title-page to be 'according to the true and perfect Coppie', was substituted in 1604. The publisher was again Ling, acting alone, and now Roberts was the printer. In 1607 Ling acquired Burby's copyrights of *Love's Labour's Lost* and *Romeo and Juliet*, and transferred them, together with *Hamlet*, to John Smethwick. An unregistered transfer of *Hamlet* from

THE PLAYS: PUBLICATION

Roberts to Ling must be assumed. In 1603 Roberts registered *Troilus and Cressida*, after the exceptional procedure of a 'full court' held by the Company, and with the proviso that 'sufficient aucthority' must be obtained. He never published the play.

By the end of Elizabeth's reign, therefore, fifteen Shakespearean texts had appeared. Of these six, and probably seven (*2, 3 Henry VI, Romeo and Juliet, Henry V, Merry Wives of Windsor, Hamlet, Love's Labour's Lost?*), were originally in bad texts, although of two and probably three (*Romeo and Juliet, Hamlet, Love's Labour's Lost?*) good ones were substituted. Of eight (*Titus Andronicus, Richard II, Richard III, 1, 2 Henry IV, Much Ado About Nothing, Midsummer-Night's Dream, Merchant of Venice*) the original texts were good. A note in the Register suggests that at one time the publication of *As You Like It*, as well as *Troilus and Cressida*, had been contemplated. But these, with *Comedy of Errors, Taming of the Shrew, Two Gentlemen of Verona, John, Julius Caesar, Twelfth Night,* and *All's Well That Ends Well*, probably all of Elizabethan date, remained unprinted. There was little more fresh publication before the time of the First Folio. In 1607 Busby and Nathaniel Butter registered *King Lear* and Butter published it in 1608. Edward Blount registered both *Anthony and Cleopatra* and *Pericles* in 1608. He published neither of them. But *Pericles* was published in the next year by Henry Gosson, to whom no transfer is recorded. *King Lear* and *Pericles* cannot be called good texts, although they are not of the same type as the bad texts of the early publishers. In 1609 Richard Bonian and Henry Walley registered and published a good text of *Troilus and Cressida*, with the unusual feature, in Shakespearean quartos, of an epistle, in which they complained of the unwillingness of 'the grand possessors' to allow publication. Either the earlier registration by Roberts had been overlooked, or his copyright had lapsed through failure to publish before he left business about 1608. Finally, on the eve of the First Folio, Thomas Walkley registered *Othello* in 1621 and published it in 1622.

Meanwhile several of the plays had been reprinted from time to time, notably those in the hands of Law (*Richard II, Richard III, 1 Henry IV*) and Smethwick (*Romeo and Juliet, Hamlet*). A scene omitted from the Elizabethan editions of *Richard II* was added in 1608. With this exception, there is not much to be said about the reprints. The distribution of them may be a measure either of the popularity of the plays or of the energy of the copyright-owners. There was, however, one reprinting enterprise of a special nature. Examples have been preserved together, in half a dozen different collections, of ten plays which have certain features in common. They are rather taller than most Quartos, and their imprints are exceptionally short. They are as follows:

2, 3 Henry VI (*The Whole Contention betweene . . . Lancaster and Yorke*). Printed at London, for T. P.
Pericles. Printed for T. P. 1619.
A Yorkshire Tragedy. Printed for T. P. 1619.
Merry Wives of Windsor. Printed for Arthur Johnson, 1619.
Merchant of Venice. Printed by J. Roberts, 1600.
King Lear. Printed for Nathaniel Butter 1608.
Henry V. Printed for T. P. 1608.
1 Sir John Oldcastle. London printed for T. P. 1600.
Midsummer-Night's Dream. Printed by Iames Roberts, 1600.

The Contention and *Pericles* have continuous signatures and were clearly designed for issue together. It will be observed that two of the plays, *Sir John Oldcastle* and *A Yorkshire Tragedy*, are not Shakespeare's. It has been demonstrated that, in spite of the apparent variation in the dates, all the ten reprints really appeared in 1619. They came from the press of William and Isaac Jaggard, no doubt by arrangement with the publisher Thomas Pavier, to whom several of the copyrights had passed. The shortened imprints suggest that the title-pages were originally meant for half-titles in a comprehensive volume, which would naturally begin with a general and more explicit title-page. On the other hand, the absence of continuous signatures after *Pericles* and the obsolete dates '1600' and '1608' seem to bear witness to departure from the original purpose. And the most plausible explanation of this may, perhaps, be found in an intervention by the King's men. It was nothing to Pavier and Jaggard that they were reprinting bad texts and ascribing to Shakespeare plays that were not his. Perhaps Shakespeare's fellows viewed such proceedings with less equanimity. At any rate, on 3 May 1619, a letter was addressed by the Lord Chamberlain to the Stationers' Company directing that none of the King's men's plays should be printed 'without some of their consents'.

But, whatever the events of 1619, they can have left no enduring malice between the King's men and the Jaggards, since it was again from their press that the collection of Shakespeare's plays known as the First Folio came, with the active co-operation of Heminges and Condell, in 1623. This contained eighteen of the nineteen plays already published in Quarto. *Pericles* was omitted. Good texts of *2, 3 Henry VI*, *Henry V*, and *Merry Wives of Windsor* appeared for the first time. Eighteen plays were added, and of these sixteen were covered by the following registration entry:

8° Nouembris 1623.

Mr Blounte Isaak Jaggard. Entred for their Copie vnder the hands of Mr Doctor Worrall and Mr Cole, warden, Mr William

Shakspeers Comedyes Histories, and Tragedyes soe manie of the said Copies as are not formerly entred to other men. vizt. Comedyes. The Tempest. The two gentlemen of Verona. Measure for Measure. The Comedy of Errors. As you Like it. All's well that ends well. Twelft night. The winters tale. Histories. The thirde parte of Henry the sixt. Henry the eight. Coriolanus. Timon of Athens. Julius Caesar. Tragedies. Mackbeth. Anthonie and Cleopatra. Cymbeline.

The play here described as 'The thirde part of Henry the sixt' is clearly *1 Henry VI*. The *Taming of the Shrew* and *King John* must have been allowed to pass as reprints of older plays on which they were founded. The title-page of the Folio runs:

M^r. William Shakespeares Comedies, Histories, & Tragedies Published according to the True Originall Copies. [*Portrait, signed* Martin Droeshout sculpsit London] London. Printed by Isaac Iaggard, and Ed. Blount. 1623.

There is a head-title:

The Workes of William Shakespeare, containing all his Comedies, Histories, and Tragedies: Truely set forth, according to their first Originall.

The Second Folio was printed in 1632, and the Third Folio in 1663, and to a second issue of 1664 were appended reprints of *Pericles* and of the 'apocryphal' *London Prodigal, Thomas Lord Cromwell, 1 Sir John Oldcastle, Puritan, Yorkshire Tragedy*, and *Locrine*. The Fourth Folio was printed in 1685. These later Folios and the post-1623 Quartos are of little value for textual criticism.

Upon the nature of the copy which reached the publishers, first for the Quartos and afterwards for the First Folio, the amount of authority to be attached to the traditional texts, as representative of what Shakespeare actually wrote, must in the last resort depend. The claim of the First Folio, on its title-page and in its head-title, that its

THE PLAYS: PUBLICATION 75

plays are derived from the author's 'originals', receives some expansion in an epistle to the readers, where Heminges and Condell profess—

so tő haue publish'd them, as where (before) you were abus'd with diuerse stolne, and surreptitious copies, maimed, and deformed by the frauds and stealthes of iniurious impostors, that expos'd them: euen those, are now offer'd to your view cur'd, and perfect of their limbes; and all the rest, absolute in their numbers, as he conceiued them.

An epistle, like a title-page, is an advertisement, and need not be read literally. But while a desire to exalt the merit of the Folio is apparent, it would be unreasonable to ignore altogether the stress laid upon the fidelity of the texts to the original intentions of the author. The statement of Heminges and Condell has been sometimes pressed too far and sometimes unduly disregarded. It has been interpreted as meaning that all the Quarto texts were surreptitiously obtained against the will of the company; and, on the other hand, it has been asserted that even the Folio texts were based, not upon the author's 'originals', but upon transcripts in the private possession of actors or 'fair copies' presented to friends and patrons. The best modern scholarship, however, wisely refrains from any such sweeping generalizations, and attempts to consider the origin of the printers' copy for each play as a separate problem, in the light of such literary, scenic, and bibliographical indications as it may yield. A summary treatment is alone feasible here.

An isolated group is formed by the corrupt editions of the early publishers, *2, 3 Henry VI* (the *Contention*), *Romeo and Juliet, Henry V, Hamlet, Merry Wives of Windsor*. These have been conveniently designated the 'Bad Quartos'. They differ in detail, and each presents features of special difficulty. But they have in common a measure of textual corruption, far beyond anything which a combination of bad transcription and bad printing could explain. Many passages are only intelligible in the light of the better texts which followed. There are constant omissions leaving *lacunae* in the sense, constant paraphrases, constant inversions of the order of sentences, and dislocations in the sequence of dialogue and episodes. The metre is bungled; verse lines are wrongly divided; prose is printed as verse and verse as prose. The diction betrays a substitution of synonyms or loose verbal equivalents or of variant inflections for the wording intended by the author. The total effect is one of perversion and vulgarization. It cannot be doubted that these are primarily the versions which Heminges and Condell stigmatized as 'surreptitious'. Certain features of some or all of the bad texts suggest that the copy for them was obtained, not by transcription from originals, but from stage performances by some process of reporting. There are errors which may be due to mishearing, although these are not unlike some which are made by printers and transcribers. There are unmetrical ejaculations and connective words, such as actors introduce to accompany their gestures and demonstrate their indifference to the blank verse. There are bits of gag. The confusion tends to be greatest in bustling episodes or in the rapid interchange of dialogue between a number of speakers. In *Romeo and Juliet* and *Hamlet* there are stage-directions which look like the attempts of a spectator to describe the action seen on the stage. In *Hamlet*, conversely, bits of action seem to have been translated into dialogue. One naturally asks what kind of reporter can have been at work. A note-taker in the audience would almost inevitably have attracted attention. Moreover, there is one singular feature, apparent in all the texts except *Henry V*, which by itself seems to exclude such a

THE PLAYS: PUBLICATION 77

note-taker. The dislocation of matter extends to the incorporation in scenes of phrases which really belong to earlier scenes or even to later scenes. A long interval may separate these from their rightful positions. Such 'anticipations and recollections' imply a reporter who has throughout some knowledge of the play as a whole, and point to a process, not of direct note-taking, but of reproduction from memory, probably by an actor or a prompter. The possibilities of memorization as a method of textual transmission have been shown to be fully equal to the production of such results as the bad Quartos exhibit. An alternative theory to that of memorization is the use of shorthand. But no system of shorthand, adequate for the purpose, is known to have existed before about 1602, which is too late for most of the 'Bad Quartos'. Nor would shorthand account for the dislocations.

There are fourteen plays for which we have parallel Quarto and Folio texts. They include at least two, *Romeo and Juliet* and *Hamlet*, for which the Quartos had replaced reported ones. *Love's Labour's Lost* may be a third. All the fourteen Quartos may reasonably claim the epithet 'Good', in contradistinction to the six admittedly 'Bad' ones. They are not all of equal merit, and Heminges and Condell would probably have claimed that *Troilus and Cressida* and *King Lear*, if not also *Othello*, fell within the category of 'stolne and surreptitious' texts. There is no reason to suppose that the eleven others were not issued with the assent of the company. It is the existence of parallel texts in these fourteen cases which gives us our closest insight into the nature of the copy which reached the printers. Only a summary account of the conclusions to be drawn from a study of the differences between them can here be given. Of the fourteen Quartos, *King Lear* may rest upon a report, *Richard III* upon a theatrical transcript of a cut version, and *Troilus and Cressida* and *Othello* also upon transcripts, which may, however, have been made for private collectors, and not for stage purposes. *Othello*, but not *Troilus and Cressida*, again represents a cut version. *Love's Labour's Lost* and *Romeo and Juliet* may rest in the main on originals, but it is possible that the former and probable that the latter was in part set up on a corrected example of a bad Quarto, and if so, an element of transcription is involved. The text of *Romeo and Juliet* is not good enough to exclude the possibility of more extensive transcription. The other eight may all be from originals. *Titus Andronicus* is not very likely to have been in Shakespeare's hand throughout. The rest—*Richard II*, *1, 2 Henry IV*, *Midsummer-Night's Dream*, *Merchant of Venice*, *Much Ado About Nothing*, *Hamlet*—all might have been. It is hardly possible to say more than this in any case. The probability is highest for *Hamlet*, since the Quarto version shows no signs of adaptation for the stage, and it is therefore difficult to see why a transcript, at any rate for theatrical purposes, should ever have been made. Stage-directions of the type which suggest an author's hand might of course be preserved by a transcriber. So too, although with less justification, might duplications of matter, such as we find in *Love's Labour's Lost* and *Romeo and Juliet*, as well as in *Midsummer-Night's Dream*. Nor can one attach much importance to the presence of abnormal spellings, analogous to those found in three pages of a manuscript play called *Sir Thomas More* which was believed by many to have been written by Shakespeare. These, too, might survive a transcriber, since *ex hypothesi* they must have survived a compositor. Could we be sure that Shakespeare's hand is in *Sir Thomas More*, the recurrence of the spellings in some of the Quartos would be consistent with his hand being also in the copy for these.

It would not be proof, for we could not in any event take it for granted that he had a monopoly of such spellings. At the same time, we know that originals, as well as transcripts, were used for stage purposes; and there is no reason to assume that transcripts were made without need. *Hamlet* is apart, but although all the other six texts in question bear the evidence of intrusive actor-names or of cuts and other stage alterations, that their manuscripts had been used as prompt copies, there is nothing which could not be provided for on the originals, at the most with the help of an additional leaf for *Midsummer-Night's Dream* and an appended slip for *Merchant of Venice*. Transcripts, for anything that we can trace, would be quite superfluous.

From a comparison of the fourteen Good Quarto texts with their Folio counterparts two generalizations emerge. The first is that, in spite of the apparent wholesale repudiation of the Quartos by Heminges and Condell, nearly all the Folio texts were in fact set up from examples of the Quartos. As a rule, the Quarto used was the latest that had been issued. The evidence for this consists partly in a general resemblance of orthographical and typographical detail, and partly in the repetition of obvious errors. It is at its strongest where the errors have been introduced in Quartos later than the first. It is less conclusive where there is only one Quarto, and a possibility remains that the common errors may derive from a common manuscript source. It has indeed been doubted whether Quartos were used for *2 Henry IV* and *Troilus and Cressida*, although in *Troilus and Cressida* the argument from general resemblance seems strong. The only certain exceptions are *Othello* and *Hamlet*. The Quarto (1622) of *Othello* indeed may hardly have been in existence when the copy for the Folio was prepared. Here the texts are independent, but clearly represent the same original, with cuts in the Quarto and accidental omissions in the Folio. In *Hamlet*, on the other hand, the Folio gives a cut version, in which theatrical alterations have been made. The second generalization is that most and probably all of the reprinted texts have undergone some modification beyond what can be attributed to the compositors. Even where there is no general textual divergence, there is theatrical alteration. Passages are cut or added; stage-directions and speech-prefixes are revised; actor-names, which must be due to the book-keeper, make their appearance. Invariably there seems to be some elimination, often very slight, of profanity, as a result of an Act of Parliament in 1606. The total amount of departure from the Quarto basis varies considerably. There is very little in *Romeo and Juliet*, *Love's Labour's Lost*, *Midsummer-Night's Dream*, *Merchant of Venice*, *Much Ado About Nothing*, and *1 Henry IV*, and in these it may be regarded as wholly theatrical. To *Titus Andronicus* a whole scene, possibly of late origin, has been added. In *Richard II* cuts have been restored and the scene which was recovered in 1608 is more regularly printed. But in this play textual differences also begin to occur. There is a reversion to some readings of the First Quarto departed from by its successors. The changes in *2 Henry IV* also include the restoration of cuts, but although numerous, they are again mainly theatrical. Textual divergence, however, is persistent in *Richard III*, *Troilus and Cressida*, and *King Lear*, in all of which we get independent versions of a common original, analogous to those of *Othello*. In these cases at least we must assume that the Quarto used as a basis was altered from a theatrical manuscript which was regarded as authoritative. It does not, of course, follow that the alteration was always complete and accurate.

There is less to be said about the eighteen plays for

THE PLAYS: PUBLICATION

which the only texts are in the Folio, and the four for which the only alternative is a bad Quarto. There is no obvious reason why most of them should not have been set up from originals. That of *1 Henry VI* is not likely to have been for the most part in Shakespeare's hand. Both this and *2, 3 Henry VI* may contain some scenes of comparatively late date. There are probably some theatrical interpolations in *As You Like It* and *Cymbeline*, and perhaps *Tempest*, and both interpolations and cuts in *Macbeth*. An original ending may have gone from *Taming of the Shrew*. On the other hand, it is improbable that *Timon of Athens*, which appears to be unfinished, was ever staged. The known history of *Winter's Tale* makes it likely that it was printed from a transcript, and this is confirmed by some typographical features. The badness of the text in *Measure for Measure* and *All's Well* suggests that here too transcripts may have intervened.

We come back to the claim of Heminges and Condell and the Folio publishers to have given the plays 'according to the True Originall Copies' and 'absolute in their numbers, as he conceiued them'. It is clear that this cannot be quite literally pressed. It may reasonably be admitted that genuine pains were taken, according to the standard of the times, to secure reliable texts. The bad Quartos were quite properly disregarded. The labour spent on glossing good Quartos from manuscripts must have been considerable. We could wish that First Quartos and not later ones had been chosen, but perhaps Heminges and Condell were not so familiar as we are with the progressive deterioration of successive reprints. Doubtless the use of transcripts was sometimes inevitable; we know that the original of *Winter's Tale* was lost. Perhaps we could hardly expect that interpolations should have been removed; still less that they should have been placed in square brackets. Some hint might have been given of the occasional presence of non-Shakespearean scenes. A fuller text of *Macbeth* would have been welcome; that of *Romeo and Juliet* could probably have been improved. Something must have gone wrong with the directions for the treatment of cuts, as a result of which *Richard II* and *King Lear* show *lacunae* in the Folio, which are not in the corresponding Quartos. The greatest lapse is of course the complete failure to make any use of the full Second Quarto of *Hamlet*.

IV
THE PLAYS: AUTHENTICITY AND CHRONOLOGY

THE canon of Shakespeare's plays rests primarily on the authority of title-pages. Thirty-six are included in the First Folio. Quartos, good and bad, of fifteen of these also bear his name; it is not on those of *Titus Andronicus*, *Romeo and Juliet*, or *Henry V*. Quartos also ascribe to him *Pericles* and a share in *Two Noble Kinsmen*, which are not in the Folio. The registration entries of *2 Henry IV* and *King Lear*, which name him, probably themselves rest on the title-pages. There is confirmation for some of the plays in contemporary references. The most important is the list given by Francis Meres in his *Palladis Tamia* of 1598. This, on the assumption that *Love Labours Won* is an alternative title for *Taming of the Shrew*, contains twelve plays, but not *Henry VI*, which must be early work.[1] John Weever in 1599 speaks of *Romeo and Juliet* and either *Richard II* or *Richard III* as Shakespeare's, Gabriel Harvey in or before 1601 of *Hamlet*, Ben Jonson in 1619 and later of *Julius Caesar* and *Winter's Tale*.[2] The Revels Accounts of 1604–5 assign to him *Measure for Measure*, *Comedy of Errors*, and *Merchant of Venice*, but leave the *Moor of Venice*, *Merry Wives of Windsor*, *Henry V*, and *Love's Labour's Lost* anonymous.[3] This evidence is of a kind which is ordinarily accepted as determining the authorship of early literature. It is better than anything which we have for many of Shakespeare's dramatic contemporaries. *The Spanish Tragedy*, for example, is only attributed to Kyd on the basis of a casual reference by Nashe, and of Marlowe's authorship of *Tamburlaine* there is no direct

---

[1] p. 191. [2] pp. 194, 195, 201, 205. [3] p. 178.

contemporary record at all. But of course title-pages are capable of rebuttal, on sufficient external or internal grounds shown. Publishers are not always well-informed or even honest. Shakespeare's name is also in the registration entry and on the title-page of *A Yorkshire Tragedy* and on those of *The London Prodigal* and Jaggard's reprint of *Sir John Oldcastle*, and the initials 'W. S.' are on those of *Locrine* (1595), *Thomas Lord Cromwell* (1602), and *The Puritan* (1607); and these six plays, with *Pericles*, were added as his to the Third Folio in 1664. All six can be safely rejected from the canon. But the reason for the appearance of the name may not be the same in all cases. It is conceivable that Shakespeare or another W. S. 'oversaw' the printing of the old court play *Locrine*. Three of the other plays belonged to his company, and the publishers may have been ignorant of their authorship. The same charitable supposition will not cover *The Puritan* or *Sir John Oldcastle*, a distinct play from *Henry IV*, which also sometimes went under that name. The 'W. S.' is similarly found on the Q2 of the *Troublesome Reign*, Shakespeare's source-play for *King John*. This never got into a Folio. Other misascriptions are due to Commonwealth and Restoration booksellers. The only bit of external evidence against the authority of the First Folio itself is the statement of Edward Ravenscroft in 1687 that Shakespeare only touched up *Titus Andronicus*.[1] But the inclusion of an individual play under the comprehensive title of that collection must not be pressed too far. Heminges and Condell and their publishers were not attempting a modern 'critical' edition, and no doubt their methods were imperfect. It is quite possible that they saw no harm in including without comment a play which Shakespeare had only revised, one or two for which he had a collaborator,

[1] p. 231.

and one to which he had contributed little, but which had long been linked to other 'parts' of an historical series. It follows, of course, that alien matter may be present in other plays than *Titus Andronicus*, *Taming of the Shrew*, *Henry VIII*, and *1 Henry VI*. Contrariwise the possibility that Shakespeare may have had a hand in some uncollected plays cannot be wholly disregarded. Nevertheless the Folio must be regarded as the chief authority for the main range of Shakespeare's dramatic responsibility, and it requires deference as coming from men who were in the best position to know the facts. A desire to do justice to a dead 'fellow' and some care taken in the work are apparent enough in the epistles to Pembroke and to 'the great variety of readers'. The corroborative testimony of Meres cannot be disposed of by the repeated assertion that his list was 'derived from the theatre'. We do not know whence he derived it. He was a literary clergyman, resident in London, and evidently interested in writers for the stage, about whom he tells us other things not recorded elsewhere. Many sources of information may have been open to him. His style tends to parallelism, and he balances six comedies of Shakespeare against six tragedies. He does not mention *Henry VI*. It would have upset the balance. But Meres did not complete his university career until 1593, and *Henry VI* may not have been played in London between his arrival and the compilation of his list.

In so far as the authority of the Folio is departed from, it must, except for the isolated case of *Titus Andronicus*, be upon internal and not external evidence. At present many students hold, and with varying degrees of stress on the different issues, that the Quarto and Folio texts have often been altered or abridged by other hands than Shakespeare's; that he revised his plays, with the result that variant texts, and even a single text, may contain fragments of different recensions; that he also revised the work both of predecessors and contemporaries, whose writing remains entangled with his in the texts. There are certain practices of Elizabethan dramaturgy which have helped to create a prepossession in favour of such theories. Collaboration and revision are both *verae causae*. Collaboration, rarely found in other forms of contemporary literature, was very common in drama. This can be established on records alone, without regard to the findings of conjecture. It begins with the courtly and legal amateurs of the 'sixties. *Gorboduc*, *Tancred and Gismund*, *Jocasta*, and later *Locrine* and *The Misfortunes of Arthur* had all from two to seven collaborators. It is traceable among the University wits. The *Looking Glass* bears the names of Greene and Lodge; *Dido* those of Marlowe and Nashe. Greene, in 1592, addresses a 'young Juvenal, that biting satirist, that lastly with me together writ a Comedy'. Probably we find the practice at its maximum in Henslowe's accounts for the Admiral's and Worcester's men during 1597–1604. Fees were paid for about 130 new plays, and of these well over half were written in collaboration by from two to as many as five hands. We may speculate as to the reasons for a method which cannot have made for good workmanship, and we hardly get beyond speculation. Many of the plays were ephemeral productions. Plays did not have long runs. One which did not draw was quickly discarded, and a new one called for, often at short notice. Even for the court, Munday had to bind himself to furnish a play within a fortnight. The playwrights themselves were needy, and presumably small but frequent returns suited their purses. We have little information as to the men, other than Shakespeare and Jonson, who wrote for the Chamberlain's company. Probably they were the same who wrote for Henslowe. There is no reason to suppose that, as a rule, a playwright, who was not himself an actor, was anything but a free lance. Jonson wrote two unaided plays for the Chamberlain's, but for his *Sejanus* of 1603 he had a collaborator, whose work, with a compliment, he replaced by his own, before it went to press.¹ There is no recorded parallel to this proceeding, which must be set down to Jonson's conscious pride of artistry. In the seventeenth century we get the familiar and enduring partnership of Beaumont and Fletcher, although certainly Fletcher and probably Beaumont also wrote independently. Much has been written as to the way in which labour was divided in joint plays. It is not necessary to assume that the same method was always followed. Presumably an outline was agreed upon and some sort of a *scenario* prepared. Thereafter the actual writing might be distributed according to the interweaving of a plot and sub-plot, of which one might be tragic and the other comic. Or each author might follow up particular characters, which would come to much the same thing. Or one author might start all the main themes, and the rest carry them forward on his lines. There are certainly cases of a rough-and-ready partition by acts. Daborne gave Tourneur an act of his *Arraignment of London* to write, and Dekker contributed the first act of *Keep the Widow Waking* and one speech in the last act. There is no evidence at all for anything of the nature of a line-by-line collaboration, which certainly would not have made for expedition.

Clearly there need be no reason for surprise if Shakespeare occasionally had a collaborator. The problem of revision is more complicated. Plays which had been laid aside were often revived. A stock favourite was called a

¹ 'This Booke, in all numbers, is not the same with that which was acted on the publike Stage, wherein a second Pen had good share: in place of which I have rather chosen, to put weaker (and no doubt lesse pleasing) of mine own, then to defraud so happy a *Genius* of his right by my lothed usurpation.'—Epistle to *Sejanus*.

'get-penny'. When the Chapel resumed their activities in 1600, it was complained that 'the vmbrae, or ghosts of some three or foure playes, departed a dozen yeeres since, haue bin seen walking on your stage heere'.[1] And revival was sometimes accompanied by revision. Even with a familiar play, it was a fairly obvious device to increase the attraction. Sometimes a forgotten play was passed off as new. It may be that higher entrance fees could be charged for a play called new. Revision does not seem to have been regarded as very exalted dramatic work. Dekker speaks of 'a Cobler of Poetrie called a play-patcher', and in Jonson's *Poetaster* Demetrius Fannius, who is probably Dekker himself, is 'a dresser of plaies about the towne, here'. It is difficult to estimate the extent of the practice.

There is little evidence, so far as the records go, for any widespread theatrical practice of what may be called stylistic revision, the systematic line-by-line correction or rewriting of old dialogue, either by the original author or by another. The nearest approach to the same sort of thing in a theatrical text is the rewriting of parts of *Sir Thomas More*. It probably came before production, if there was a production. When, therefore, one finds stylistic revision brought forward again and again, as a conjectural factor in the literary history of one after another in a series of plays, one is justified in expressing a profound scepticism as to whether the practice, if it existed at all, can have been anything like so universal as the theorists assume. All the probabilities are against it. The ordinary Elizabethan audience is not likely to have been very critical of style, and it is difficult to see how the process contemplated could have resulted in any increase of drawing power commensurate with the cost and trouble involved. Even if the rewriting could be done on the margins of an existing

[1] Jonson, *Cynthia's Revels*; Induction.

prompt-copy, which is hardly credible, the reviser would have to be paid and new parts made out. These any actors already familiar with the old version would learn with reluctance. Minor alterations or even the addition of scenes would not cause quite the same inconvenience, and no doubt some adaptation to changing conditions of cast, theatre, and audience may be taken for granted. There are, of course, texts which have not come down to us in their original form. Some are reported; some have been interpolated; some have been abridged. Abridgement, like interpolation, is a form of revision, and it may involve consequential adjustment of context. Again we must assume that it would not be lightly undertaken. The motives which prompted it are obscure. It has been held that plays were abridged for court performance. There is no obvious reason why this should have been so. Court entertainments often lasted for three hours, and a full-length play of 3,000 lines would not require more.[1] It is true that in Elizabethan, although not in Jacobean days, a mask often followed. For the matter of that, a jig often followed on the public stage. Some of the shorter plays may have originally been written to go with an afterpiece. It has also been held that abridgement was for provincial performance. But again, while we do not know much about provincial conditions, it is a mere assumption that a country audience would want a particularly short entertainment. There is plenty of leisure in the country. It is true that, if a travelling company was a small one, the cutting of superfluous parts and *spectacle* might incidentally lead to shortening. But such companies were often ten or more strong, and

---

[1] Cf. *Mid. N. Dr.* v. 1. 32.
what masques, what dances shall we have,
To wear away this long age of three hours
Between our after-supper and bedtime?

probably many London plays could be found to fit them without going to the trouble and expense of extensive adaptation. It is just possible that conditions of lighting tied the London public theatres themselves to shorter performances in the winter than in the summer, and that this may be one explanation of abridgement.

To return to the topic of stylistic revision. It has been argued that Shakespeare could and would revise for his company any play that came into his hands. This argument has been treated as axiomatic for the interpretation of internal evidence. He could and would have done so, therefore he did; and what, on that argument, he did is a proof that he could and would have done it. But the only fact behind the argument, apart from such interpretation, is the isolated statement of Ravenscroft about an exceptional play. One need not altogether reject that statement, but it is not much on which to establish a conception of Shakespeare's habitual method of work. 'His mind and hand went together; and what he thought, he uttered with easiness', say Heminges and Condell. 'He flowed with facility', says Ben Jonson. The last man, one would suppose, in the absence of rigid proof, to tie himself to the painful following up and meticulous correction of the thoughts and words of another. So far as facts go, it is the Admiral's and not the Chamberlain's company which we know to have had cobblers of poetry ready to hand, in Chettle and in Dekker, the 'dresser of plaies' chaffed by Jonson, who between them did most of the small amount of revision required. Few critics will think that Shakespeare went on dressing up alien plays well into his mid-career, even if they believe him to have had a fancy for rewriting his own work. It is, however, very commonly held that such was the occupation of his apprenticeship. Even this is hardly a certainty. Two things, besides Ravenscroft's statement, seem to have con-

AUTHENTICITY AND CHRONOLOGY

tributed to form the notion. One is the long-standing belief in the derivation of *2, 3 Henry VI* through a line-by-line revision of the *Contention*. That support must go, when it is realized that the *Contention* is a reported text, and could never have been written as it stands. The other is the reference to Shakespeare in Robert Greene's address of 1592 to his fellow dramatists.[1]

The phrase 'beautified with our feathers', helped by the parody of *3 Henry VI*, i. 4. 137, has been regarded as a charge of appropriating the plays of Greene and his fellows, and in particular the *Contention*, by rewriting them. With the fall of the *Contention*, this interpretation at once becomes less plausible. And a closer examination of the passage shows that there is really no charge of appropriation at all. It is an attack by a disgruntled poet on the players who have profited by him and now have no further use for his services, and one of whom thinks that he can do everything himself, and is taking the job of writing out of the mouths of better men. There is a charge of imitation at the end, no doubt, but imitation is not rewriting. The 'beautified with our feathers' cannot be dissociated from the 'garnisht in our colours' applied just before to the actors as such, of which it is a mere variation. It was Greene's prospect of further employment, not his property in what he had already written, that he bewailed.

Shakespeare did not as a rule invent his plots; that is to say, the narratives to which he gave dramatic form. This we know, because for many plays we have his direct sources, although for others we may suspect that we have only more remote sources which reached him in intermediate versions, perhaps themselves dramatic. The direct sources he handled very freely when they were romance, and rather less so when they were history. Often, especially

[1] p. 187.

in the histories, he adopted words and phrases from what lay before him. Shakespeare is not revising Holinshed and Plutarch, and he is not merely pruning and planing down *A Shrew*, *The Troublesome Reign*, and *King Leir*. He is taking a story, using so much of it as appeals to his sense of dramatic values, altering what does not, and giving it literary form through his command of language. The habit of stylistic revision, if it was his at all, must be established elsewhere, and on internal, not external, grounds. The observed use of sources does not reveal it. The task has been approached from two angles, that of style itself and that of bibliography. Many writers have found disparate styles in the plays of the canon. Conviction of these has led to the search for 'clues' to other dramatists, whose work it is historically possible that Shakespeare might have revised; and after canons of their plays have been satisfactorily framed, the conviction is confirmed. Here are styles consonant to those which are repudiated for Shakespeare. As a result the primary responsibility is transferred—as, for example, for *Richard III*, *Richard II*, *Henry V*, *Julius Caesar*, and *Comedy of Errors* to Marlowe, for *Romeo and Juliet* to Peele, for *Two Gentlemen of Verona* to Greene, for *Troilus and Cressida*, *All's Well that Ends Well*, and *Measure for Measure* to Chapman. There has been much collaboration between some of these and possibly with Kyd and others. At last a point is reached when it can be said of the plays as a whole, 'the great majority are simply not of Shakespeare's drafting'. Here, of course, common sense revolts. After all, we have read the plays for ourselves, and have learnt to recognize in them, through all their diversities, a continuous personality, of which style is only one aspect. A single mind and a single hand dominate them. They are the outcome of one man's critical reactions to life, which make the stuff of comedy, and of one man's emotional reactions to life, which make the stuff of tragedy. Something must be wrong with the methods which have led to such devastating conclusions.

Everything indeed is wrong with them. It would be both tedious and unprofitable to follow painstaking investigations in detail, when one's starting-point is a complete rejection of the methods by which they are governed. And it is perhaps superfluous to stress the remarkable diversity between the various reconstructions of students who work, broadly speaking, upon the same lines. The variant distributions of *Julius Caesar* among Marlowe, Shakespeare, Jonson, Beaumont, Chapman, and Drayton furnish a noteworthy example. No doubt a method may be sound, and may be more skilfully applied by one practitioner than by another. But the conflicts do not inspire any great confidence in the critical principles which underlie them. The fundamental error lies in a misconception of the limits within which the discrimination of styles, as applied to the particular subject-matter of the Elizabethan drama, must operate. The percipience of style is a very real quality. It has its origin in the same natural feeling for the value of words and the rise and fall of rhythm, which is the starting-point of literary expression itself; and it may be trained, half-unconsciously, through reading and reflection and comparison into a valuable instrument of criticism. A quasi-intuitive sense is developed. It becomes effective in the presence of a writer who has a characteristic style and has room and inclination to give that style free play. It enables one, for instance, to dismiss some of the apocryphal plays ascribed to Shakespeare without more ado. It helps at least to disentangle collaborators, if their styles are sufficiently distinct, and their separate contributions of sufficient length. It must make allowance, of course, for many things; for the gradual evolution of styles, for influences, for experiments, for variations of interest and temper, for the adaptation of manner to subject-matter. It will be at a loss when a writer, as sometimes happens with Shakespeare, is bored, or in haste, or merely careless, and fails to hold his style. Moreover dramatic writing, and Elizabethan dramatic writing in particular, contains many bits of undistinguished joiner's work which may help the action along, but are in themselves colourless. One man might have written them as well as another. The most percipient critic cannot reasonably claim to have acquired a faculty which is fine enough to identify commonplace passages or very short passages. And he will be wise if he refrains, so far as possible, from detecting the small touches of a reviser. Now and then a phrasing seems to stand out in startling distinctness from its context, like the 'poor worm' which 'casts copp'd hills towards heaven' in the normally unShakespearean part of *Pericles*.[1] But even in such cases attributions can rarely be made with conviction. It is said that the ultra-violet rays will reveal over-painting in pictures through different effects upon different pigments. The sense of style does not work like an ultra-violet ray. It must be added that the sense of style is itself ultimately dependent upon external evidence. There is no way of getting at the characteristics of an individual writer, except from work of which his authorship is acknowledged. And if the acquired sense is then used to discredit the canon wholesale, a vicious circle is set up, of which the inevitable result is chaos.

The history of Shakespeare's writing is that of the gradual development of a characteristic style or series of styles. In its matured flights it is often unmistakable. Its beginnings belong to a period in which the difficulties of style-discrimination are at their maximum. The dramatists

[1] *Per.* i. 1. 100.

of the 'eighties may reasonably be called a school. They have largely a common style and a common vocabulary, which owe much to Spenser, to the Elizabethan translators of the classics, to Seneca and his court imitators. Marlowe is the dominant figure, with Peele, Greene, Lodge, and Nashe as his satellites; Kyd stands a little apart. There is a mass of anonymous work. There were other prolific writers, such as Thomas Watson, of whose plays we know nothing. Probably we should be able to differentiate some of the personalities a little better, if we had reliable canons. Even now, Marlowe's is more distinct than the rest. But there are no such canons. Only from two to seven plays are ascribed to any one man, and of these many have been transmitted in such corrupt texts that they are valueless. The style of non-dramatic work may be compared; the translations of Marlowe, the pamphlets of Greene, the ceremonial poems of Peele. But these only give limited help in judging the handling of dialogued verse. It is illegitimate to expand the canons by adding first one anonymous play, and then on the basis of this another, and then again another. There is no certainty in this process, which mainly rests on parallels, and the chain becomes weaker at every link. This school was Shakespeare's early environment, and his first plays were inevitably in its manner. The influence of Marlowe is discernible until well on in his career. Young writers, even when they have done good work, remain subject to influences, especially if they are of receptive, as well as creative, temperaments. There is no reason why Shakespeare should have been an exception.

Cutting certainly was a theatrical practice, for authors themselves have told us so. That Shakespeare's plays were not immune is shown both by the condition of the bad Quartos and by some of the omissions in parallel-text plays, for which cuts are the most plausible explanation.[1] The latter are not extensive; they do not amount to the replacement of a three-hour play by a two-hour play. Two or three hundred lines go, to prevent normal limits from being exceeded, or merely to prevent particular scenes or speeches from dragging. Probably *Hamlet* was always too long for performance as a whole. Shakespeare may have been more intent upon his poetry, than upon getting it over the stage-rails. One hopes that he remained unperturbed when some of his best lines were sacrificed. Cutting may be suspected also in plays for which we have not parallel-texts. The very short *Macbeth* possibly represents a substantial abridgement. An argument for abridgement has been found in personages to whom reference is made, but who do not appear at all. A good example of a personage, whom we should naturally have looked to see but do not, is Petruchio's cousin Ferdinand in *Taming of the Shrew*.[2] Petruchio, when he gets home, sends for Ferdinand to make Katharina's acquaintance, and he never comes. Perhaps the audience were not exactly on the tip-toe of expectation for him, but it is a badly dropped thread, all the same. In the *Tempest*, the Duke of Milan's 'brave son' is said to have been seen in the wreck.[3] He does not appear with the other rescued travellers, and there is no lamentation for him. An introduction of Maudlin Lafeu would seem obvious in the last scene of *All's Well that Ends Well*, but she remains absent.[4] In these and in countless other cases, we have probably a deliberate dramatic device. Persons and incidents are alluded to, but kept out of the action. The effect is one of solidity, as if life were passing on all

---

[1] *Rich. III* (Q), *Tit. Andr.* (Q), *Rich. II* (F), *2 Hen. IV* (Q), *Ham.* (F), *Oth.* (Q), *K. Lear* (F).
[2] *Tam. of Shrew*, iv. 1. 154.
[3] *Temp.* i. 2. 438. [4] *All's Well*, v. 3.

AUTHENTICITY AND CHRONOLOGY

the time behind the stage. Characters, again, are sometimes named in initial stage-directions, but have no share in the dialogue. Violenta enters with Diana in a scene of *All's Well that Ends Well*, and is forgotten throughout.[1] Juliet is unexpectedly dumb on her first appearance in *Measure for Measure*.[2] We must of course allow for mutes, especially in court or processional scenes. But sometimes the silence is clearly unnatural. Leonato is accompanied by 'Innogen his wife' at the beginning of *Much Ado About Nothing*.[3] She recurs in one later scene, but has not a word throughout the play. A lady, whose daughter is successively betrothed, defamed, repudiated before the altar, taken for dead, and restored to life, ought not to be a mute. It is not motherly. Abridgement is a possible explanation. But did Shakespeare sometimes write down initial entries before he had thought out the dialogue, and omit through carelessness to correct them by eliminating characters for whom he had found nothing to say, and ought to have found something to say, if they were to be on the stage at all?

Internal evidence makes it necessary to accompany a general acceptance of the traditional Shakespearean canon with certain qualifications, which may be set out in summary form. Collaboration must be admitted in *Henry VIII* and probably in *Taming of the Shrew*, as well as in the uncanonical *Pericles* and *Two Noble Kinsmen*, and possibly in *Edward III*. Of replacement of the work of a collaborator, which was presumably suggested by Ben Jonson's treatment of *Sejanus*, there is no sign. Apart from the touching-up of *Titus Andronicus*, which rests primarily on external evidence, and the insertion of two late scenes into the

---
[1] *Ibid.* iii. 5.
[2] *Meas. for Meas.* i. 2. 120.
[3] *Much Ado*, i. 1. 1; ii. 1. 1. Some modern editions omit her.

heterogeneous structure of *1 Henry VI*, there is nothing substantial which points to the dressing-up of alien plays. Some afterthoughts written into *Love's Labour's Lost*, *Romeo and Juliet*, *Julius Caesar*, and *Troilus and Cressida*, are revealed by failures to delete the original wordings. Mislineations in *The Shrew* and *Timon of Athens* may indicate others. Such alterations are no proof of complete rewriting, and for this the evidence is of the scantiest. An exception may be made for *Midsummer-Night's Dream*, which looks as if it had been converted from a wedding entertainment into a play for the public stage, by some changes in the last act and the provision of an alternative ending. Some passages in *2, 3 Henry VI* may owe their origin to a revival. We know, again on external evidence, that a line not now found in *Julius Caesar* met with criticism from Jonson. It would be absurd to lay down categorically that there has been no touching-up anywhere else. But that the great majority of the plays are Shakespeare's from beginning to end, and that, broadly speaking, when he had once written them, he left them alone, there is little doubt. These are propositions which, so far, disintegrating criticism has entirely failed to shake.

That most of the texts have undergone some adaptation for theatrical purposes is obvious. But this does not involve any substantial rewriting. There has clearly been some shortening, and although the existence of alternative versions sometimes makes it possible to restore the omitted passages, this is not so for all the plays. Whether Shakespeare himself exercised any discretion as to the cuts we cannot tell; they are not all equally judicious. A few interpolations can also be traced; bits of *spectacle*, a growing feature of the seventeenth-century stage, in *As You Like It*, *Cymbeline*, *Tempest*, and notably *Macbeth*; bits of clowning in *Merchant of Venice*, *Hamlet*, *King Lear*, and possibly *Othello*.[1] It is not always certain that the songs used were Shakespeare's own. Traces of the censorship are not very numerous. The Chamberlain's and King's men were, of all companies, in the closest relation to the court through their patrons, and the least likely to run counter to authority, except by inadvertence. An episode capable of political misrepresentation was removed from *Richard II* before it was printed, and restored in Jacobean editions. Possibly two passages, at which Anne of Denmark might be likely to take offence, were similarly removed from *Hamlet*. These point to press censorship, rather than stage censorship. Indiscreet nomenclature has been reformed in *Henry IV* and *Merry Wives of Windsor*, and possibly in *Hamlet*. A jest on German and Spanish costume has disappeared from the Folio version of *Much Ado About Nothing*, and one on a Scottish lord from that of the *Merchant of Venice*. An intervention of the censor may also account for the absence of the 'four nations' scene, with its Captain Jamy, from the reported text of *Henry V*. We know that James resented the girding at Scotland in English plays. Conceivably the absence of Shallow's 'dozen white louses' from the reported *Merry Wives of Windsor* may be no mere accident. There seems to have been some pruning of social and political criticism in *King Lear*, which has differently affected the Quarto and the Folio; of pathological details, with a similar divergence, in *Troilus and Cressida*; and of an unpatriotic sentiment and some bits of indelicacy in *2 Henry IV*.

A recognition of the substantial homogeneity of most of the plays simplifies the approach to the problem of

---

[1] Cf., however, Gildon's tradition as to Shakespeare's responsibility for incongruous clowning in *Othello* (p. 235). Sheer gag, of which the bad Qq show evidence, would presumably not get into the prompt-book, unless it was exceptionally successful.

chronology, since it makes it reasonable to assume, in the absence of any special ground for suspecting an insertion, that datable allusions have not been added by a reviser, and that the mention of a play by name implies its existence much in the form in which it is preserved to us. It will again be well to attach primary weight to external evidence, and a convenient starting-point is provided by the list of plays in the *Palladis Tamia* of Francis Meres, which was presumably compiled before the registration of that book on 7 September 1598.[1] This at once enables us to segregate a considerable group of comparatively early works. There are six comedies, *Two Gentlemen of Verona, Comedy of Errors, Love's Labour's Lost,* 'Loue labours wonne', *Midsummer-Night's Dream, Merchant of Venice*; four histories, *Richard II, Richard III, Henry IV, King John*; and two tragedies, *Titus Andronicus* and *Romeo and Juliet.* Meres names them in the order here followed, but it is not necessary to suppose that he paid attention to their respective dates of production. On the other hand, the list is so long as to suggest that it includes all that were known to him, and that it was only by a happy accident that he was able, by treating the histories as tragedies, to balance six of these against six comedies in accordance with his artificial manner of writing. Meres took his M.A. degree at Cambridge in 1591 and by incorporation at Oxford on 10 July 1593. It was probably after that date that he came to London, where he was dwelling in Botolph Lane by 1597, and if so, *Henry VI* or any other play not on the stage between 1593 and 1598 may have been unknown to him. His mention of *Henry VI* leaves it uncertain whether he knew both parts, and the identity of *Love Labours Won* must for the present be left aside.

Terminal dates before which production must have

[1] p. 191.

AUTHENTICITY AND CHRONOLOGY

occurred can be established for a good many plays. The commonest sources are entries in the *Stationers' Register*, or the title-pages of printed editions. The former give precise dates, the latter years only, which are best taken as calendar years. Twice the Register specifically notices a court performance during the preceding Christmas. The lists of such performances for 1604–5 and 1611–12 give some help. So does the *Diary* of Philip Henslowe. A few performances at the Inns of Court or in public theatres are independently recorded in contemporary documents. And there are a few literary notices, some of which are not capable of very exact dating. Echoes cannot be relied on, but Jonson's quotation of *Julius Caesar* in *Every Man Out of his Humour*, 'Reason long since is fled to animals, you know', is more than an echo. Only one play carries its own evidence. This is *Henry V*, where a chorus indicates not only a terminal date, but also an initial date, after which the production can be placed. As a rule the initial dates are much less certain than the terminal ones. An account of the Globe fire shows that *Henry VIII* was then a new play. For the rest we can only rely upon the dates at which 'sources' became available, in most cases too remote to be helpful, and upon allusions in the plays themselves to datable historical events. These require handling with great caution. Few are so definite as to be primary evidence; others at the most come in as confirmatory, after a provisional date has been arrived at on safer grounds. We can be pretty sure that the references to Scottish kings of England in *Macbeth* are Jacobean, and if so, the reference to equivocators in the same play is likely to be to the equivocators of the Gunpowder Plot. We can be a little less sure that the bit about the currish wolf in *Merchant of Venice* reflects the Lopez conspiracy, but if so, a phrase about a coronation may echo that of Henri IV. Yet both equivocation and coronations were common phenomena, to which any dramatist might refer at any date. So too were the plague and tempests and even eclipses, although an allusion is fairly plausible in *Midsummer-Night's Dream* to the rather unusual bad weather of 1594–5, which impressed the chroniclers, and an allusion in *King Lear* to the double eclipse of sun and moon in 1605, which was heralded by the astrological prophets. But Shakespeare does not seem to have been greatly given to 'topical' allusions, and the hunt for them becomes dangerous, especially if it is inspired by a desire to link the plays with contemporary literary controversies in which he may have taken but little interest, or with incidents in the chequered careers of the Earls of Southampton and Essex, revealed to us by the ransacking of political archives, but of doubtful familiarity to the Elizabethan populace or its playwrights.

It is, however, possible, on external evidence alone, to draw up a trial-table of primary indications limiting initial and terminal dates for nearly but not quite all of the plays. They are not all equally convincing, but a good many others which are less so have been excluded. They are put in columnar form, the 'initial' indications on the left, the 'terminal' indications on the right. The order, for convenience of reference, is that of the final table.[1]

2 Henry VI.
>Registration (12 March 1594).
>Print (1594).

3 Henry VI.
>Parody by Greene[2] (ob. 3 September 1592).
>Print (1595).

---
[1] Cf. p. 116.
[2] Cf. i. 4. 137: 'O tiger's heart wrapp'd in a woman's hide.' See p. 187.

AUTHENTICITY AND CHRONOLOGY

1 Henry VI.

Production by Henslowe (3 March 1592).	Production by Henslowe (3 March 1592). Allusion by Nashe in *Pierce Penilesse* (8 August 1592).[1]

Richard III.

Registration (20 October 1597).
Print (1597).

Comedy of Errors.

Performance at Gray's Inn (28 December 1594).[2]

Titus Andronicus.

Production by Henslowe (24 January 1594).	Production by Henslowe (24 January 1594). Registration (6 February 1594). Print (1594).

Two Gentlemen of Verona.

Notice by Meres (7 September 1598).[3]

Love's Labour's Lost.

Allusion to Chapman's *Shadow of Night* (1594).[4]	Performance at court (Christmas 1597–8 at latest). Print (1598).

Romeo and Juliet.

Print (1597).

---

[1] p. 187. [2] p. 172. [3] p. 192.
[4] iv. 3. 346–7.
  Never durst poet touch a pen to write
  Until his ink were tempered with Love's sighs.
Cf. *Shadow of Night: Hymnus in Noctem*, ll. 376–7
  No pen can anything eternal write
  That is not steep'd in humour of the Night.

Richard II.

No parallels in 1st edition of Daniel's *Civil Wars* (1595).

Parallels in 2nd edition of Daniel's *Civil Wars* (1595)
Performance for Sir Edward Hoby (9 December 1595).[1]
Registration (29 August 1597).
Print (1597).[2]

Midsummer-Night's Dream.

Allusion to weather of 1594.[3]
Allusion to baptism of Henry of Scotland (30 August 1594).[4]

Notice by Meres (7 September 1598).[5]

King John.

Notice by Meres (7 September 1598).[6]

Merchant of Venice.

Allusion to death of Lopez (7 June 1594).[7]

Use of Gobbo as nickname for Sir Robert Cecil (27 October 1596).[8]
Registration (22 July 1598).

---

[1] p. 173.

[2] The abdication scene was cut and only added in the fourth Quarto (1608).

[3] ii. 1. 81–117. Bad weather began in March 1594, prevailed during the greater part of the year, and ushered in a long period of corn shortage.

[4] iii. 1. 33. A projected lion had been abandoned at the baptismal feast, *A True Reportarie* of which was registered 24 Oct. 1594.

[5] p. 192. If the play was written for a wedding the most likely possibilities are that of William Earl of Derby and Elizabeth Vere at Greenwich, 26 Jan. 1595, or that of Thomas Berkeley and Elizabeth Carey at Blackfriars, 19 Feb. 1596.   [6] p. 192.

[7] The Jew Roderigo Lopez was hanged for the attempted poisoning of Elizabeth and of Don Antonio of Portugal. Cf. iv. 1. 134.

[8] Francis Davison refers to an unnamed enemy of the Earl of Essex who can only be Robert Cecil: 'all the world shall never make me confess, but that bumbasted legs are a better fortification than bulwarks, and St. Gobbo a far greater and more omnipotent saint than either St. Philip or St. Diego.'

AUTHENTICITY AND CHRONOLOGY

1 Henry IV.

    Registration (25 February 1598).
    Print (1598).

2 Henry IV.

    Survival of name Oldcastle (abandoned by 25 February 1598).[1]

Much Ado About Nothing.

No notice by Meres (7 September 1598).	'Stay' in *Stationers' Register* (4 August 1600). Registration (23 August 1600). Print (1600).

Henry V.

Allusion to campaign of Essex in Ireland (begun 27 March 1599).[2] No notice by Meres (7 September 1598).	Allusion to campaign of Essex in Ireland (ended 28 September 1599).

---

[1] There is no doubt of the alteration. Cf. pp. 173–4. Cf. also Part I, i. 2. 47, and the Epilogue to Part II. Sir John Oldcastle had married an ancestress of the Lords Cobham. The alteration had clearly been made before the play was registered and almost equally clearly not before production, since 'Oldcastle' lingered in popular usage as the name of the character. Perhaps it was made when the play was reviewed by the Revels officers for court performance. The Lord Chamberlain's players must have played *Henry IV* and not the *Sir John Oldcastle* of the rival Admiral's men: which in 1599 has in its prologue:

    It is no pampered glutton we present,
    Nor aged Councellor to youthful sinne.

[2] v. Chor. 30. The Quarto of 1600, among other cuts, omits the choric matter—possibly because the unsuccessful return of Essex made the reference unsuitable.

Julius Caesar.

No notice by Meres (7 September 1598).	Performance seen by Thomas Platter [1] (21 September 1599.)
	Quotation in Jonson's *Every Man out of his Humour* (1599).[2]
	Echo in Weever's *Mirror of Martyrs* (1599).[3]

As You Like it.

No notice by Meres (7 September 1598).	'Stay' in *Stationers' Register* (4 August 1600).

Twelfth Night.

Use of Robert Jones's *First Book of Airs* (1600) for the song-scraps in II.iii.109–21.	Performance at Middle Temple (2 February 1602).[4]
No notice by Meres (7 September 1598).	

Hamlet.

Allusion to revival of boy actors (1599): II. ii. 352–79.	Notice by Gabriel Harvey (before 25 February 1601).[5]
No notice by Meres (7 September 1598).	Registration (26 July 1602). Print (1603).

Merry Wives of Windsor.

No notice by Meres (7 September 1598).	Registration (18 January 1602). Print (1602).

Troilus and Cressida.

Echo in prologue of Jonson's *Poetaster* (1601).[6]	Registration (7 February 1603).

[1] p. 173.
[2] iii. 2. 109:
    O judgement, thou art fled to brutish beasts
    And men have lost their reason;
in Jonson (iii. 4. 33): 'Reason long since is fled to animals, you know.'
[3] p. 195.   [4] p. 177.   [5] p. 194.
[6] Prol. 23. The Prologue to the *Poetaster* had entered 'armed'.

AUTHENTICITY AND CHRONOLOGY

No notice by Meres (7 September 1598).
[Meres names no later plays, but his list is getting too remote to be worth citation.]

Measure for Measure.

Performance at court (26 December 1604).

Othello.

Performance at court (1 November 1604).

King Lear.

Registration of source-play Leire (8 May 1605).
Allusions to eclipses (27 September (moon) and 2 October (sun) 1605).[1]

Performance at court (26 December 1606).
Registration (26 November 1607).
Print (1608).

Macbeth.

Allusion to equivocation of Gunpowder conspirators (Jan.–March 1606).[2]
Allusion to reign of James I (25 March 1603).[3]

Performance seen by Forman (20 April 1611).[4]

Antony and Cleopatra.

Registration (20 May 1608).

---

[1] i. 1. 112.   [2] ii. 3. 10.
[3] iv. 1. 121. The 'two-fold' balls must be the 'mounds' borne on the English and Scottish crowns, and 'the treble sceptres' the two used for investment in the English and the one in the Scottish coronation. James was 'touching' for the 'King's evil' (iv. 3. 141) in Nov. 1604.
[4] p. 180.

Pericles.

> Performance seen by Venetian ambassador (5 January 1606⟨⟩23 November 1608).
> Print of derivative novel by G. Wilkins (1608).
> Print (1609).

Cymbeline.

> Performance seen by Forman (21⟨⟩29 April 1611).[1]

Winter's Tale.

> Performance seen by Forman (15 May 1611).[2]
> Performance at court (5 November 1611).

Tempest.

> Performance at court (1 November 1611).

Henry VIII.

Performance, as 'new' play (29 June 1613).   Performance (29 June 1613).

Two Noble Kinsmen.

Use of dance from mask by Beaumont (20 February 1613).

The table is a mere scaffolding. Four plays, *Taming of the Shrew*, *All's Well That Ends Well*, *Coriolanus*, and *Timon of Athens*, do not appear in it at all; and for many others, especially in the Jacobean period, a considerable range of dating remains open. On the other hand, it provides confirmation of the *Palladis Tamia* list for the early

[1] p. 182.   [2] p. 184.

years, except as regards the *Two Gentlemen of Verona* and *King John*. It establishes fixed points for *1 Henry VI*, *Titus Andronicus*, *Henry V*, and *Henry VIII*; and fairly narrow limits for *Much Ado About Nothing*, *Julius Caesar*, *Merry Wives of Windsor*, *As You Like It*, *Twelfth Night*, and *Hamlet*, on the reasonable assumption that if these had existed when Meres wrote, he would have named them. It points to an early run of Yorkist histories and a later run of Lancastrian histories. And it at least suggests several other tentative groupings. There is a common lyrical quality in *Love's Labour's Lost*, *Romeo and Juliet*, *Midsummer-Night's Dream*, and *Richard II*, which are all in Meres's list. There is a common vein of realistic comedy in *Henry IV* and the *Merry Wives of Windsor*, which are further linked by the recurrence of identical characters. There is a common vein of courtly comedy in *As You Like It* and *Twelfth Night*. Both of these groups must come very near the end of the sixteenth century. *Julius Caesar*, *Hamlet*, and *Troilus and Cressida* again must all be late Elizabethan tragedies, and *Othello* seems to begin a series of Jacobean tragedies, to which *King Lear*, *Macbeth*, and *Antony and Cleopatra*, coming in no certain order, belong. Finally *Cymbeline*, *Winter's Tale*, and *Tempest*, which emerge in rapid succession at the tail-end of the list, have again a common quality of romantic tragi-comedy, which makes it probable that they were not far apart in origin. These are not all equally valid inferences, since some of them rest, not so much upon positive indications, as upon the absence of earlier indications. But if they are provisionally accepted and the plays studied in accordance with the time-order of the groups, it is possible to arrive at an outline conception of Shakespeare's development, as regards both dramatic temper and the use of language, which in its turn makes a starting-point for further progress. It is not necessary here to retrace in detail an argument which has been already worked out by many writers. Instead one may draw upon the admirable treatment of Professor Dowden. He distinguishes four stages in Shakespeare's career, which he calls respectively 'In the workshop', 'In the world', 'Out of the depths', and 'On the heights'. The first is the period of 'dramatic apprenticeship and experiment', the second that of the later historical plays and the mirthful and joyous comedies, the third that of grave or bitter comedies and of the great tragedies, the fourth that of 'the romantic plays, which are at once grave and glad, serene and beautiful poems'. He has a corresponding 'impression' of changes in diction.

In the earliest plays the language is sometimes as it were a dress put upon the thought—a dress ornamented with superfluous care; the idea is at times hardly sufficient to fill out the language in which it is put; in the middle plays (*Julius Caesar* serves as an example) there seems a perfect balance and equality between the thought and its expression. In the latest plays this balance is disturbed by the preponderance or excess of the ideas over the means of giving them utterance. The sentences are close-packed; 'there are rapid and abrupt turnings of thought, so quick that language can hardly follow fast enough; impatient activity of intellect and fancy, which, having once disclosed an idea, cannot wait to work it orderly out'; 'the language is sometimes alive with imagery'.[1]

Of course Professor Dowden has a great deal more to say about Shakespeare's mental and stylistic history than this; only so much is here given as can be justified from a

---

[1] Dowden, *Shakespeare Primer*, 37, 47. It is possible to feel that the balance of thought and expression is recovered in the magnificent phrasing of *Antony and Cleopatra*; and that in the romances too, the intricate weaving of clauses is a closely fitting vesture for the involutions and qualifications of the ideas.

grouping of the plays on external evidence alone. A full literary and psychological analysis can only follow and not precede the establishment of a chronology. And in the meantime we are bound to a circular process. A preliminary dating sets up impressions of temper and style, and the definition of these helps to elaborate the dating. This is inevitable, once we depart from the external evidence. The chronology can only become a complex hypothesis, pieced together from materials not in themselves conclusive, and depending for its acceptance on the success with which it combines convergent and reconciles conflicting probabilities. General impressions, such as Professor Dowden formulates, make it at once possible to give some expansion to the groups already realized. *Two Gentlemen of Verona* finds its natural affinities with the experimental plays, *King John* with the later histories, *All's Well That Ends Well* with *Measure for Measure*, *Coriolanus* and *Timon of Athens* with the Jacobean tragedies, *Pericles* with the romances. *Merchant of Venice* and *Much Ado About Nothing* approximate, perhaps rather less closely, to the joyous comedies.

Obviously the mere grouping of plays is only the first stage of the chronological problem. There remain the more difficult tasks of determining an order of succession within the groups and between the members of overlapping groups, and of fitting this order into the time allowed by the span of Shakespeare's dramatic career. Here it is legitimate to make some cautious use of minor topical allusions and echoes forwards and backwards, which were rejected as not sufficiently convincing to furnish primary evidence. The cumulative results can at the most only support conclusions of higher or lower degrees of probability. The main effort of recent scholarship has been to supplement external evidence by a closer analysis of style, and to establish chronological 'tests' analogous to those which have often been used as determinative of authorship. The outcome is not without value, although a doubt must be expressed at the outset whether it is ever possible to determine an order for work of more or less level date upon stylistic considerations alone. The style of every writer has its intelligible development, no doubt. But it is not always a matter of smooth progression. Subject-matter has its reaction upon style. During all the first half of Shakespeare's career, he moves more freely in comedy than in history. Moreover, allowance has to be made for the influence of moods and for deliberate experiment. The resultant leaps forward and set-backs become apparent when a chronological order is already known, but may be very misleading as material from which to reconstruct one. Certainly particular aspects of style can be singled out and studied in isolation, and by such a process the general impression of characteristic style and of its phases is naturally both strengthened and refined. There is the aspect of structure, for example, in the types of character employed and the choice of dramatic situations. One may note that in the earlier plays comic relief is often afforded by the use of a lout and that in the later plays a court fool takes his place; or again that a rather artificial balancing between pairs of young men or young women tends to disappear after the experimental stage. On the other hand, such features are not always purely stylistic; they depend in part on the nature of the story adapted for the plot, and probably in part also on the succession of actors available. Nor are they all significant of period. The favourite device of concealed identity runs through the plays from beginning to end. One may take, again, Shakespeare's imagery, and compare its range at different periods. No doubt similes and metaphors from country sights and sounds prevail in his earliest and perhaps his latest plays and those from urban life in his middle plays, although it must not be forgotten that the unconscious memory is a reservoir, giving up from its store things both new and old. There are aspects of diction, too, to be observed; an early habit of ringing the changes upon some particular word, a later habit of coining new words, and so forth. All such investigations make for a closer and more confident grouping of plays, but they do not really help us to get beyond the grouping.

A great deal of work has been done upon what are roughly called 'verse' or 'metrical' tests. Differences in the handling of blank verse afford units which readily lend themselves to statistical treatment. Variations in the length of lines, in the number of syllables carried by lines, in the value given to unstressed vowels, in the distribution of stresses and pauses, can all be enumerated and tabulated. The extent of departure from the blank verse form by the introduction of prose and rhyme can also be measured. These tests are by no means all of equal value, and much caution is required in drawing inferences from them. In the first place the variations occur discontinuously, and the law of averages must be respected. The greater the number of variations, and the greater the number of opportunities for variation, the more reliable an average figure, such as a percentage, is likely to be. In the present investigation, the measure of opportunities for variation is generally the number of lines, sometimes the number of speeches, taken into account. Percentages for total plays are therefore far more comparable than those for single acts; those for individual scenes or shorter passages have little meaning, because they do not leave room for the discontinuities to average out. Some passages in a play may show a continuous or nearly continuous series of overflows or double endings; in others there may be none over a considerable stretch. It is futile to point out that the former show an exceptionally high percentage of the variations, and to use this as an argument in favour of a diversity of authorship or a diversity of date.

A second caution is that variations which become part of the unconscious or subconscious instinct of a writer are more likely to be significant of a chronological development than those which involve deliberation. It has been assumed that the proportion of rhyme was a measure of earliness: *Midsummer Night's Dream* has been made the first of the comedies, so has *Love's Labour's Lost*. But no man can substitute rhyming for blank-verse dialogue without realizing what he is doing, and it is most reasonable to suppose that at some date Shakespeare decided to make a deliberate experiment in lyrical drama. A very natural stimulus would be afforded by his experience of lyrical work in the narrative poems. The actual percentage of rhyme in the plays affected by such an experiment is of no importance. There seems to have been a notion that rhyme was a characteristic of the pre-Shakespearean drama, which Shakespeare gradually discarded. It is true that mid-Elizabethan popular plays were written in various forms of doggerel. These, and not heroic couplets, were the 'iygging vaines of riming mother wits', which Marlowe repudiated. There is little use of the heroic metre in the plays of Shakespeare's immediate predecessors. Marlowe has only a few sporadic couplets, including some curious ones in which a line of blank verse interrupts the rhyme. Kyd's *Spanish Tragedy* has one continuous scene, and there are some passages in Greene's *James IV*, in Greene and Lodge's *Looking-Glass*, and in scenes of *1 Henry VI*, which may not be Shakespeare's. There is more in the anonymous *Selimus*, and by Peele, mainly in *Arraignment of*

Paris. But this is a court play for boys, and so, if it is of early date at all, is the anonymous *Maid's Metamorphosis*, which only uses heroics. Substantially, the medium of Shakespeare's models was blank verse. The rhyme of the lyric plays represents a fresh start and not a looking backwards. Conscious variation of metre is further illustrated by prologues and epilogues, by inserted plays and masks, and by the characteristic bombast of Pistol. These are meant to contrast with the ordinary dialogue, and should be left out of account in computing the variations of its blank verse.

Probably the variations that most easily become unconscious are those of pausation. But here a third caution must be observed. A test, to be reliable, must be uniformly applied throughout, and this is difficult, unless it is objective; rests, that is to say, upon units which can be identified and enumerated with certainty. But the overflow test is extremely subjective; much depends upon the personal equation of the enumerator. It may be thought that this does not much matter, so long as the enumerator is the same throughout, since only one personal equation can be in question. It is not really so. Nothing can be more difficult, as any one who has dealt with large batches of literary examination papers will know, than to maintain a continuous subjective standard through a long series of qualitative judgements. Even Rhadamanthus has his moods. And there is the effect of environment to be reckoned with. The same man may well be impressed by an overflow in a play comparatively free from them, which he would certainly pass over where they come more thickly.

In view of all the uncertainties attaching to the metrical tests, it would be unwise to conclude that any one of them or any combination of them can be taken as authoritative in determining the succession of plays which come near to each other in date; and they are best used as controls for the indications of external evidence. The following table attempts to bring together the results of such external evidence as can be gathered concerning the separate plays and to fit them into the facts of Shakespeare's dramatic career as given in chapter ii. There is much of conjecture, even as regards the order, and still more as regards the ascriptions to particular years. These are partly arranged to provide a fairly even flow of production when plague and other inhibitions did not interrupt it. It is on the whole more practicable to take theatrical seasons, roughly from early autumn to the following summer, rather than calendar years, as a basis. Some slackening is assumed towards the end of Shakespeare's career, and Ward's statement that he supplied his company with two plays a year is not taken literally.[1]

1590–1.
2 Henry VI.
3 Henry VI.

1591–2.
1 Henry VI.

1592–3.
Richard III.
Comedy of Errors.

1593–4.
Titus Andronicus.
Taming of the Shrew.

1594–5.
Two Gentlemen of Verona
Love's Labour's Lost.
Romeo and Juliet.

[1] p. 227.

1595–6.
Richard II.
Midsummer-Night's Dream.

1596–7.
King John.
Merchant of Venice.

1597–8.
1 Henry IV.
2 Henry IV.

1598–9.
Much Ado About Nothing
Henry V.

1599–1600.
Julius Caesar.
As You Like It.
Twelfth Night.

1600–1.
Hamlet.
Merry Wives of Windsor.

1601–2.
Troilus and Cressida.

1602–3.
All's Well That Ends Well.

1603–4.
———

1604–5.
Measure for Measure.
Othello.

1605–6.
King Lear.
Macbeth.

1606–7.
Antony and Cleopatra.
1607–8.
Coriolanus.
Timon of Athens.
1608–9.
Pericles.
1609–10.
Cymbeline.
1610–11.
Winter's Tale.
1611–12.
Tempest.
1612–13.
Henry VIII.
Two Noble Kinsmen.

Something may be added about the main points of difficulty. The first is as to the position of *Taming of the Shrew*. It has often been put nearer to 1598 than to 1594, because of the resemblance of its provincial environment to that of *2 Henry IV*. The neighbourhood of Stratford must, however, always have been within the scope of Shakespeare's memory. The problem is complicated by that of identifying the *Love Labours Won* of Meres's list. It is most natural to take this as an alternative title for some extant play. Such alternative titles, which may sometimes be no more than unofficial descriptions, are not uncommon, although the only ones which have got into the prints of the plays are *The Contention of York and Lancaster* for *2, 3 Henry VI* and *What You Will* for *Twelfth Night*. But elsewhere we get, certainly or probably, *Robin Goodfellow*

AUTHENTICITY AND CHRONOLOGY

for *Midsummer-Night's Dream*, *Oldcastle*, *Falstaff* and *Hotspur* for *Henry IV*, *Benedicte and Betteris* for *Much Ado About Nothing*, *Malvolio* for *Twelfth Night*, *All is True* for *Henry VIII*. Claims have been made for the equation of *Love Labours Won* with *Love's Labour's Lost*, *Midsummer-Night's Dream*, *Twelfth Night*, *Much Ado About Nothing*, *All's Well That Ends Well*, *Tempest*, and *Taming of the Shrew* itself. The two first may be at once dismissed; they assume that Meres meant to attach a second title to the entries which follow and precede that of *Love Labours Won*, and this his wording makes impossible. There is little to go upon, except the implications of the title itself, and the possibility of finding a play of early date not otherwise named by Meres. The titles of Shakespeare's comedies have rarely any significance; *As You Like It* and *What You Will* are floutingly vague. Almost any love comedy might bear the title in question; it is least appropriate to *Much Ado About Nothing*, which is, however, on the border of Meres's range, and might fall within it. The wit-combats between Benedick and Beatrice, resembling those between Berowne and Rosaline in *Love's Labour's Lost*, have been called in aid, and the references which the two plays have in common to Cupid as the god of love and to Hercules, who no doubt performed labours. Similarly, it is pointed out that the resemblance of twins is a motive common to *Twelfth Night* and the *Comedy of Errors*. But is it not more likely that an interval would have been allowed to expire before such situations were repeated? The 'labours' found in *The Tempest* are Ferdinand's athletic wrestlings with the logs. There is really no reason for assuming an early version of *Twelfth Night* or of *The Tempest*. It is upon the assumption of such a version that the case for *All's Well That Ends Well* has been defended, and this also is here rejected. A suggestion of an old as well as a new title might indeed be found in 'All is well ended, if this suit be won', and in Helena's statement just before that Bertram is 'doubly won'. *Taming of the Shrew* also has several references to winning, although more obviously the winning of Petruchio's wager than of his wife's love.¹ If we set aside *Much Ado About Nothing* as too remote in theme from the title, *Taming of the Shrew* is the only comedy which, as it stands, could fill a gap in Meres's list. And the stylistic evidence, so far as one can judge it through the uncertainty as to the extent of Shakespeare's authorship, is in favour of a quite early date. With some hesitation *Merry Wives of Windsor* is put at a little distance from the other Falstaff plays, largely on account of the borrowing from *Hamlet* in a report which must rest on early performances, since the obnoxious name Brooke still survived. And if an explanation is necessary for the continuance of light-hearted comedy after the period of gloom had begun, the need to obey a royal behest may supply it. The time-relation of *King Lear* and *Macbeth* is not very clear. The verse-tests, as shown by Dr. Bradley, confirm the priority here given to *King Lear*, but one cannot put much confidence in their application to a play like *Macbeth*, which can hardly be in its original form. Nor is the dating of *Timon of Athens* at all clear. Dr. Bradley would place it between *King Lear* and *Macbeth*, partly because of the resemblance of its temper to that of *King Lear*, and partly again on metrical grounds. But an unfinished play is even less likely than an abridged play to answer to the metrical tests, and it would be hard to find room for *Timon of Athens* in the already rather full

---

¹ *All's Well*, v. 3. 315, 336; *Tam. of Shrew*, iv. 5. 23; v. 2. 69, 112, 116, 186. But the winning of love's labour connotes an unsuccessful suit in *Two Gent. of Ver.* i. 1. 32,

> If haply won, perhaps a hapless gain;
> If lost, why then a grievous labour won.

year 1605-6. One may agree as to the temper. Both *King Lear* and *Timon of Athens* seem to show symptoms of mental disturbance. But mental disturbance may come in waves. It may very likely be only a personal whimsy of the writer's that during the attempt at *Timon of Athens* a wave broke, that an illness followed, and that when it passed, the breach between the tragic and the romantic period was complete.

V
THE SONNETS

THE *Sonnets* were issued in 1609 by Thomas Thorpe; there was another edition by John Benson in 1640, which contains minor poems by Shakespeare and others interspersed. The 1609 text is not a very good one. It may rest upon a fairly authoritative manuscript, but there are sufficient misprints, including misprints of punctuation not explicable upon any theory of rhetorical punctuation, to make it clear that the volume cannot have been 'overseen', as *Venus and Adonis* and *Lucrece* may have been, by Shakespeare. The absence of any author's epistle is a further indication of this. The 1640 text does not rest upon any fresh reference to a manuscript, although the sonnets, of which eight are omitted, have been regrouped in a new order under fancy headings, and the pronouns altered so as to suggest that those really written to a man were written to a woman. In this respect at least they cannot be, as Benson claimed, 'of the same purity, the Authour himselfe then living avouched'.[1] For what it is worth, however, the phrase seems to imply a belief that the original publication was not contrary to Shakespeare's desire, and perhaps the same inference might be drawn from William Drummond's statement about 1614[2] that Shakespeare had lately published his works. Drummond may not have been in a position to know much about it.

Shakespeare was known to Meres as a writer of 'sugred Sonnets among his private friends' in 1598, and versions of two (cxxxviii, cxliv) of those in the 1609 volume had already appeared in the *Passionate Pilgrim* (1599). It does not follow that all those now extant were already written.

[1] p. 223.   [2] p. 213.

A traditional interpretation, from the days of Malone, has taken the arrangement of the 1609 volume at its face value, and treated the bulk of its contents (i–cxxvi) as forming a single continuous series, written to a single recipient. If so, this recipient was a man, since the pronouns show that some of the sonnets were certainly written to a man. He was a 'lovely boy', whose hair recalled buds of marjoram and his face the lovely April of his mother's prime; and he was of higher social position than the poet's own. The earliest sonnets (i–xvii) urge him to marriage and progeny. The rest take on a more personal note. The boy is at once a patron, to be immortalized by the poet's verse, and an object of close affection, to be spoken of in language which, but for the pronouns, one would have taken to be addressed to a woman. In some of the sonnets he is called 'You'; in others the more intimate 'Thou' is used. There is not likely to be any significance in this. There are many fluctuations of mood. Sometimes the boy is reproached for scandal and wantonness. Sometimes the poet is conscious of his own unworthiness, his 'tann'd antiquity', his 'disgrace with fortune and men's eyes', his 'bewailed guilt', a 'brand' upon his name, due to 'public means which public manners breeds'. He is lame; a literal criticism takes this for autobiography. He is tired of life and obsessed with thoughts of death. There are estrangements and neglects on both sides. Some of these themes are dropped and recur again. At an early stage the friend steals the poet's mistress and is forgiven. Other poets compete in praising the boy. One in particular is a serious rival. The remaining sonnets (cxxvii–cliv) are less homogeneous. They have been called 'a disordered appendix'. But several of them record the poet's love for a dark beauty, who is faithless to him, and who is not unreasonably supposed to be the stolen mistress of the main series. It is in favour of the traditional theory that there is evidently some grouping in the sonnets, and that, if they are read in the light of the theory, there is no obvious lack of coherence. It is certainly not imperative to accept the theory as a whole. The unity of the sonnets is one of atmosphere. The thread of incident is a frail one. Each sonnet is generally self-contained. A few are linked. On the other hand, there is occasionally a jar in the continuity, which may suggest misplacement. There is room for subjective interpretations; and the licence has been freely used. It has been held that the sonnets of the main series were not written to the same person; that some of them were after all to a woman, Elizabeth or Anne Hathaway or another; that they were written for another man to give to a woman, or for a woman to give to a man; that their intention is dramatic and not personal; that they are a dialogue between 'You' and 'Thou'; that they are allegorical; that they are mere literary exercises in the Petrarchan convention. There is much absurdity in many of these views. More folly has been written about the sonnets than about any other Shakespearean topic. No doubt there is a convention. The attitudes and language of the sonnets can be abundantly paralleled from other Renaissance poems, Italian, French, and English. But the use of a convention is not inconsistent with the expression of personal feeling. The level of poetic value is far from even. It has been thought that the work of other men has been intermingled with Shakespeare's. It is impossible to be dogmatic on the evidence available. But on the whole, it does not seem likely, in view of the character of some of the sonnets in the second series, that the whole collection can have been kept together by any one but Shakespeare himself. And if so, it is most likely that the arrangement of 1609 was his. It does not, of course, follow that in putting them together he made no departure from the chronological order of composition. One might suppose, for example, that cxxvi, which now ends the first series, originally ended the group i–xvii. But clearly, if it was so, the strict chronological order is irrecoverable. Nor does it much matter, so far as the very slight indications of external biography are concerned. And indeed these would remain unaltered, even if it could be shown that some of the sonnets were not Shakespeare's, and that some of the first series were written to a woman. The boy would still be there, and the stolen mistress, and the rival poet. And we should still know little more about them than that they existed, and for a time counted for much in Shakespeare's personal life. It is not surprising that great pains have been spent upon attempts to identify them. The date of the sonnets is, of course, material. Their wording does not give us much help. In xxvii–xxviii, and again in xlviii and l–li the poet is travelling. It is rather futile to relate these absences to the known provincial tours of the Chamberlain's men. Shakespeare may have had many other opportunities of leaving London. In lxvi he speaks of 'art made tongue-tied by authority'. If the reference is to theatrical art, the troubles of 1596 or 1597 (cf. p. 44) are more likely to be in point than those of 1600, by which the Chamberlain's men at least did not stand to lose much. In c we learn that there has been some interval in the sonnetteering; in civ that three years have elapsed since the 'fair friend' was first met. In cxxiv is a very vague allusion to

> thralled discontent,
> Whereto the inviting time our fashion calls.

There should be something more specific in cvii.

> Not mine own fears, nor the prophetic soul
> Of the wide world dreaming on things to come,
> Can yet the lease of my true love control,
> Supposed as forfeit to a confined doom.
> The mortal moon hath her eclipse endured,
> And the sad augurs mock their own presage;
> Incertainties now crown themselves assured
> And peace proclaims olives of endless age.
> Now with the drops of this most balmy time
> My love looks fresh, and Death to me subscribes,
> Since, spite of him, I'll live in this poor rime,
> While he insults o'er dull and speechless tribes:
>   And thou in this shalt find thy monument,
>   When tyrants' crests and tombs of brass are spent.

But even this proves difficult to date. There can be no reference, as has been thought, to anybody's imprisonment. The 'confined doom' can only be the limited duration to which a lease is subject. The 'mortal moon' is doubtless Elizabeth, and the sonnet has been placed in 1603, when James succeeded to the throne, without the opposition which had been anticipated, in the balmy days of spring, and a prospect of peace with Spain opened. Apart from the lateness of the date, an objection to this is that, while death may be called an eclipse, it is not so easy to think that to 'endure' an eclipse can mean to die. The year 1596 has been suggested when an illness of Elizabeth, in the year of her 'grand climacteric', had caused some alarm at court, which seems to have soon been dispelled, and when a fresh alliance with Henri IV was ratified at Rouen in October, with a royal entry in which Henri was presented by an angel with a sword of peace. He may have been, but the whole object of the alliance was to avoid peace and keep Henri at war with Spain. The augurs, no doubt, had been

THE SONNETS 127

busy at the end of 1595, and a *Prognostication* printed by Abel Jeffes was suppressed. It seems to have foretold a sea-battle, rather than any special danger to Elizabeth's life. Nor can we suppose that the 'peace' of the sonnet was the Peace of Vervins, made between France and Spain in 1598, since this when it came was still contrary to English interests. A more plausible date is 1599–1600. In August 1599 there was an alarm of Spanish invasion. Elizabeth was again ill, and the gathering of troops led to 'wilde conjectures' that her life was in danger and even that she was dead. Negotiations for peace had already been opened. They soon became matter of public knowledge, and continued to 28 July 1600, when they broke down at Boulogne. This sonnet cvii comes late in the first series, and for the dating as a whole we are thrown back upon internal evidence. This mainly consists of a large accumulation of parallels. Many of these, of course, are individually slight; it is the mass effect which is relied upon. It may be thought that the sonnets began as a continuation of the lyrical impulse represented by *Venus and Adonis* and *Lucrece*, in the former of which the invitation to marriage theme is already, rather inappropriately, found; that the three-years' range of civ was probably 1593–6; that the bulk of the sonnets belong to this period; and that others were added more sparsely up to 1599 or so. Some reflection of the sentiments which occupied the poet's mind may be traceable in the structure of the plays of 1595 and 1596. It has been generally assumed that the boy-friend was some young noble to whom Shakespeare was devoted. Robert Devereux, Earl of Essex, Henry Wriothesley, Earl of Southampton, William Lord Herbert, from 1601 Earl of Pembroke, have had their champions. Essex, born in 1566 and married in 1590, is chronologically impossible. The careers of Southampton and Herbert show curious analogies. Both are known to have shown favour to Shakespeare. Both were good-looking and had beautiful mothers. Both were much in the public eye. Both were the subjects of early negotiations for marriages which came to nothing. Both had amorous relations with ladies of Elizabeth's court and suffered disgrace and imprisonment as a result, although Southampton married his Elizabeth Vernon in 1598, whereas Herbert declined to marry his Mary Fitton in 1601. Neither of these can, of course, be the Dark Lady, a married woman, who broke her bed-vow (clii) to take first Shakespeare and then his friend. Southampton, born in 1573, was perhaps young enough to be called a 'boy' by Shakespeare in 1593–6, and to him *Venus and Adonis* and *Lucrece* were dedicated. The case for him as the friend of the sonnets is now very generally accepted, but it is hardly a convincing one. If it were sound, one would expect to find some hints in the sonnets of the major interests of Southampton's early life; his military ambitions, his comradeship with Essex, the romance of his marriage. There are none. It has, of course, been apparent that the volume of 1609 is dedicated to 'Mr W. H.', and that Southampton's initials were H. W. Attempts have been made to turn this issue by suggesting that, since 'begetter' in Elizabethan English may mean 'procurer' as well as 'inspirer', the dedication is not to the friend but to the person who furnished Thorpe with copy. If so, perhaps the best guess which has been made at a 'Mr W. H.' by the believers in Southampton is Sir William Harvey, who married his mother in 1598. Lee offered William Hall. He found a W. H. who wrote a dedication to the *Foure-fold Meditation* printed as Robert Southwell's in 1606, assumed that both were the William Hall, who was a printer in 1609, but did not print the *Sonnets*, and gave a blessing to a further assumption that this was also a William Hall who married

THE SONNETS

at Hackney in 1608 and might therefore be congratulated on the birth of a child in 1609. He did not go so far as to suggest with others that 'M^r. W. H. ALL . HAPPINESSE' might be read in a double sense by the omission of a full stop. But all his equations seem quite unwarrantable, in view of the commonness of the initials W. H. and the name Hall. And there is some unconscious humour in the notion of Thorpe's dedicating the volume to a printer whom he had not employed. The actual terms of the dedication make it difficult to believe that, even in Thorpe's affected phrasing, the person to whom he wished eternity was any other than the person to whom the 'ever-living poet' promised eternity. Nor can one feel that in such a document there would be anything very out of the way either in the inversion of initials or in the suppression of an actual or courtesy title. If Southampton was meant by 'Mr W. H.' both these things have been done; if Herbert, one only. The case for Herbert was elaborately argued by Thomas Tyler and others thirty years ago, and it was rather mishandled. Obsessed by Mary Fitton, they put the bulk of the sonnets in 1598–1601, after Herbert had come to live in London, and related the early group, urging marriage upon the friend, to an abortive match between him and Lady Bridget Vere, which was under discussion in 1597. If the sonnets are of 1593–6, it might well be thought that Herbert, born in 1580, was too young to be their subject, even though he was more naturally to be called a 'boy' at that time than Southampton. But oddly enough, although Tyler used the *Sydney Papers*, he apparently failed to notice the evidence which they contain that an attempt, probably due to his father's failing health, had already been made as early as 1595 to betroth Herbert at the tender age of 15. On October 8 Rowland Whyte writes to Sir Robert Sydney (i. 353):

My Lord ⟨Pembroke⟩ hymself, with my Lord *Harbart*, ⟨is⟩ come vp to see the Queen, and (as I heare) to deale in the Matter of a Marriage with Sir *George Careys* Daughter.

The visit was in fact put off, but had taken place, probably by October 29 and certainly by November 3 (i. 355, 356, 357, 361), and on December 5 Whyte reports (i. 372):

Sir *George Carey* takes it very unkindly, that my Lord of *Pembroke* broke of the Match intended between my Lord *Herbart* and his Daughter, and told the Queen it was becawse he wold not assure him 1000¹· a Yeare, which comes to his Daughter, as next a Kinne to Queen *Ann Bullen*. He hath now concluded a Marriage between his Daughter and my Lord *Barkleys* Sonne and Heire.

It is, perhaps, relevant that Sir George Carey was son to the patron of the Chamberlain's men in 1595, and that the ultimate marriage of Elizabeth Carey to Thomas Berkeley is perhaps at least as likely as any other to have been honoured by the production of *Midsummer-Night's Dream*. And it is a striking fact that, although Southampton was still alive, it was not to him, but to Herbert and his brother, that the Folio was dedicated. On the whole, therefore, if we are to look in the ranks of the higher nobility, it is Herbert, rather than Southampton, who affords the most plausible identification for Shakespeare's friend. It is by no means clear that the conditions might not be satisfied by some young man of good birth and breeding, but of less degree than an earl. But there is no candidate to propose. The Rival Poet, from whom we should desire light, only adds to the obscurity. The 'precious phrase by all the Muses filed' (lxxxv) and 'the proud full sail of his great verse' (lxxxvi) ought to mean Spenser, or failing him, Daniel or perhaps Drayton. Marlowe's death in 1593 probably puts him out of question. Daniel, who was Herbert's tutor at Wilton, dedicated more than one book to his mother Lady Pembroke, but nothing to Herbert himself before his *Defence of Rhyme* of 1603. He is perhaps as likely as any one to have praised him in unpublished verse. His *Epistles* of 1603 include one to Southampton. There are no extant poems by Spenser or Drayton either to Herbert or Southampton. Indeed, Southampton was not a great mark for dedications until he came into favour under James. There are sonnets, in which he is only ranked with others, by Barnabe Barnes (1593), Gervase Markham (1595), Henry Lok (1597), and John Florio (1598). It is difficult to agree with Lee that 'all the conditions of the problem are satisfied' by Barnes. Nashe addresses to Southampton his prose tale of *The Unfortunate Traveller* (1594). The same writer's indecent *Choice of Valentines* was for a 'Lord S', but Southampton had no claim to be spoken of as the 'fairest bud the red rose euer bare'. The rival has been identified with Chapman, and his *Shadow of Night* (1594) has phrases about his inspiration which might be echoed, although not very closely, in the rival's 'affable familiar ghost' and 'compeers by night' (lxxxvi). Only the courtesy of a rival, however, could represent the uncouth manner of his 'hymns' as a 'proud full sail'. And Chapman again dedicated nothing Elizabethan to Herbert, or to Southampton, or to a 'Mr W. H.'. One other clue proves equally elusive. A poem called *Willobie his Avisa* was registered on 3 September 1594 and printed in the same year. In fluent but undistinguished verse it describes the successive and fruitless assaults upon the virtue of Avisa by 'a Nobleman' before her marriage, and after by 'a Caveleiro', by 'D. B. a French man', by 'Dydimus Harco, Anglo-Germanus', and finally by 'Henrico Willobego, Italo-Hispalensis'. The last of these has (cf. p. 190) a 'familiar friend W. S. who not long before had tryed the curtesy of the like passion, and was now newly recouered of the like infection', and who 'vewing a far off the course of this louing Comedy, determined to see whether it would sort to a happier end for this new actor, then it did for the old player'. The 'like passion' does not necessarily mean a passion for Avisa herself. There is a dialogue between W. S. and H. W. in which W. S. says (cf. *Sonn.* xli; *1 Hen. VI*, v. 3. 78; *Tit. Andr.* ii. 1. 83; *Rich. III*, i. 2. 229):

> She is no Saynt, She is no Nonne,
> I thinke in tyme she may be wonne.

It seems natural to see some sort of allusion to Shakespeare's love affair here; the more as his *Lucrece* is cited in a set of commendatory verses. Another set by Abell Emet tells us nothing. Henry Willobie is said in an epistle, subscribed 'Hadrian Dorrell', and dated at Oxford on an October 1, to be himself the author of the poem. But no inferences can be drawn, not even from the fact that Willobie's inverted initials would make W. H.

APPENDIX I

RECORDS

1. CHRISTENINGS, MARRIAGES, AND BURIALS

(*a*) *Stratford-on-Avon.*

1558, Sept. 15. C. Jone Shakspere daughter to John Shakspere.
1562, Dec. 2. C. Margareta filia Johannis Shakspere.
1563, Apr. 30. B. Margareta filia Johannis Shakspere.
1564, Apr. 26. C. Gulielmus filius Johannes Shakspere.

[There is no record of the actual birthday. All that can be inferred from the present entry and the words of the monumental inscription '*obiit anno . . . aetatis* 53' is that the birth was on a day not earlier than 24 Apr. 1563 or later than 23 Apr. 1564, since otherwise Shakespeare would have died either in his 54th or his 52nd year. This of course rests on two assumptions. One is that the draftsman of the inscription understood by an *annus aetatis* a current and not a completed year. He probably did in this case, as an interval of a year is not likely between birth and baptism, although the practice is by no means uniform in old datings. The other is that he followed the present legal convention by which a new year of life is treated as beginning at the first moment of the anniversary of the day of birth, without regard to the time of day at which the birth took place.]

1566, Oct. 13. C. Gilbertus filius Johannis Shakspere.
1569, Apr. 15. C. Jone the daughter of John Shakspere.
[It must be inferred that the elder Joan had died.]
1571, Sept. 28. C. Anna filia magistri Shakspere.
1574, Mar. 11. C. Richard sonne to Mr John Shakspeer.
1579, Apr. 4. B. Anne daughter to Mr John Shakspere.
1580, May 3. C. Edmund sonne to Mr John Shakspere.

1583, May 26. C. Susanna daughter to William Shakespeare.

1585, Feb. 2. C. Hamnet & Judeth sonne and daughter to William Shakspere.

[It is idle to guess at the origin of common names, such as William. But the conjunction of unusual names here suggests that the god-parents were Shakespeare's legatee, Hamnet Sadler, a baker of High Street, and his wife Judith Staunton of Longbridge. The name was also used as a surname. An inquisition was taken on 11 Feb. 1580 upon the body of Katherine Hamlett of Tiddington, spinster, who was drowned in the Avon while fetching water in a pail. The resemblance of the name to that of the hero of Shakespeare's tragedy, which has a different Scandinavian origin, can hardly be more than a coincidence.]

1596, Aug. 11. B. Hamnet filius William Shakspere.

1600, Aug. 28. C. Wilhelmus filius Wilhelmi Hart.

[The marriage of Joan Shakespeare to William Hart is not recorded in the *Register*, but can be inferred from later entries and the mention in Shakespeare's will of 'my sister Johane Harte'. Nothing is known of Hart, except that he was a hatter and had some cases in the Court of Record.]

1601, Sept. 8. B. Mr Johannes Shakspeare.

1603, June 5. C. Maria filia Wilhelmi Hart.

1605, July 24. C. Thomas fil. Wilhelmus Hart Hatter.

1607, June 5. M. John Hall gentleman & Susanna Shaxspere.

[John Hall has recently been shown to have been the son of William Hall of Acton, Middlesex, who died in 1607. His monument shows him a gentleman of coat-armour, bearing *Three talbots' heads erased*, and aged 60 at his death on 25 Nov. 1635. His own record (cf. p. 136) gives him as *circa aetatis annum 57 Die August. 27 anno Salutis 1632*. We may take it that he was born in the summer or autumn of 1575. The editor of the *Observations* (cf. p. 136) says that he had been a traveller

CHRISTENINGS, MARRIAGES, AND BURIALS

and knew French. Very possibly he took a foreign medical degree. But he is also described as *generosus in Artibus Magister* in a Stratford document of 1632, and this fact, with the coincidence of age, may bear out an identification of him with the John Haule of Worcestershire, *generosi filius*, who matriculated from Balliol, Oxford, aged 16, on 4 Feb. 1592, and took his B.A. in 1595 and his M.A. from St. Edmund Hall in 1598. It is, of course, possible that William Hall of Acton was of Worcestershire origin.]

1607, Dec. 17. B. Mary dawghter to Willyam Hart.
1608, Feb. 21. C. Elizabeth dawghter to John Hall gentleman.
1608, Sept. 9. B. Mayry Shaxspere, wydowe.
1608, Sept. 23. C. Mychaell sonne to Willyam Hart.
1612, Feb. 3. B. Gilbert Shakspere, adolescens.

[Little is known of Gilbert. He took delivery for his brother of the conveyance of land at Old Stratford in May 1602, and appended a well-written 'Gilbart Shakespere' as witness to a Stratford lease on 5 Mar. 1610. Gilbert is not in the poet's will. The term *adolescens*, applied to a man of 45, need not trouble us. *Adolescens, adolocentulus, adolocentula* appear several times in the *Register* during 1603–11. They may mean no more than 'bachelor' and 'spinster'.]

1613, Feb. 4. B. Rich: Shakspeare.
1616, Feb. 10. M. Tho Queeny tow Judith Shakspere.

[Thomas Quiney was a vintner at The Cage in Stratford from 1616 to about 1652, when he may have left the town. He was a man of some education and a competent chamberlain to the corporation. But in 1633 he was in financial difficulties, and John Hall and Thomas Nash acted as trustees for his wife and children. He was alive in 1655; the date and place of his death are unknown.]

1616, Apr. 17. B. Will. Hartt, hatter.
1616, Apr. 25. B. Will. Shakspere, gent.

1616, Nov. 23. C. Shaksper fillius Thomas Quyny gent.
1617, May 8. B. Shakspere fillius Tho. Quyny, gent.
1618, Feb. 9. C. Richard fillius Thomas Quinee.
1618, Nov. 1. B. Micael filius to Jone Harte, widowe.
1620, Jan. 23. C. Thomas filius to Thomas Queeney.
1623, Aug. 8. B. Mrs Shakspeare.

[Dowdall records a tradition that Anne desired to be laid in her husband's grave, but that the sexton feared the poet's curse. Her grave is in fact to the left of his in the chancel of Stratford church, below his monument.]

1626, Apr. 22. M. Mr Thomas Nash to Mrs Elizabeth Hall.
1634, Apr. 13. C. Thomas filius Thomæ Hart.
1635, Nov. 26. B. Johannes Hall, medicus peritissimus.

[His gravestone, the second to the right of Shakespeare's in the chancel at Stratford, bears the arms of Hall, *Three talbots' heads erased*, impaling Shakespeare, and an inscription. Hall left a selection from his case-books, which was translated from the Latin and published by James Cooke, a Warwick surgeon, as *Select Observations on English Bodies* (1657). Hall notes illnesses of his wife and daughter and his own in 1632. There is no mention of Shakespeare. Hall had a wide practice, not only at Stratford, but among families of position in Warwickshire and the neighbouring counties. One of his patients was Mr. Drayton, 'an excellent poet', whom he cured of a tertian fever by an infusion of violets. Hall writes like a Protestant, but we are told in the prefatory matter to the *Observations* that even 'such as hated his religion' were glad to use him as a doctor. He lived in a house in Old Stratford, but moved to New Place upon Shakespeare's death.]

1636, Sept. 18. C. Georgius filius Tho: Hart.
1639, Jan. 28. B. Thomas filius Thomæ Quiney.
1639, Feb. 26. B. Richardus filius Tho: Quiney.

CHRISTENINGS, MARRIAGES, AND BURIALS

1639, Mar. 29. B. Willielmus Hart.
1646, Nov. 4. B. Joan Hart, widow.
1647, Apr. 5. B. Thomas Nash, Gent.

[His stone, to the right of Shakespeare's in the chancel, has under the arms of Nash (⟨*Az.*⟩ *on a chevron between three ravens' heads erased* ⟨*arg.*⟩ *a pellet between four crosses crosslet* ⟨*sa.*⟩), quartered with Bulstrode, and impaling Hall quartered with Shakespeare.]

1649, July 16. B. Mrs Sussanna Hall, widow.

[Her stone, to the right of her husband's in the chancel, has under the arms of Hall impaling Shakespeare in a lozenge:

> HEERE LYETH Y^{E}. BODY OF SVSANNA
> WIFE TO IOHN HALL, GENT: Y^{E}. DAVGH
> TER OF WILLIAM SHAKESPEARE, GENT:
> SHEE DECEASED Y^{E}. ijth OF IVLY. A^{o}.
> 1649, AGED 66.

Witty above her sexe, but that's not all,
Wise to salvation was good Mistris Hall,
Something of Shakespeare was in that, but this
Wholy of him with whom she's now in blisse.
Then, Passenger, hast nere a teare,
   To weepe with her that wept with all;
That wept, yet set her self to chere
   Them up with comforts cordiall.
Her love shall live, her mercy spread,
   When thou has't ner'e a teare to shed.

This, however, was erased for another interment in the 18th century and has been recut from a copy in Dugdale's *Warwickshire*.

Susanna's reputation did not escape calumny. In July 1613 she brought an action for slander in the Consistory Court at Worcester against John Lane, junior, of Stratford, who had reported that she 'had the runninge of the raynes & had bin naught with Rafe Smith at John Palmer'. Robert Whatcott, afterwards a witness to Shakespeare's will (no. 13), appeared for the plaintiff. The defendant did not appear and was excommunicated. Ralph Smith was a hatter of Stratford. The culprit was a first cousin of Thomas Nash.]

1662, Feb. 9. B. Judith, vxor Thomas Quiney Gent.

[Judith's grave is unknown. All her children had predeceased her, presumably unmarried; and with the death of the childless Elizabeth Hall, remarried to John, later (1661) Sir John, Bernard, of Abington, Northants, at Billesley on 5 June 1649, and buried at Abington on 17 Feb. 1670, the descent from Shakespeare was extinct.]

2. THE GRANTS OF ARMS

[1596, 20 Oct. There are two versions. The following seems to give the final intention.]

Shakespere

non sanz droict
[Trick of coat and crest]

To all and singuler Noble and Gentilmen: of what Estate, degree, baring Arms to whom these presentes shall come. William Dethick Garter principall king of Arms sendethe greetinges. Knowe yee that whereas, by the authorite and auncyent pryveleges perteyning to my office from the Queenes most excellent Maiestie and by her highnesse most noble & victorious progenitours, I am to take generall notice & record and to make declaration & testemonie for all causes of Arms and matters of Gentrie thorough all her maiesties kingdoms, dominions, principalites, Isles and provinces, To the'nd that, as manie gentillmen by theyr auncyent names of families, kyndredes, & descentes have & enioye certeyne enseignes & cottes of arms, So it is v⟨erie⟩ expedient in all Ages that some men for theyr valeant factes, magnanimite, vertu, dignites & des⟨ertes⟩ maye vse & beare suche tokens of honour and worthinesse, Whereby theyr name & good fame may be the better knowen & divulged and theyr children & posterite (in all vertue to the service of theyr prynce & contrie) encouraged. Wherefore being solicited and by credible report ⟨info⟩rmed, That John Shakespeare of Stratford vppon Avon, ⟨in⟩ the count⟨e of⟩ Warwike, ⟨whose⟩ parentes ⟨& late⟩ grandfather for his faithfull & va⟨leant service was advanced & rewar⟩ded ⟨by the most prudent⟩ prince King Henry the seventh of ⟨famous memorie, sithence which tyme they have⟩ continewed in those partes being of good reputacon ⟨& credit, and that the s⟩aid John hath maryed the daughter ⟨& one of the heyres of Robert Arden of Wilmcoote in the said⟩ Counte esquire, and for the encouragement of his posterite to whom ⟨these achivmentes by the a⟩uncyent custome of the Lawes of Arms maye descend. I the Said G⟨arter king⟩ of Arms have assigned, graunted, and by these presentes confirmed: This sh⟨ield⟩ or ⟨cote of⟩ Arms, viz. Gould, on a Bend Sables, a Speare of the first steeled argent. And for his creast or cognizaunce a falcon his winges displayed Argent standing on a wrethe of his coullers: suppo⟨rting⟩ a Speare Gould steeled as aforesaid sett vppon a helmett with mantelles & tasselles as hath ben accustomed and doth more playnely appeare depicted on this margent: Signefieing hereby & by the authorite of my office aforesaid ratefieing that it shalbe lawfull for the said John Shakespeare gentilman and for his children yssue & posterite (at all tymes & places convenient) to beare and make demonstracon of the same Blazon or Atchevment vppon theyre Shieldes, Targetes, escucheons, Cotes of Arms, pennons, Guydons, Seales, Ringes, edefices, Buyldinges, vtensiles, Lyveries, Tombes, or monumentes or otherwise for all lawfull warlyke factes or ciuile vse or exercises, according to the Lawes of Arms, and customes that to gentillmen belongethe without let or interruption of any other person or persons for vse or bearing the same. In witnesse & perpetuall remembrance hereof I have herevnto subscribed my name & fastened the Seale of my office endorzed with the signett of my Arms. At the office of Arms London the xx daye of October the xxxviii[th] yeare of the reigne of our Soueraigne Lady Elizabeth by the grace of God Quene of England, France and Ireland Defender of the Fayth etc. 1596.

> This John shoeth A patierne herof vnder Clarent Cookes hand.
>
> —paper. xx years past.
>
> A Justice of peace And was Baylyue The Q officer & cheff of the towne of Stratford vppon Avon xv or xvi years past.
>
> That he hath Landes & tenementes of good wealth, & substance 500[li].
>
> That he ma⟨rried a daughter and heyre of Arden, a gent. of worship⟩.

3. SHAKESPEARE'S MARRIAGE

(*a*) [1582, Nov. 27. Entry of Licence from the Bishop of Worcester's Register.]

Item eodem die similis emanavit licencia inter Willelmum Shaxpere et Annam Whateley de Temple Grafton.

(*b*) [1582, Nov. 28. Bond of Sureties from the Bishop of Worcester's Register.]

Noverint vniversi per presentes nos Fulconem Sandells de Stratford in comitatu Warwicensi agricolam et Johannem Rychardson ibidem agricolam teneri et firmiter obligari Ricardo Cosin generoso et Robert Warmstry notario publico in quadraginta libris bone et legalis monete Anglie Soluendis eisdem Ricardo et Roberto, heredibus executoribus vel assignatis suis, ad quam quidem solucionem bene et fideliter faciendam obligamus nos et vtrumque nostrum per se pro toto et in solidum, heredes executores et administratores nostros, firmiter per presentes sigillis nostris sigillatas. Datum 28 die novembris Anno Regni Domine nostre Elizabethe Dei gratia Anglie Francie et Hibernie Regine fidei defensoris etc., 25° ⟨1582⟩.

The condicion of this obligacion ys suche that if herafter there shall not appere any Lawfull Lett or impediment by reason of any precontract consanguinitie affinitie or by any other lawfull meanes whatsoeuer but that William Shagspere on thone partie, and Anne Hathwey of Stratford in the Dioces of Worcester maiden may lawfully solemnize matrimony together and in the same afterwardes remaine and continew like man and wiffe according vnto the lawes in that behalf prouided, and moreouer if there be not at this present time any action sute quarrell or demaund moved or depending before any iudge ecclesiasticall or temporall for and concerning any such lawfull lett or impediment, And moreouer if the said William Shagspere do not proceed to solemnizacion of mariadg with the said Anne Hathwey without the consent of hir frindes, And also if the said William do vpon his owne proper costes and expenses defend & save harmles the right Reverend father in god Lord John bushop of Worcester and his offycers for Licencing them the said William and Anne to be married togither with once asking of the bannes of matrimony betwene them and for all other causes which may ensure by reason or occasion therof, That then the said obligacion to be voyd and of none effect or els to stand & abide in full force and vertue.

(c) [1601, Mar. 25. Extracts from Will of Thomas Whittington of Shottery, husbandman.]

Item I geve and bequeth unto the poore people of Stratford

40^s. that is in the hand of Anne Shaxspere, wyf unto Mr Wyllyam Shaxspere, and is due debt unto me, beyng payd to myne Executor by the sayd Wyllyam Shaxspere or his assigns, accordyng to the true meanyng of this my wyll ... Item I geve to Thomas, sonne to Edward Cottrell, my godson, 12^d ... Item I geve and bequeth unto John Pace, of Shottre, the elder, with whom I sojorne, 20^s ... Item, I geve to Thomas Hathaway, sonne to the late decessed Margret Hathway, late of Old Stratford, 12^d. [*Schedule*.] Imprimis John Hathway and Wylliam Hathway executours unto the late decessed Jone Hathway theyr mother do owe me that is due to me by her last will iiij marks iij^s viij^d: Item the sayd John and Wyllyam Hathway owe me more lv^s vij^d. Item the forsayd John Hathway oweth me more iij^s iiij^d. Item the sayd Wyllyam Hathway oweth me iij^s. Item I owe the sayd John and Wyllyam Hathway for a quarter of an yeares bord.

4. THE GLOBE AND BLACKFRIARS

[1635, *c.* Aug. 1. From *Answer* of Cuthbert Burbadge, Winifred Robinson, and William Burbadge to *Petition* of Robert Benfield and Heliard Swanston to the Lord Chamberlain.]

The father of vs Cutbert and Richard Burbage was the first builder of Playhowses, and was himselfe in his younger yeeres a Player. The Theater hee built with many Hundred poundes taken vp at interest. The players that liued in those first times had onely the profitts arising from the dores, but now the players receaue all the commings in at the dores to themselues and halfe the Galleries from the Houskepers. Hee built this house vpon leased ground, by which meanes the landlord and Hee had a great suite in law, and by his death, the like troubles fell on vs, his sonnes; wee then bethought vs of altering from thence, and at like expence built the Globe with more summes of money taken vp at interest, which lay heauy on vs many yeeres, and to our selues wee ioyned those deserueing men, Shakspere, Hemings, Condall, Philips and others partners in the profittes of that they call the House, but makeing the leases for twenty-one yeeres hath beene the destruction of our selues and others, for they dyeing at the expiration of three or four yeeres of their lease, the subsequent yeeres became dissolued to strangers, as by marrying with their widdowes, and the like by their Children. Thus, Right Honorable, as concerning the Globe, where wee our selues are but lessees. Now for the Blackfriers that is our inheritance, our father purchased it at extreame rates and made it into a playhouse with great charge and troble, which after was leased out to one Euans that first sett up the Boyes commonly called the Queenes Majesties Children of the Chappell. In processe of time the boyes growing vp to bee men, which were Vnderwood, Field, Ostler, and were taken to strengthen the Kings service, and the more to strengthen the service, the boyes dayly wearing out, it was considered that house would bee as fitt for our selues, and soe purchased the lease remaining from Evans with our money, and placed men Players, which were Hemings, Condall, Shakspeare, &c.

5. SHAKESPEARE AND HIS FELLOWS

(a) [1598, before 20 Sept. Note after text of *Every Man In his Humour* in *First Folio* of Ben Jonson's *Workes* (1616). A contemporary letter shows that *E.M.I.* was 'a new play' shortly before 20 Sept.]

This Comoedie was first Acted, in the yeere 1598. By

the then L. Chamberlayne his Seruants. The principall Comœdians were.

Will. Shakespeare.	Ric. Burbadge.
Aug. Philips.	Ioh. Hemings.
Hen. Condel.	Tho. Pope.
Will. Slye.	Chr. Beeston.
Will. Kempe.	Ioh. Duke.

(*b*) [1603, May 19. From Licence for King's men.]

Wee . . doe licence and aucthorize theise our Servauntes Lawrence Fletcher, William Shakespeare, Richard Burbage, Augustyne Phillippes, Iohn Heninges, Henrie Condell, William Sly, Robert Armyn, Richard Cowly, and the rest of theire Assosiates freely to vse and exercise the Arte and faculty of playing Comedies, Tragedies, histories, Enterludes, moralls, pastoralls, Stageplaies and Suche others like as theie haue alreadie studied or hereafter shall vse or studie aswell for the recreation of our lovinge Subjectes as for our Solace and pleasure when wee shall thincke good to see them duringe our pleasure.

(*c*) [1603, *c*. Christmas. Note after text of *Sejanus* in *First Folio* of Ben Jonson's *Workes* (1616).]

This Tragœdie was first acted, in the yeere 1603. By the Kings Maiesties Seruants. The principall Tragœdians were,

Ric. Burbadge.	Will. Shake-Speare.
Aug. Philips.	Ioh. Hemings.
Will. Sly.	Hen. Condel.
Ioh. Lowin.	Alex. Cooke.

(*d*) [1604, *c*. Mar. 15. From *Account* of Sir George Home, Master of the Great Wardrobe, for the Proceeding of King James through London on 15 Mar. 1604.]

Red Clothe bought of sondrie persons and giuen by his

Maiestie to diuerse persons against his Maiesties sayd royall proceeding through the Citie of London, viz:— ...

The Chamber ...	
Fawkeners &c. &c.	Red cloth
William Shakespeare	iiij yardes di.
Augustine Phillipps	,,
Lawrence Fletcher	,,
John Hemminges	,,
Richard Burbidge	,,
William Slye	,,
Robert Armyn	,,
Henry Cundell	,,
Richard Cowley	,,

(e) [1605, May 4. Extract from *Will* of Augustine Phillips (*P.C.C.* 31 Hayes, proved 16 May 1605).]

Item I geve and bequeathe unto and amongste the hyred men of the Company which I am of, which shalbe at the tyme of my decease, the some of fyve pounds of lawfull money of England to be equally distributed amongeste them, Item I geve and bequeathe to my Fellow William Shakespeare a thirty shillings peece in gould, ...

(f) [1623. From ninth preliminary leaf to the First Folio.]

The Names of the Principall Actors in all these Playes.

William Shakespeare.	Samuel Gilburne.
Richard Burbadge.	Robert Armin.
John Hemmings.	William Ostler.
Augustine Phillips.	Nathan Field.
William Kempt.	John Vnderwood.
Thomas Poope.	Nicholas Tooley.
George Bryan.	William Ecclestone.
Henry Condell.	Joseph Taylor.
William Slye.	Robert Benfield.

Richard Cowly.	Robert Goughe.
John Lowine.	Richard Robinson.
Samuell Crosse.	Iohn Shancke.
Alexander Cooke.	Iohn Rice.

6. SHAKESPEARE'S LONDON RESIDENCES

(a) [1597, Nov. 15. From *Certificate* of London Commissioners for second instalment of third subsidy granted by Parliament of 1593.]

The petty collectors ... within the warde of Byshopsgate ... upon their corporall othes upon the holye Evangelists of Allmighty God ... dyd saye and affirme that the persons hereunder named are all ether dead, departed, and gone out of the sayde warde or their goodes soe eloigned or conveyd out of the same or in suche a pryvate or coverte manner kept, whereby the severall sommes of money on them severallye taxed and assessed towards the sayde secound payment of the sayde last subsydye nether mighte nor coulde by anye meanes by them the sayde petty collectors, or ether of them, be levyed of them, or anye of them, to her Majesties use.

St Ellen's parishe.
... William Shackspere v^{li}–v^s.

(b) [1598, Oct. 1. From *Indenture* between London Commissioners for first subsidy granted by Parliament of 1597–8 and petty collectors for Bishopsgate ward, with list of persons assessed for payment.]

S^t: Hellens parishe.
Affid. William Shakespeare—v^l.—xiii^s. $iiij^d$.

(c) [1598–9. From list (*Exchequer L.T.R. Enrolled Accounts of Subsidies*, no. 56) furnished for Bishopsgate and five other wards, showing defaulters for the first subsidy granted by Parliament in 1597–8, who had no goods or chattels, lands or tenements

SHAKESPEARE'S LONDON RESIDENCES

within the limits of the collection on which the collector could distrain, and for whom answer will be due.]

In Warda de Bishopsgate . . . In parochia Sancte Helene . . . Willelmus Shakespeare ibidem xiij.^{s}. iiij^d.

(*d*) [1599, Oct. 6. From list of persons owing sums to the Exchequer.]

Surr R

Willelmus Shakspeare in parochia sancte Helene in Warda predicta debet xiij.^{s} iiij.^{d} de eodem subsidio ibidem. [*Added*] Respondebit in rotulo sequente in Residuum Sussex.

(*e*) [1600, Oct. 6. From list of persons owing sums to the Exchequer.]

London R:
o n^l Episcopo
Wintonensi T

Willelmus Shakspeare in parochia sancte Helene xiij.^{s} iiij^d de primo integro subsidio predicto Anno xxxix^{no} concesso Qui requiritur super eundem ibidem.

[Subsidies were imposed from time to time by statute, at the alternative rates of 4*s*. on the annual value of lands or 2*s*. 8*d*. on the value of personal property. The valuations were low and there was much evasion. The collection was entrusted to local commissioners with collectors under them. Defaulters were reported to the Exchequer, who instructed the sheriffs of counties to recover arrears and answer for them at the annual view of their accounts on the octave of Michaelmas in each year. Two payments by Shakespeare as a resident in St. Helen's Bishopsgate were not forthcoming. The first was a sum of 5*s*. due as a second instalment of the last of three subsidies granted by the parliament of 1593. The assessment was made in October 1596 and payment should have been made by February 1597. But the collectors reported in the following November (*a*) that they had been unable to collect it. A new subsidy was granted by the parliament of 1597. Shakespeare was assessed, again in St. Helen's, on 1 Oct. 1598 (*b*) at 13*s*. 4*d*. on goods valued £5, and should have paid in the following winter. 'Affid⟨avit⟩' was subsequently written in the margin of the assessment against his name, which indicates that again the collectors swore to their inability to collect. The arrear was reported to the Exchequer (*c*) and entered on the *Pipe Roll* for 1598–9, with the marginal notes 'Surr⟨ey⟩' and 'R', probably for 'R⟨espondebit⟩'. These were intended for reference at the sitting of the Court of Exchequer in October 1599, and at this sitting a note seems to have been added to the main entry, directing the sheriff for Surrey and Sussex, which were combined for fiscal purposes, to answer for the amount on the *Roll* for 1599–1600. The marginal 'R' was then cancelled. Accordingly the amount appears on the Sussex membrane of the *Roll* for 1599–1600. And here there are these marginal notes, (i) London R, (ii) o⟨neratur⟩ n⟨is⟩i, (iii) Episcopo Wintonensi, (iv) T⟨ot⟩. Presumably (i) indicates the origin of the entry as an amount to be answered from the London membrane for 1598–9; (ii) that the sheriff for Surrey and Sussex was to be charged with the amount unless he showed cause to the contrary; (iii) that the amount was referred for collection to the Bishop of Winchester, who had a liberty, the Clink, in Surrey, outside the sheriff's jurisdiction; and (iv), probably a later addition, that the amount was collected and would be accounted for. And in fact the Bishop of Winchester did account in the *Roll* of 1600–1 for a lump sum received from various persons referred to him by the sheriff. This probably includes Shakespeare's 13*s.* 4*d.*, although names are not given. Shakespeare has not so far been traced in any other subsidy rolls, either for London or Surrey or Stratford, where his name certainly does not appear, or for the Royal Household, of which he became an officer in 1603.

So far as his residence is concerned, the inference is that at some date before October 1596 he had lived in St. Helen's, Bishopsgate; that by 1599, and possibly by the winter of 1596–7, he had ceased to do so, and that by October 1599 he was resident in the Clink on the Surrey Bankside. The *Belott* v. *Mountjoy* papers (no. 7) make it improbable that Shakespeare was continuously resident in Southwark up to as late a date as 1608.]

7. THE BELOTT-MOUNTJOY SUIT

[1612, 11 May, 19 June. From *Depositions* in suit of *Belott* v. *Mountjoy* (Court of Requests).]

(*a*) [11 May 1612. *Depositions to Interrogatories on behalf of Belott.*]

[(1) *Deposition of Johane Johnsone.*]

3 To the thirde interrogatory this deponent sayth ... there was a shewe of goodwill betweene the plaintiff and defendantes daughter Marye, which the defendantes wyffe did geue countenaunce vnto and thinke well of. And as she remembereth the defendant did send and perswade one Mr Shakespeare that laye in the house to perswade the plaintiff to the same marriadge.

[(2) *Deposition of Daniell Nicholas.*]

3 To the thirde interrogatory this deponent sayth he herd one W^m: Shakespeare saye that the defendant did beare a good opinion of the plaintiff and affected him well when he served him, and did move the plaintiff by him the said Shakespeare to haue ⟨a⟩ marriadge betweene his daughter Marye Mountioye ⟨and⟩ the plaintiff, and for that purpose sent him the said Sh⟨akespeare⟩ to the plaintiff to perswade the plaintiff to the same, as Shakespere tould him this deponent, which was effected and solempnized vppon promise of a porcion with her. And more he cannott depose.

4 To the iiijth interrogatory this deponent sayth that the plaintiff did requeste him this deponent to goe with his wyffe to Shakespe⟨are⟩ to vnderstande the truthe howe muche and what the defendant did promise ⟨to⟩ bestowe on his daughter in marriadge with him the plaintiff, who did soe. And askinge Shakespeare therof, he answered that he promissed yf the plaintiff would marrye with

Marye his the defendantes onlye daughter, he the defendant would by his promise as he remembered geue the plaintiff with her in marriadge about the some of ffyftye poundes in money and certayne houshould stuffe.

(3) [*Deposition of William Shakespeare.*] William Shakespeare of Stratford vpon Aven in the Countye of Warwicke gentleman of the age of xlviij yeres or thereaboutes sworne and examined the daye and yere abouesaid deposethe & sayethe

1 To the first interrogatory this deponent sayethe he knowethe the partyes plaintiff and deffendant and hathe know⟨ne⟩ them bothe as he now remembrethe for the space of tenne yeres or thereaboutes.

2 To the second interrogatory this deponent sayeth he did know the complainant when he was servant with the deffendant, and that duringe the tyme of his the complainantes service with the said deffendant he the said complainant to this deponentes knowledge did well and honestly behaue himselfe, but to this deponentes remembrance he hath not heard the deffendant confesse that he had gott any great profitt and comodytye by the service of the said complainant, but this deponent saithe he verely thinkethe that the said complainant was a very good and industrious servant in the said service. And more he canott depose to the said interrogatory.

3 To the third interrogatory this deponent sayethe that it did evydentlye appeare that the said deffendant did all the tyme of the said complainantes service with him beare and shew great good will and affeccion towardes the said complainant, and that he hath hard the deffendant and his wyefe diuerse and sundry tymes saye and reporte that the said complainant was a very honest fellow: And this deponent sayethe that the said deffen-

(*a*) Deposition

(*b*) Conveyance

(*c*) Mortgage

SHAKESPEARE'S SIGNATURES

dant did make a mocion vnto the complainant of marriadge with the said Mary in the bill mencioned beinge the said deffendantes sole chyld and daughter, and willinglye offered to performe the same yf the said complainant shold seeme to be content and well like thereof: And further this deponent sayethe that the said deffendantes wyeffe did sollicitt and entreat this deponent to move and perswade the said complainant to effect the said marriadge, and accordingly this deponent did moue and perswade the complainant thervnto :And more to this interrogatorye he cannott depose.

4 To the ffourth interrogatory this deponent sayth that the defendant promissed to geue the said complainant a porcion in marriadg⟨e⟩ with Marye his daughter, but what certayne porcion he rememberethe not, nor when to be payed, nor knoweth that the defendant promissed the plaintiff twoe hundered poundes with his daughter Marye at the tyme of his decease. But sayth that the plaintiff was dwellinge with the defendant in his house, and they had amongeste them selues manye conferences about there marriadge which ⟨afterwardes⟩ was consumated and solempnized. And more he cann⟨ott depose.⟩

5 To the vth interrogatory this deponent sayth he can saye noth⟨inge⟩ touchinge any parte or poynte of the same interrogatory, for he knoweth not what implementes and necessaries of houshould stuffe the defendant gaue the plaintiff in marriadge with his daughter Marye.

Willm Shakp

(b) [19 June 1612. *Depositions to further Interrogatories on behalf of Belott.*]

(1) [*Deposition of Daniell Nicholas.*]

4 To the iiijth interrogatory this deponent sayth that the defendant did never send him this deponent vnto the complainant to make mocion of marriadge betwixte the

complainant and the said Marye Mountioye beinge the
defendantes sole daughter and childe, but M^r: William
Shakespeare tould him this deponent that the defendant
sent him the said Mr Shakespeare to the plaintiff about
suche a marriadge to be hadd betweene them, and Shakespeare tould this deponent that the defendant tould him
that yf the plaintiff would marrye the said Marye his
daughter he would geue him the plaintiff a some of
monney with her for a porcion in marriadge with her.
And that yf he the plaintiff did not marry with her the
said Marye and shee with the plaintiff shee should never
coste him the defendant her ffather a groat. Where-
vppon, and in regard Mr Shakespeare hadd tould them
that they should haue a some of monney for a porcion
from the father, they weare made suer by Mr Shakespeare by geuinge there consent, and agreed to marry
and did marrye. But what some yt was that Mr Mount-
yoye promissed to geue them he the said Mr Shakespeare
could not remember, but said yt was ffyftye poundes
or theraboutes to his best rememberaunce. And as he
rememberith Mr Shakespeare said he promissed to geue
them a porcion of his goodes: but what, or to what
valewe he rememberithe not. And more he cannott
depose.

(2) [*Deposition of William Eaton.*]

4 To the iiijth interrogatory this deponent sayth he hath
herd one Mr Shakespeare saye that he was sent by the
defendant to the plaintiff to move the plaintiff to haue
a marriadge betweene them the plaintiff and the defend-
entes daughter Marye Mountioye, and herd Mr Shakespeare saye that he was wished by the defendant to make
proffer of a certayne some that the defendant said he
would geue the plaintiff with his daughter Marye Mount-

ioye in marriage, but he had forgott the some. And more he cannott depose touching the same interrogatory.

(3) [*Deposition of Nowell Mountjoy.*]
4 To the iiij^th interrogatory this deponent sayth he was never sent by the defendant vnto the complainant to make a mocion to him of a marriadge to be hadd betwixte the complainant and Mary Mountioy the defendantes sole child and daughter, nor knoweth of any other that was by the defendant sent vnto the plaintiff vppon that messiage: but the plaintiff tould this deponent that one Mr Shakespeare was imployed by the defendant about that buysnes: in what manner: or to what effecte he knoweth not: ...

[Shakespeare was not a party to this suit, which was discovered with other related documents by Professor Wallace. Christopher Mountjoy was a French Huguenot, who had apparently been resident in London for some years before 1600, when he was of St. Olave's parish. Probably then, and certainly in 1612, he occupied a house at the corner of Silver and Monkwell Sts., close to St. Olave's church, in Cripplegate ward, within the NW. corner of the city walls. His business was that of a tiremaker, and he had an apprentice, Stephen Belott, also of French extraction. On 19 Nov. 1604 Belott married Mountjoy's daughter Mary. Some years later he quarrelled with his father-in-law, and brought the suit of 1612, in which he alleged that Mountjoy had broken promises to pay a portion of £60 with his daughter and to make a will leaving her a further £200. The claims were disputed, and evidence as to the negotiations leading to the marriage became relevant. Joan Johnson, once a servant in Mountjoy's house, deposed that Shakespeare 'that laye in the house' had been his agent to persuade Belott to the marriage, and this was confirmed on hearsay from Shakespeare himself, but whether in 1604 or later is not clear, by one Daniel Nicholas, who further said that Shakespeare had named the portion to him as about £50 and some household stuff.

Obviously Shakespeare's own evidence was crucial. Unfortunately his memory failed him when he was examined on 11 May 1612. He had known the plaintiff and defendant for ten years and could speak to the plaintiff's good behaviour as an apprentice and the defendant's goodwill towards him. He had persuaded Belott to the marriage at the instigation of Mountjoy's wife. A portion had been promised, but he could not remember how much, or when it was to be paid, and knew nothing as to the alleged promise of a legacy or as to what goods had been given to Belott. Shakespeare's name appears in the margin of a set of interrogatories for a second hearing on 19 June, and presumably it was intended to press his memory further; but there is no second deposition by him. Nicholas repeated his hearsay and added that Belott and Mary Mountjoy were 'made sure', i.e. betrothed, by Shakespeare. Some slight confirmation, still at second-hand, was obtained as to Shakespeare's part in the matter from William Eaton, now an apprentice to Mountjoy, and Mountjoy's brother Nowell, and the court, after hearing other evidence, referred the case for arbitration to the overseers and elders of the French church in London. They awarded Belott 20 nobles which Mountjoy had not paid a year later. Incidentally they noted 'tous 2 pere & gendre desbauchéz', and later notes also record Mountjoy as of licentious life.

What we learn of Shakespeare is that he had known the Mountjoy household since 1602, had been a lodger in it, but perhaps only temporarily, in 1604, was described as of Stratford-on-Avon in 1612 and therefore presumably had no London residence, was present at Westminster on 11 May 1612, and, perhaps, was then of failing memory.

8. SHAKESPEARE AS MALTSTER

[1598, Feb. 4. Extract from *S.A. Misc. Doct.* i. 106. Presumably the holdings, such as Shakespeare's, not specified as corn, were in malt.]

Stratforde Burrowghe, Warrwicke. The noate of corne & malte Taken the iiijth of ffebruarij 1597 in the xlth yeare

of the raigne of our moste gracious Soveraigne Ladie Queen Elizabethe etc. ...
Chapple street warde ... W^m. Shackespere. x quarters.

[Three wet summers in 1594, 1595, and 1596 had produced, not only *Mid. N. Dr.*, but also a serious dearth of corn, leading to high prices, poverty, and discontent. The position was aggravated by the engrossing and forestalling of corn—that is, holding supplies in bulk for a rise of price and purchasing direct from farmers, instead of in open market; and by the excessive use of barley for malt. The Privy Council attempted to remedy these abuses by reissuing in 1594 a set of *Orders* to Justices of the Peace originally framed in 1586. The Council's remedies, which told against the interests of many Justices and other well-to-do men, were not altogether effective. The matter was still occupying Lord Burghley in preparation for the parliament of 1597, and a Council letter of 22 August called upon the Justices for a fresh inquisition upon the engrossers, 'a number of wycked people in condicions more lyke to wolves or cormerants than to naturall men', and including, as the Council regretfully note, 'men which are of good lyvelyhoode and in estymacion of worshipp'. The dearth appears to have been particularly felt in south-west Warwickshire, which was in part dependent for its supply upon the neighbouring corn-growing districts of Worcestershire. Sturley reports to Quiney on 24 Jan. 1598, that the people were growing 'malcontent', and were approaching neighbouring Justices with complaints against 'our maltsters'. There was wild hope of leading them in a halter, and 'if God send my Lord of Essex down shortly, to see them hanged on gibbets at their own doors'. It was in these circumstances that the return of 4 February was made. There was not now much engrossed wheat in the town; only 44 quarters of wheat and practically no barley. The amount of malt was still considerable, 438 quarters belonging to townsmen and 251 to strangers. But the individual holdings were less than in 1595. The largest was 18 quarters; only a dozen men had more than Shakespeare's 10.]

9. THE QUINEY CORRESPONDENCE

(a) [1598, Jan. 24. Extract from letter of Abraham Sturley ⟨to Richard Quiney⟩.]

This is one speciall remembrance from v^r fathers motion. It semeth bj him that our countriman, Mr Shaksper, is willinge to disburse some monei vpon some od yardeland or other att Shottri or neare about vs; he thinketh it a verj fitt patterne to move him to deale in the matter of our tithes. Bj the instruccions v can geve him theareof, and bj the frendes he can make therefore, we thinke it a faire marke for him to shoote att, and not vnpossible to hitt. It obtained would advance him in deede, and would do vs muche good. Hoc movere, et quantum in te est permouere, ne necligas, hoc enim et sibi et nobis maximi erit momenti. Hic labor, hoc opus esset eximiae et gloriae et laudis sibi .... Stretfordia, Januarii 24. Abrah. Strl.

(b) [1598, Oct. 25. Richard Quiney to Shakespeare.]

Loveinge Contreyman, I am bolde of yowe as of a ffrende, craveinge yowre helpe with xxx^{ll} vppon Mr Bushells & my securytee or Mr Myttons with me. Mr Rosswell is nott come to London as yeate & I have especiall cawse. Yowe shall ffrende me muche in helpeinge me out of all the debettes I owe in London, I thancke god, & muche quiet my mynde which wolde nott be indebeted. I am nowe towardes the Cowrte in hope of answer for the dispatche of my Buysenes. Yowe shall neither loase creddytt nor monney by me, the Lorde wyllinge, & nowe butt perswade yowre selfe soe as I hope & yowe shall nott need to feare butt with all hartie thanckefullenes I will holde my tyme & content yowre ffrende, & yf we Bargaine farther yowe shalbe the paiemaster yowre self. My tyme biddes me hasten to an ende & soe I committ thys ⟨to⟩ yowre care & hope of yowre helpe. I feare I shall

THE QUINEY CORRESPONDENCE 157

nott be backe thys night ffrom the Cowrte. Haste. The Lorde be with yowe & with vs all Amen. ffrom the Bell in Carter Lane the 25 October 1598. Yowres in all kyndenes Ryc. Quyney. [*Addressed*] H⟨aste⟩ To my Loveinge good ffrend & contreymann M^r W^m. Shackespere deliver thees. [*Seal*] On a bend three trefoils slipped.

(*c*) [n.d. ⟨1598, *c*. 30 Oct.⟩. Extract from letter of Adrian Quiney to Richard Quiney.]

Yow shalle, God wylling, receve from your wyfe by ye baylye, thys brynger, aswrance of x^s. . . . Yff yow bargen with Mr Sha. . or receve money therfor, brynge your money home yf yow maye, I see howe knite stockynges be sold, ther ys gret byinge of them at Evysshome. Edward Wheat and Harrye, your brother man, were both at Evyshome thys daye senet, and, as I harde, bestow 20^{ll}. ther in knyt hosseyngs, wherefore I thynke yow maye doo good, yff yow can have money. . . . [*Addressed*] To my lovynge sonne Rycharde Qwyney at the Belle in Carter Leyne deliver thesse in London.

(*d*) [1598, Nov. 4. Extract from letter of Abraham Sturley to Richard Quiney.]

V^r letter of the 25 of October came to mj handes the laste of the same att night per Grenwaj, which imported . . . that our countriman M^r Wm. Shak. would procure vs monej, which I will like of as I shall heare when, and wheare, and howe; and I praj let not go that occasion if it may sort to any indifferent condicions. Allso that if monej might be had for 30 or 40^l, a lease, &c., might be procured. Oh howe can v make dowbt of monej, who will not beare xxx^{tie} or xl^l towardes sutch a match? . . . From Stretford Novem. 4th 1598 . . . Abrah. Sturlej. [*Addressed*] To his most lovinge brother, Mr Richard Quinej, att the Bell in Carterlane att London, geve these.

158 RECORDS

[Richard Quiney's London visits seem to have been partly occupied with the private affairs of himself, his father, their associate Sturley, and other relatives and friends, and partly with public business entrusted to him by the Corporation. Stratford, at the end of the 16th century, was a 'decaying' town. Richard was charged to negotiate with the Privy Council, and to enlist the support of Sir Edward Greville, then lord of the manor of Stratford. A new charter was not granted until 23 July 1610, but Richard did in fact succeed in securing relief from the taxes by a royal warrant of 27 Jan. 1599. Richard's relations with his 'countreyman' were, so far as we know the facts, limited to his private concerns. He wanted a loan on reaching London in October 1598, and either applied to Shakespeare or thought of applying to him. The fact that the letter was found with Richard's own correspondence suggests that it was never delivered. This loan was apparently to be spent on London debts. The later letters show an expectation of money to come from Shakespeare, which might be available for an investment.]

10. THE WELCOME ENCLOSURE

(*a*) [1614, Sept. 5. Extract from *The Particulars of Olde Stratforde; also Landes of Freeholders & where they lye.*]

5 Septembris. 1614.

Auncient ffreeholders in the ffieldes of Oldstratford and Welcombe.

Mr Shakspeare. 4. yard Land, noe common nor ground beyond gospell bushe, noe grownd in Sandfield, nor none in slowe hill field beyond Bishopton nor none in the enclosure beyond Bishopton.

(*b*) [1614, Oct. 28. Contemporary extract from Articles between Shakespeare and William Replingham.]

Vicesimo octavo die Octobris, anno Domini 1614. Articles of agreement indented made betweene William Shackespeare, of Stretford in the county of Warwicke, gent., on the one partye, and William Replingham, of Greete Harborowe in the countie of Warwicke, gent., on the other partie, the daye and yeare abouesaid. Inter alia Item, the said William Replingham, for him, his heires, executours and assignes, doth covenaunte and agree to and with the said William Shackespeare, his heires and assignes, That he, the said William Replingham, his heires or assignes, shall, uppon reasonable request, satisfie, content and make recompence unto him, the said William Shackespeare or his assignes, for all such losse, detriment and hinderance as he, the said William Shackespeare, his heires and assignes, and one Thomas Greene, gent., shall or maye be thought, in the views and judgement of foure indifferent persons, to be indifferentlie elected by the said William and William, and their heires, and in default of the said William Replingham, by the said William Shackespeare or his heires onely, to survey and judge the same, to sustayne or incurre for or in respecte of the increasinge ⟨decreasinge⟩ of the yearelie value of the tythes they the said William Shackespeare and Thomas doe joyntlie or seuerallie hold and enioy in the said fieldes, or anie of them, by reason of anie inclosure or decaye of tyllage there ment and intended by the said William Replingham; and that the said William Replingham and his heires shall procure such sufficient securitie vnto the said William Shackespeare and his heires, for the performance of theis covenauntes, as shalbee devised by learned counsell. In witnes whereof the parties abouesaid to theis presentes interchangeablie their handes and seales have put, the daye and yeare first aboue wrytten. Sealed and deliuered in the presence of us, Tho: Lucas; Jo: Rogers; Anthonie Nasshe; Mich: Olney. [*Endorsed.*] Coppy of the articles with Mr Shakspeare.

(c) [1614, Nov. 17 to 1615, Sept. 5. Extracts from memoranda of Thomas Greene.]

(1) [1614.] Jovis 17 No. At my Cosen Shakspeare commyng yesterday to towne I went to see him howe he did he told me that they assured him they ment to inclose noe further then to gospell bushe & so vpp straight (leavyng out part of the dyngles to the ffield) to the gate in Clopton hedge & take in Salisburyes peece: and that they meane in Aprill to servey the Land & then to gyve satisfaccion & not before & he & Mr Hall say they think there will be nothyng done at all. ...

(2) ⟨In margin⟩ 10 Dec. that the survey there was past, & I came from Wilson to look Mr Replingham at the beare & at new place but myssed him & on the narowe sid but he was not to be spoken with: ...

(3) 23 Dec. 1614. A Hall. L⟨ett⟩res wrytten one to Mr Manneryng another to Mr Shakespeare with almost all the com⟨panyes⟩ hands to eyther: I alsoe wrytte of myself to my Cosen Shakespeare the Coppyes of all our oathes m⟨a⟩de then alsoe a not of the Inconvenyences wold gr⟨ow⟩ by the Inclosure. ...

(4) r⟨emember⟩ ... 9 Jan. 1614. Mr Replyngham 28 Octbris articled w⟨i⟩th Mr Shakspeare & then I was putt in by T. Lucas. ...

(5) [11 Jan. 1615] On Wednesday, being the xjth day. .. At night Mr Replingham supped w⟨i⟩th me and Mr Barnes was to beare him Company, where he assured me before Mr Barnes that I should be well dealt w⟨i⟩thall, confessyng former promises by himself Mr Manneryng & his agreement for me w⟨i⟩th my cosen Shakpeare. ...

(6) 7. Apr. being goodfryday Mr Barb⟨e⟩r commyng to the colledge to M^r T C⟨ombe⟩ about a debt he stood surety for M⟨ist⟩ris Quyney W C⟨ombe⟩ willed his brother to shewe Mr Barb⟨e⟩r noe favour & threatned him that

THE WELCOME ENCLOSURE

he should be served vpp to London within a ffortnight. (and so yt fell out:). . . .

(7) 14 Aug. 1615. Mr Barb⟨e⟩r dyed.

(8) [*Inserted later*] Sept. W Shakspeares tellyng J Greene that J was not able to beare the encloseinge of Welcombe.

(9) 5 Sept. his sendyng James for the executours of Mr Barb⟨e⟩r to agree as ys sayd w⟨i⟩th them for Mr Barb⟨e⟩rs interest.

11. A PREACHER'S THIRST

[1614. From *Account* (Xmas) of Chamberlains.]

Item for one quart of sack and one quart of clarrett winne geuen to a precher at the new place. xx^d.

[Such a gift was a common courtesy to a neighbouring justice or other distinguished visitor at his inn or lodging in the town. There were notes of other preachers so refreshed between 1619 and 1630. Lee says that the preacher was 'of Puritan proclivities'. It may be so, but there is no evidence. There were three official foundation sermons each year before the Bailiff and Corporation; the Oken on election day in September, the Hamlet Smith at Easter, the Perrott at Whitsuntide. John Combe left a legacy for another in 1614.]

12. LORD RUTLAND'S IMPRESA

[1613, Mar. 31. From *Account* of Thomas Screvin, steward to Francis Manners, 6th Earl of Rutland.]

Item. 31 Martii, to Mr Shakspeare in gold about my Lorde's impreso, xliiij^s; to Richard Burbage for paynting and making yt, in gold xliiij^s.—iiij^{li}. viij^s.

[This was for the tilt upon the King's Accession day, 24 Mar. 1613.[1] There is no reason to doubt that the payment was to the poet, as the association with Burbadge, known to have been a painter, suggests.]

[1] Cf. *Eliz. Stage*, i. 148.

13. SHAKESPEARE'S WILL

[1616, Mar. 25. The original is preserved in the Principal Probate Registry at Somerset House. The writing, in an English hand, covers one side of each of three sheets. The second alone is numbered. When found, the sheets were fastened together by a narrow strip of parchment along the top margins. Now (Lee 520) each sheet has been mended with transparent material, and placed in a separate locked oaken frame between two sheets of glass, to which it is fixed. The first signature has become illegible, and a few other words are very obscure. There is practically no punctuation; I have added a minimum. Words ruled through are struck out in the original. The inventory exhibited at probate has not been found.]

⟨*Sheet 1*⟩

Vicesimo Quinto die ~~Januarij~~ **Martij** Anno Regni Domini nostri Jacobi nunc Regis Anglie &c decimo quarto & Scotie xlix° Annoque domini 1616.

T⟨*estamentum*⟩ W⟨*illel*⟩mj Shackspeare.
R⟨*ecognoscatu*⟩r. In the name of god Amen I William Shackspeare of Stratford vpon Avon in the countie of Warr gent in perfect health & memorie god be praysed doe make & Ordayne this my last will & testament in manner & forme followeing. That is to saye ffirst I Comend my Soule into the handes of god my Creator, hoping & assuredlie beleeving through thonelie merittes of Jesus Christe my Saviour to be made partaker of lyfe everlasting, And my bodye to the Earth whereof yt ys made. Item I Gyve & bequeath vnto my ~~sonne in L~~ daughter Judyth One Hundred & ffyftie poundes of lawfull English money to be paied vnto her in manner & forme followeing; That ys to saye, One Hundred Poundes **in discharge of her marriage porcion** within one yeare after my deceas, with consideracion after the Rate of twoe shillinges in the pound for soe long tyme as the same shalbe

SHAKESPEARE'S WILL

vnpaied vnto her after my deceas, & the ffyftie poundes Residewe thereof vpon her Surrendring **of**, or gyving of such sufficient securitie as the overseers of this my will shall like of to Surrender or graunte, All her estate & Right that shall discend or come vnto her after my deceas or **that shee** nowe hath of in or to one Copiehold tenemente with thappurtenaunces lyeing & being in Stratford vpon Avon aforesaied in the saied countie of Warr, being parcell or holden of the mannour of Rowington, vnto my daughter Susanna Hall & her heires for ever. Item I Gyve & bequeath vnto my saied daughter Judith One Hundred & ffyftie Poundes more if shee or Anie issue of her bodie be Lyvinge att thend of three Yeares next ensueing the daie of the date of this my will, during which tyme my executours to paie her consideracion from my deceas according to the Rate aforesaied. And if she dye within the saied terme without issue of her bodye then my will ys & I doe gyve & bequeath One Hundred Poundes thereof to my Neece Elizabeth Hall & the ffiftie Poundes to be sett fourth by my executours during the lief of my Sister Johane Harte & the vse & profitt thereof Cominge shalbe payed to my saied Sister Jone, & after her deceas the saied 1^{li} shall Remaine Amongst the children of my saied Sister Equallie to be devided Amongst them. But if my saied daughter Judith be lyving att thend of the saied three Yeares or anie yssue of her bodye, then my will ys & soe I devise & bequeath the saied Hundred & ffyftie poundes to be sett out **by my executours and overseers** for the best benefitt of her & her issue & **the stock** not **to be** paied vnto her soe long as she shalbe marryed & covert Baron ~~by my executours & overseers,~~ but my will ys that she shall have the consideracion yearelie paied vnto her during her lief & after her deceas the saied stock and consideracion to bee paied to her children if she have Anie & if not to her executours or assignes she lyving the saied terme after my deceas. Provided that yf such husbond as she shall att thend of the saied three Yeares be marryed vnto or attaine after doe sufficientlie Assure vnto her & thissue of her bodie landes Awnswereable to the porcion by this my will gyven vnto her & to be adiudged soe by my executours & overseers then my will ys that the said cl^{li} shalbe paied to such husbond as shall make such assurance to his owne vse. Item I gyve & bequeath vnto my saied sister Jone xx^{li} & all my wearing Apparrell to be paied & deliuered within one yeare after my deceas, And I doe will & devise vnto her **the house** with thappurtenaunces in Stratford wherein she dwelleth for her naturall lief vnder the yearelie Rent of xij^{d}. Item I gyve and bequeath

⟨(*In left margin now illegible*) William Shakspere⟩

⟨*Sheet 2*⟩

Vnto her three sonns Welliam Harte ⟨*blank*⟩ Hart & Michaell Harte ffyve poundes A peece to be payed within one Yeare after my deceas. ~~to be sett out for her within one Yeare after my deceas by my executours with thadvise & direccions of my overseers for her best proffit vntil her Marriage and then the same with the increase thereof to be paied vnto~~ her. Item I gyve & bequeath vnto her **the saied Elizabeth Hall** All my Plate **(except my brod silver & gilt bole)** that I now have att the date of this my will. Item I gyve & bequeath vnto the Poore of Stratford aforesaied tenn poundes, to m^{r} Thomas Combe my Sword, to Thomas Russell Esquier ffyve poundes, & to ffrauncis Collins of the Borough of Warr in the countie of Warr gent thirteene poundes Sixe shillinges & Eight pence to be paied within one Yeare after my deceas. Item I gyve & bequeath to ~~m^{r} Richard Tyler~~ thelder **Hamlett Sadler** xxvj^{s} viij^{d} to buy him A Ringe, to William Raynoldes gent xxvj^s viij^d to buy him A Ringe, to my godson William Walker xx^s in gold, to Anthonye Nashe gent xxvj^s viij^d, & to Mr John Nashe xxvj^s viij^d in gold, & to my ffellowes John Hemynge Richard Burbage & Henry Cundell xxvj^s viij^d A peece to buy them Ringes. Item I Gyve Will bequeath & Devise vnto my daughter Susanna Hall for better enabling of her to performe this my will & towardes the performans thereof All that Capitall Messuage or tenemente with thappurtenaunces in Stratford aforesaied Called the newe place wherein I nowe dwell & twoe messuages or tenementes with thappurtenaunces scituat lyeing & being in Henley streete within the borough of Stratford aforesaied, And all my barnes stables Orchardes gardens landes tenementes & hereditamentes whatsoever scituat lyeing & being or to be had Receyved perceyved or taken within the townes Hamlettes villages ffieldes & groundes of Stratford vpon Avon Oldstratford Bushopton & Welcombe or in anie of them in the saied countie of Warr, And alsoe All that Messuage or tenemente with thappurtenaunces wherein one John Robinson dwelleth, scituat lyeing & being in the blackfriers in London nere the Wardrobe, & all other my landes tenementes and hereditamentes whatsoever; To Have & to hold All & singuler the saied premisses with their Appurtennaunces vnto the saied Susanna Hall for & during the terme of her naturall lief, & after her Deceas to the first sonne of her bodie lawfullie yssueing & to the heires Males of the bodie of the saied first Sonne lawfullie yssueing, & for defalt of such issue to the second Sonne of her bodie lawfullie issueing and ~~so~~ to the heires Males of the bodie of the saied Second Sonne lawfullie yssueinge, & for defalt of such heires to the third Sonne of the bodie of the saied Susanna Lawfullie yssueing and of the heires Males of the bodie of the saied third sonne lawfullie yssueing, And for defalt of such issue the same soe to be & Remaine to the ffourth sonne ffyfth sixte & Seaventh sonnes of her bodie lawfullie issueing one after Another & to the heires

2   Willm̃ Shakspere

⟨*Sheet 3*⟩

Males of the bodies of the said fourth fifth Sixte & Seaventh sonnes lawfullie yssueing, in such manner as yt ys before Lymitted to be & Remaine to the first second and third Sonns of her bodie & to their heires Males; And for defalt of such issue the said premisses to be & Remaine to my sayed Neece Hall & the heires males of her bodie Lawfullie yssueing, and for defalt of issue to my daughter Judith & the heires Males of her bodie lawfullie yssueing, And for defalt of such issue to the Right heires of me the saied William Shackspere for ever. **Item I gyve vnto my wief my second best bed with the furniture** Item I gyve & bequeath to my saied daughter Judith my broad silver gilt bole. All the Rest of my goodes chattels Leases plate Jewels & householde stuffe whatsoever, after my dettes and Legasies paied & my funerall expences discharged, I gyve devise & bequeath to my Sonne in Lawe John Hall gent & my daughter Susanna his wief whom I ordaine & make executours of this my Last will and testament. And I doe intreat & Appoint **the saied** Thomas Russell Esquier & ffrauncis Collins gent to be overseers hereof. And doe Revoke All former wills & publishe this to be my last will and testament. In witnesse whereof I have hereunto put my ~~Seale~~ **hand** the daie & Yeare first aboue Written.

witnes to the publishing hereof. Fra: Collyns	By me William Shakspeare.
Julyus Shawe	Hamnet Sadler
John Robinson	Robert Whattcott

(d) Will (1)

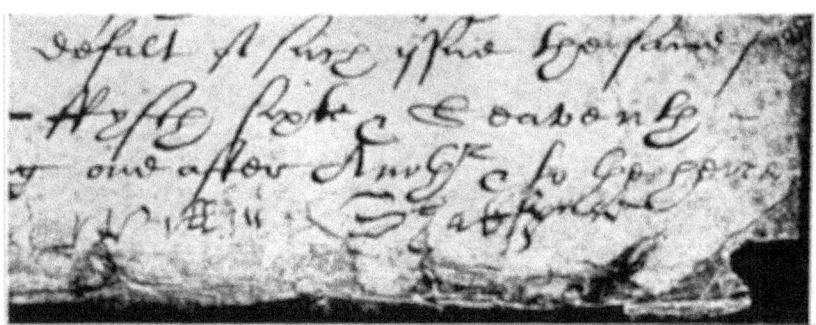

(e) Will (2)

(f) Will (3)

SHAKESPEARE'S SIGNATURES

[*Endorsed*] Probatum coram magistro Willielmo Byrde legum doctore Comissario &c xxij^{do} die mensis Junij Anno domini 1616. Juramento Johannis Hall vnius executoris &c Cui &c de bene &c Jurato. Reservata potestate &c Susanne Hall alteri executori &c cum venerit &c petitura

Inventorium exhibitum

[The text is probably in the hand of a clerk employed by Francis Collins, a solicitor of Warwick, who no doubt drafted the will. The following hypothesis seems best to fit the facts. In or before a January, probably of 1616, Shakespeare gave instructions for a will. Collins prepared a complete draft for execution in that month. It was not then executed, but on 25 Mar. 1616 Shakespeare sent for Collins. The changes he desired in the opening provisions were so substantial that it was thought best to prepare a new sheet 1. The heading and initial formulas as to health and religious expectation were adapted by the clerk from the old draft. He gave correctly the calendar year which had begun on the very day on which he wrote, and the regnal year which had begun on the day before; and this of itself shows that the present sheet 1 cannot be earlier than 25 Mar. 1616. But he made, and afterwards corrected, the slip of transcribing 'Januarij' from the old draft Then the opening provisions were dictated afresh with one or two corrections, such as the elimination of 'sonne in L', during the process, and proved so much longer than those they replaced, as to crowd the writing and necessitate the carrying of two lines on to the old sheet 2, where they were inserted before a cancelled passage. The rest of this sheet and sheet 3 were allowed to stand, with some alterations; and in this form it was signed on each sheet by Shakespeare, 'published' by his declaration to the witnesses that it was his will, and signed by them. Sheet 1 is mainly occupied with bequests in favour of Shakespeare's daughter Judith, and it is reasonable to suppose that it was her marriage on 10 Feb. 1616 which determined the principal changes, as her marriage 'porcion', and £50 more contingently on her resignation to her sister of any right in

Shakespeare's Rowington copyhold. Of another £150 she was to have the interest. If she died without issue in three years, the capital was to be divided between Shakespeare's grand-daughter Elizabeth Hall, whom he calls his 'neece', and his sister Joan Hart. If not, and if any husband, whom Judith might have at the end of the three years or might thereafter 'attaine', had made a settlement upon her and her issue of lands answerable to her portion, it was to be paid to him. If no such settlement had been made, the sum was to be held in trust for her and her heirs. Palaeographically the word 'attaine' might also be read, and has been read, 'att anie'. But this would involve a *lacuna*, while 'attaine' gives an adequate and complete sense. The scribe of an old copy at the P.C.C., cited by Staunton, wrote 'attayne'. Possibly the elaborate provisions with regard to Judith indicate a lack of confidence in Thomas Quiney. Some students have thought that the will also indicates displeasure with Judith herself, either at her marriage or at its accompanying excommunication, and have suggested that Shakespeare originally left all his plate to Judith, and in the end cut her off with his silver-gilt bowl. This implies that the 'her' in the cancelled passage at the top of sheet 2, and the cancelled 'her' in the next line, which clearly go together, referred in the first draft to Judith. But it is possible that they referred to Elizabeth Hall; and if so the inference may be, not that Judith was less tenderly treated in the revision, but that a trust fund originally meant, wholly or in part for Elizabeth, was transferred to make better provision for Judith, and Elizabeth left with only a reversion. Moreover, the specific bequest of the silver-gilt bowl to Judith is unaltered in sheet 3 from the original draft, and would have been superfluous there if sheet 2 had already given her all the plate. Probably the bulk of the plate was always for Elizabeth, although, curiously enough, an inconsistent mention of 'plate' appears in the residuary bequest to John and Susanna Hall.

And now as to the 'second best bed'. A good deal of sheer nonsense has been written about this. Wills have been ransacked, for cases, none quite analogous, of other bequests of solitary or inferior household articles. And baseless theories of domestic discord or infirmity have been devised to account for the absence of any further provision in the will for Shakespeare's wife. No such provision was needed. If no equivalent jointure had been substituted, as to which there is no evidence, Mrs. Shakespeare would have been entitled by common law to her dower of a life interest in one-third of any of the testator's heritable estates on which dower had not been legally barred; and to residence in his principal mansion house. Whether she would also be entitled to 'free-bench' in copyhold property would depend on the custom of the manor. The normal Rowington custom was to admit the widow on payment of 1d.; otherwise the estate passed to sons or daughters according to the rule of primogeniture. It is doubtful whether this applied to the outlying property in Stratford, and Mrs. Shakespeare does not appear to have paid her 1d. Whether the widow was entitled to a third of personalty similarly depended upon local custom; the Warwickshire custom is unknown. Such legal or customary rights are sometimes incorporated in the provisions of wills, sometimes not; they would be operative in either event. A best bed might be treated as an heirloom.[1] To regard the interlineated bequest as a deliberate slight is absurd. If an explanation is wanted, let us guess that, when the draft will was read over, Mrs. Shakespeare asked for the bed; it had come from her old home at Hewland.

Why was the will executed in the form of a much-corrected draft, unpunctuated and unparagraphed, instead of in a fair copy? One answer is that such was the practice of Francis Collins. John Combe's will, made by Collins long before his death, is in the same condition. Lawyers, indeed, are never fond of relying on punctuation. Elizabethan probate courts were not particular as to the form of a will, where only personal property was involved. But where there was real property, the will had to be in writing and evidence of its publication forth-

---

[1] Thomas Combe in 1608 left all bedsteads to his wife 'except the best', which 'with the best Bedd and best furniture thereunto belonging', was left to his son William.

coming. This ordinarily took the form of testimony by two or three witnesses to the testator's signature. On this point Collins was careful enough, and as two of the witnesses were legatees, whose legacies would be invalidated if they had to give testimony, he secured five. Even then the rough form of the will might give rise to legal questions, and Dr. Tannenbaum is probably right in thinking that a fair copy was dispensed with because of some need for haste, such as the serious illness of the testator. It is not inconsistent with this that Shakespeare in fact lived for nearly a month after his will was signed, or that the preamble describes him as 'in perfect health and memorie'. No doubt invalid testators are often described as 'sick in body, but of perfect mind and memory', but the phrase may have been allowed to stand from the original sheet 1, and would be of little importance, so long as the testator was mentally of testamentary capacity. Dr. Tannenbaum finds further evidence of failing powers in the character of Shakespeare's signatures, and of haste in certain ambiguities in the terms of the bequest to Judith. These are not very serious, and a court would probably find no great difficulties of interpretation. It is not, perhaps, quite clear whether the 'porcion' to be met by a husband's assurance of 'answerable' lands was the specific marriage 'porcion' of £100 or the whole bequest of £300.

Surprise has been felt that the will contains no mention of books or manuscripts. There was no reason why it should, unless the testator wished to make a special bequest of such articles. A will is a legal instrument for devising property, and not a literary autobiography. Books and manuscripts may have appeared in the lost inventory. In any case, they would pass to John and Susanna Hall under the residuary bequest of 'goods'. In fact Hall, by his will of 1635, left his 'study of bookes' and his manuscripts to Thomas Nash, and under Nash's will of 1642 any that remained probably passed to his wife as his residuary legatee. Whether books belonging to Shakespeare were among them, and whether he kept any manuscripts of his plays, or handed them all to the King's men, we do not know.

14. SHAKESPEARE'S EPITAPHS

(a) [From gravestone in chancel of Stratford Church, between that of Anne Shakespeare, which is next the north wall bearing the monument, and that of Susanna Hall. The stone bears no name.]

> GOOD FREND FOR IESVS SAKE FORBEARE,
> TO DIGG THE DVST ENCLOASED HEARE!
> BLESTE BE Y^E MAN Y^T SPARES THES STONES,
> AND CVRST BE HE Y^T MOVES MY BONES.

[Dowdall in 1693 first records a tradition (p. 233) that Shakespeare wrote these lines himself, and says that the curse prevented the opening of the grave for his wife and daughters. Hall in 1694 adds that the grave was seventeen feet deep—most improbable so near the Avon—and that Shakespeare was in fear of a transfer of his bones to the charnel-house. This has now been pulled down.]

(b) [1616⟨⟩1623. From tablet in monument on north wall of chancel.]

IVDICIO PYLIVM, GENIO SOCRATEM, ARTE MARONEM:
   TERRA TEGIT, POPVLVS MÆRET, OLYMPVS HABET.

STAY PASSENGER, WHY GOEST THOV BY SO FAST?
READ IF THOV CANST, WHOM ENVIOVS DEATH HATH PLAST,
WITH IN THIS MONVMENT SHAKSPEARE: WITH WHOME,
QVICK NATVRE DIDE: WHOSE NAME DOTH DECK Y^S TOMBE,
FAR MORE THEN COST: SIEH ALL, Y^T HE HATH WRITT,
LEAVES LIVING ART, BVT PAGE, TO SERVE HIS WITT.
              OBIIT AÑO DO^I 1616
           ÆTATIS . 53 DIE 23 AP^R.

[The authorship of the lines is unknown. Hall would hardly have spoken of the burial as 'within this monument'. It was no very accurate scholar who shortened the first vowel of 'Socratem'. Steevens conjectured 'Sophoclem', but the stone-cutter, who put 'sieh' for 'sith', would be less capable of the classical substitution.]

15. PERFORMANCES

1594. Court ⟨Greenwich⟩.

Dec. 26, 27. William Kempe William Shakespeare & Richarde Burbage seruantes to the Lord Chamberleyne.

1594. London.

[Dec. 28. Gray's Inn. From *Gesta Grayorum*.]

The next grand Night was intended to be upon *Innocents-Day* at Night.... The Ambassador ⟨of the Inner Temple⟩ came ... about Nine of the Clock at Night ... there arose such a disordered Tumult and Crowd upon the Stage, that there was no Opportunity to effect that which was intended.... The Lord Ambassador and his Train thought that they were not so kindly entertained, as was before expected, and thereupon would not stay any longer at that time, but, in a sort, discontented and displeased. After their Departure the Throngs and Tumults did somewhat cease, although so much of them continued, as was able to disorder and confound any good Inventions whatsoever. In regard whereof, as also for that the Sports intended were especially for the gracing of the *Templarians*, it was thought good not to offer any thing of Account, saving Dancing and Revelling with Gentlewomen; and after such Sports, a Comedy of Errors (like to *Plautus* his *Menechmus*) was played by the Players. So that Night was begun, and continued to the end, in nothing but Confusion and Errors; whereupon, it was ever afterwards called, *The Night of Errors*.... We preferred Judgments ... against a Sorcerer or Conjuror that was supposed to be the Cause of that confused Inconvenience ... And Lastly, that he had foisted a Company of base and common Fellows, to make up our Disorders with a Play of Errors and Con-

PERFORMANCES 173

fusions; and that that Night had gained to us Discredit, and itself a Nickname of Errors.

1595. London.

[Dec. 7. From *Letter* of Sir Edward Hoby, who had a house in Canon Row, Westminster, to Sir Robert Cecil.]

Sir, findinge that you wer not convenientlie to be at London to morrow night I am bold to send to knowe whether Teusdaie ⟨Dec. 9⟩ may be anie more in your grace to visit poore Channon rowe where as late as it shal please you a gate for your supper shal be open: & K. Richard present him selfe to your vewe. Pardon my boldnes that ever love to be honored with your presence nether do I importune more then your occasions may willingly assent unto, in the meanetime & ever restinge At your command Edw. Hoby.
[*Endorsed*] 7 Dec. 1595 [*and*] readile.

1599. London.

[From account of travels of Thomas Platter.]

'After dinner on the 21st September, at about two o'clock, I went with my companions over the water, and in the strewn roof-house saw the tragedy of the first Emperor Julius with at least fifteen characters very well acted. At the end of the comedy they danced according to their custom with extreme elegance. Two in men's clothes and two in women's gave this performance, in wonderful combination with each other.'

1600. London.

[1600, Mar. 6. From *Letter* (March 8) of Rowland Whyte to Sir Robert Sidney (*Sydney Papers*, ii. 175). The play was probably at Hunsdon House, Blackfriars.]

All this Weeke the Lords haue bene in London, and past away the Tyme in Feasting and Plaies; for Vereiken dined vpon Wednesday, with my Lord Treasurer, who made hym a Roiall Dinner; vpon Thursday my Lord Chamberlain feasted hym, and made him very great, and a delicate Dinner, and there in the After Noone his Plaiers acted, before Vereiken, Sir John Old Castell, to his great Contentment.

1601. London.

[1601, Feb. 7. Globe. The performances referred to in (*a*) must date back to 1595–6. Apparently that of 1601 was arranged on Friday, February 6, and given on the next day. It was on the same day that Essex received a summons to appear before the Privy Council. This interrupted his plans for securing possession of the Queen's person and arresting her ministers, and precipitated his futile outbreak of February 8.]

(*a*) [1600? n.d., clearly before the events of 1601. The document is in tabular form, not preserved here.]

The Erle of Essex is charged with high Treason, namely, That he plotted and practised with the Pope and king of Spaine for the disposing and settling to himself Aswell the Crowne of England, as of the kingdome of Ireland. This is prooved fyue wayes . . . 5. By the Erle of Essex owne Actions. In some matters concerning this cause apparantly confirming ye intent of this Treason. His vnderhand permitting of that most treasonous booke of ⟨John Hayward's⟩ Henry the fourth to be printed and published, being plainly deciphered not onely by the matter, and by the Epistle itself, for what ende and for whose behoof it was made, but also the Erle himself being so often present at the playing thereof, and with great applause giving countenance and lyking to the same. . . . [*Endorsed*. An Abstract of the Erl of Essex his Treasons.]

(*b*) [1601, Feb. 17. From *Examination* of Sir Gelly Meyricke.]

Sir Gelly Meyricke 17th Feb. 1600.

The Examination of Sr Gelly Merick Knyght taken the xvijth of Februarij, 1600. He sayeth that vpon Saterday

PERFORMANCES 175

last was sennyght he dyned at Gunter's in the Company of the L. Monteegle, Sr Christoffer Blont, Sr Charles Percye, Ellys Jones, and Edward Busshell, and who else he remembreth not and after dynner that day & at the mocyon of Sr Charles Percy and the rest they went all together to the Globe over the water wher the L. Chamberlens men vse to play and were ther somwhat before the play began, Sr Charles tellyng them that the play wold be of Harry the iiijth. Whether Sr John Davyes were ther or not thys examinate can not tell, but he sayd he wold be ther yf he cold. He can not tell who procured that play to be played at that tyme except yt were Sr Charles Percye, but as he thyncketh yt was Sr Charles Percye. Thenne he was at the same play and Cam in somwhat after yt was begon, and the play was of Kyng Harry the iiijth, and of the kyllyng of Kyng Richard the second played by the L. Chamberlen's players

Gelly Meyricke

(c) [1601, Feb. 18. From *Examination* of Augustine Phillips.]

Augustine Phillipps 18 Feb., 1600.

The Examination of Augustine Phillypps servant vnto the L Chamberlyne and one of hys players taken the xviijth of Februarij 1600 vpon hys oth

He sayeth that on Fryday last was sennyght or Thursday Sr Charles Percy Sr Josclyne Percy and the L. Montegle with some thre more spak to some of the players in the presans of thys examinate to have the play of the deposyng and kyllyng of Kyng Rychard the second to be played the Saterday next promysyng to gete them xl*s*. more then their ordynary to play yt. Wher thys Examinate and hys fellowes were determyned to have played some other play, holdyng that play of Kyng Richard to be so old & so long out of vse as that they shold have small or no Company at yt. But at their request this Examinate and his fellowes were Content to play yt the Saterday and had their xl*s*. more then their ordynary for yt and so played yt accordyngly

Augustine Phillipps

(*d*) [1601. From ⟨Francis Bacon's⟩ *A Declaration of the Practises and Treasons . . . by Robert late Earle of Essex.*]

The afternoone before the rebellion, Merricke, with a great company of others, that afterwards were all in the action, had procured to bee played before them, the play of deposing King Richard the second. Neither was it casuall, but a play bespoken by Merrick. And not so onely, but when it was told him by one of the players, that the play was olde, and they should haue losse in playing it, because fewe would come to it: there was fourty shillings extraordinarie giuen to play it, and so thereupon playd it was. So earnest hee was to satisfie his eyes with the sight of that tragedie which hee thought soone after his lord should bring from the stage to the state, but that God turned it vpon their owne heads.

(*e*) [1601, Aug. 4. *Memorandum.*]

That which passed from the Excellent Majestie of Queen Elizabeth, in her Privie Chamber at East Greenwich, 4° Augusti 1601, 43° Reg. sui, towards WILLIAM LAMBARDE.

He presented her Majestie with his Pandecta of all her rolls, bundells, membranes, and parcells that be reposed in her Majestie's Tower at London; whereof she had given to him the charge 21st January last past.... She proceeded to further pages, and asked where she found cause of stay.... He expounded these all according to their original diversities ... so her Majestie fell upon the reign of King Richard II. saying, 'I am Richard II. know ye not that?'

PERFORMANCES

W. L. 'Such a wicked imagination was determined and attempted by a most unkind Gent. the most adorned creature that ever your Majestie made.'

Her Majestie. 'He that will forget God, will also forget his benefactors; this tragedy was played 40^{tie} times in open streets and houses.'

1601–2. London.

[1601, Dec. 29. From *Letter* of Dudley Carleton to John Chamberlain.]

The Q: dined this day priuatly at my Ld Chamberlains; I came euen now from the Blackfriers, where I saw her at the play with all her *candidae auditrices*.

[1602, Feb. 2. Middle Temple. From *Diary* of John Manningham.]

At out feast wee had a play called 'Twelue Night, or What You Will', much like the Commedy of Errores, or Menechmi in Plautus, but most like and neere to that in Italian called *Inganni*. A good practise in it to make the Steward beleeve his Lady widdowe was in love with him, by counterfeyting a letter as from his Lady in generall termes, telling him what shee liked best in him, and prescribing his gesture in smiling, his apparaile, &c., and then when he came to practise making him beleeue they tooke him to be mad.

1603. Court ⟨Wilton⟩.

[1865, Aug. 5. From a journal note of a visit to Wilton House in F. W. Cornish, *Extracts from the Letters and Journals of William Cory* (1897), 168. The Court was at Wilton in 1603.]

The house (Lady Herbert said) is full of interest: above us is Wolsey's room; we have a letter, never printed, from Lady Pembroke to her son, telling him to bring James I from Salisbury to see *As You Like It*; 'we have the man

Shakespeare with us'. She wanted to cajole the King in Raleigh's behalf—he came.

1604–5. Court ⟨Whitehall⟩ and London.
(*a*) [From *Revels Account*.]

The plaiers.		The poets which mayd the plaies.
By the Kings Maiesties plaiers.	Hallamas Day being the first of Nouembar A Play in the Banketinge house att Whit Hall Called The Moor of Venis.	
By his Maiesties plaiers.	The Sunday ffollowinge ⟨Nov. 4⟩ A play of the Merry wiues of winsor.	
By his Maiesties plaiers.	On St Stiuens night in the Hall A play Caled Mesur for Mesur.	Shaxberd.
By his Maiesties plaiers.	On Inosents night The plaie of Errors.	Shaxberd.
By his Maiesties plaiers.	Betwin Newers Day and Twelfe day A play of Loues Labours Lost.	
By his Maiesties plaiers.	On the 7 of January was played the play of Henry the fift.	
By his Maiesties plaiers.	The 8 of January A play Cauled Euery on out of his Vmor.	
By his Maiesties plaiers.	On Candlemas night A playe Euery one In his Vmor.	

The plaiers.		The poets which mayd the plaies.
	The Sunday ffollowing ⟨Feb. 3⟩ A playe provided And discharged.	
By his Maiesties plaiers.	On Shrousunday ⟨Feb. 10⟩ A play of the Marthant of Venis.	Shaxberd.
By his Maiesties plaiers.	On Shroumonday A Tragidye of The Spanishe Maz.	
By his Maiesties players.	On Shroutusday A play Cauled the Martchant of Venis Againe Commanded By the Kings Maiestie.	Shaxberd.

(b) [*Letter* of Sir Walter Cope to Robert Cecil, Lord Cranborne.]

I have sent and bene all thys morning huntyng for players Juglers & Such kinde of Creaturs, but fynde them harde to finde, wherfore Leavinge notes for them to seeke me, Burbage ys come, & Sayes ther ys no new playe that the quene hath not seene, but they have Revyved an olde one, Cawled *Loves Labore lost*, which for wytt & mirthe he sayes will please her excedingly. And Thys ys apointed to be playd to Morowe night at my Lord of Sowthamptons, unless yow send a wrytt to Remove the Corpus Cum Causa to your howse in Strande. Burbage ys my messenger Ready attendyng your pleasure.

1607-8. The High Seas.

[From T. Rundall, *Narratives of Voyages towards the North-West* (1849, Hakluyt Soc.), 231. These entries are included for convenience, although the performances were not by the King's. They were taken from a journal of William Keeling, captain of the East India Company's ship *Dragon*, bound with the *Hector*

(Capt. William Hawkins) and *Consent* to the East Indies. In September 1607 the ships were off Sierra Leone. The 'interpreter' was Lucas Fernandez, a converted negro, brother-in-law of the local king Borea. The third entry was dated in Rundall's print September 31, but corrected, probably by him, in the India Office copy.]

1607, Sept. 5. I sent the interpreter, according to his desier, abord the Hector whear he brooke fast, and after came abord mee, wher we gaue the tragedie of Hamlett.

30. Captain Hawkins dined with me, wher my companions acted Kinge Richard the Second.

⟨1608, Mar. 31⟩. I envited Captain Hawkins to a ffishe dinner, and had Hamlet acted abord me: which I permitt to keepe my people from idleness and unlawful games, or sleepe.

1611. London.

[From Simon Forman's *Booke of Plaies*.]

(*a*) In Mackbeth at the Glob, 1610 ⟨1611⟩, the 20 of Aprill ♄ ⟨Saturday⟩, ther was to be obserued, firste, howe Mackbeth and Bancko, 2 noble men of Scotland, Ridinge thorowe a wod, the⟨r⟩ stode before them 3 women feiries or Nimphes, And saluted Mackbeth, sayinge, 3 tyms vnto him, haille Mackbeth, king of Codon; for thou shalt be a kinge, but shalt beget No kinges, &c. Then said Bancko, What all to Mackbeth And nothing to me. Yes, said the nimphes, haille to thee Bancko, thou shalt beget kinges, yet be no kinge. And so they departed & cam to the Courte of Scotland to Dunkin king of Scotes, and yt was in the dais of Edward the Confessor. And Dunkin bad them both kindly wellcome, And made Mackbeth forth with Prince of Northumberland, and sent him hom to his own castell, and appointed Mackbeth to prouid for him, for he would sup with him the next dai at night, & did soe. And Mackebeth contrived to kill Dunkin, & thorowe the persuasion of his wife did that night Murder the kinge in his own Castell, beinge his guest. And ther were many prodigies seen that night & the dai before. And when Mack Beth had murdred the kinge, the blod on his handes could not be washed of by Any meanes, nor from his wiues handes, which handled the bloddi daggers in hiding them, By which means they became both moch amazed & Affronted. The murder being knowen, Dunkins 2 sonns fled, the on to England, the ⟨other to⟩ Walles, to saue them selues, they being fled, they were supposed guilty of the murder of their father, which was nothinge so. Then was Mackbeth crowned kinge, and then he for feare of Banko, his old companion, that he should beget kinges but be no kinge him selfe, he contriued the death of Banko, and caused him to be Murdred on the way as he Rode. The next night, beinge at supper with his noble men whom he had bid to a feaste to the which also Banco should haue com, he began to speake of Noble Banco, and to wish that he wer ther. And as he thus did, standing vp to drincke a Carouse to him, the ghoste of Banco came and sate down in his cheier behind him. And he turninge About to sit down Again sawe the goste of Banco, which fronted him so, that he fell into a great passion of fear and fury, Vtterynge many wordes about his murder, by which, when they hard that Banco was Murdred they Suspected Mackbet.

Then MackDove fled to England to the kinges sonn, And soe they Raised an Army, And cam into Scotland, and at Dunston Anyse overthrue Mackbet. In the meantyme whille Macdouee was in England, Mackbet slewe Mackdoues wife & children, and after in the battle Mackdoue slewe Mackbet.

Obserue Also howe Mackbetes quen did Rise in the night in her slepe, & walke and talked and confessed all, & the docter noted her wordes.

(*b*)   Of Cimbalin king of England.

Remember also the storri of Cymbalin king of England, in Lucius tyme, howe Lucius Cam from Octauus Cesar for Tribut, and being denied, after sent Lucius with a greate Arme of Souldiars who landed at Milford hauen, and Affter wer vanquished by Cimbalin, and Lucius taken prisoner, and all by means of 3 outlawes, of the which 2 of them were the sonns of Cimbalim, stolen from him when they were but 2 yers old by an old man whom Cymbalin banished, and he kept them as his own sonns 20 yers with him in A cave. And howe ⟨one⟩ of them slewe Clotan, that was the quens sonn, goinge to Milford hauen to sek the loue of Innogen the kinges daughter, whom he had banished also for louinge his daughter, and howe the Italian that cam from her loue conveied him selfe into A Cheste, and said yt was a chest of plate sent from her loue & others, to be presented to the kinge. And in the depest of the night, she being aslepe, he opened the cheste, & cam forth of yt, And vewed her in her bed, and the markes of her body, & toke awai her braslet, & after Accused her of adultery to her loue, &c. And in thend howe he came with the Romains into England & was taken prisoner, and after Reueled to Innogen, Who had turned her self into mans apparell & fled to mete her loue at Milford hauen, & chanchsed to fall on the Caue in the wodes wher her 2 brothers were, & howe by eating a sleping Dram they thought she had bin deed, & laid her in the wodes, & the body of Cloten by her, in her loues apparell that he left behind him, & howe she was found by Lucius, &c.

PERFORMANCES 183

(c) In Richard the 2 At the Glob 1611 the 30 of Aprill ♂ ⟨Tuesday⟩¹.

Remember therin howe Jack Straw by his overmuch boldnes, not being pollitick nor suspecting Anye thinge: was Soddenly at Smithfield Bars stabbed by Walworth the major of London, & soe he and his wholle Army was overthrowen. Therfore in such a case or the like, never admit any party, without a bar betwen, for A man cannot be to wise, nor kepe him selfe to safe.

Also remember howe the duke of Gloster, The Erell of Arundell, Oxford and others, crossing the kinge in his humor, about the duke of Erland and Bushy, wer glad to fly and Raise an hoste of men, and beinge in his Castell, howe the d. of Erland cam by nighte to betray him with 300 men, but hauing pryuie warninge thereof kept his gates faste, And wold not suffer the Enimie to Enter, which went back Again with a flie in his eare, and after was slainte by the Errell of Arundell in the battell.

Remember also, when the duke and Arundell cam to London with their Army, king Richard came forth to them and met them and gaue them fair wordes, and promised them pardon and that all should be well yf they wold discharge their Army, vpon whose promises and faier Speaches they did yt, and Affter the king byd them all to A banket and soe betraid them And Cut of their heades, &c, because they had not his pardon vnder his hand & sealle before but his worde.

Remember therin Also howe the ducke of Lankaster pryuily contryued all villany, to set them all together by the ears, and to make the nobilyty to Envy the kinge and mislyke of him and his gouernmentes, by which meanes he made his own sonn king, which was Henry Bullinbrocke.

¹ This is certainly not Shakespeare's.

Remember also howe the duke of Lankaster asked A wise man, wher him self should ever be kinge, And he told him no, but his sonn should be a kinge. And when he had told him, he hanged him vp for his labor, because he should not brute yt abrod or speke therof to others. This was a pollicie in the common wealthes opinion. But I sai yt was a villaines parte, and a Judas kisse to hange the man for telling him the truth. Beware by this Example of noble men, and of their fair wordes, & sai lyttell to them, lest they doe the like by thee for thy good will.

(*d*) In the Winters Talle at the glob 1611 the 15 of maye ♀ ⟨Wednesday⟩.

Obserue ther howe Lyontes the kinge of Cicillia was overcom with Jelosy of his wife with the kinge of Bohemia his frind that came to see him, and howe he contriued his death and wold haue had his cup berer to haue poisoned, who gaue the king of Bohemia warning therof & fled with him to Bohemia.

Remember also howe he sent to the Orakell of Appollo & the Annswer of Apollo, that she was giltles and that the king was jelouse &c. and howe Except the child was found Again that was loste the kinge should die without yssue, for the child was caried into Bohemia & ther laid in a forrest & brought vp by a sheppard And the kinge of Bohemia his sonn maried that wentch & howe they fled into Cicillia to Leontes, and the sheppard hauing showed the letter of the nobleman by whom Leontes sent a was ⟨away?⟩ that child and the jewells found about her, she was knowen to be Leontes daughter and was then 16 yers old.

Remember also the Rog that cam in all tottered like coll pixci and howe he feyned him sicke & to haue bin Robbed of all that he had and howe he cosened the por

PERFORMANCES

man of all his money, and after cam to the shep sher with a pedlers packe & ther cosened them Again of all their money And howe he changed apparrell with the kinge of Bomia his sonn, and then howe he turned Courtier &c. Beware of trustinge feined beggars or fawninge fellouss.

1611-12. Court ⟨Whitehall and Greenwich⟩.

[From *Revels Account*.]

By the Kings players:	Hallomas nyght was presented att Whithall before ye kinges Maiestie a play Called the Tempest.
The Kings players:	The 5th of nouember A play Called ye winters nightes Tayle.

1612-13. Court ⟨Whitehall⟩.

[From *Chamber Account*.]

Item paid to John Heminges upon the Cowncells warrant dated att Whitehall xx° die Maij 1613, for presentinge before the Princes Highnes the Lady Elizabeth and the Prince Pallatyne Elector fowerteene severall playes, viz: one playe called Filaster, One other called the Knott of Fooles, One other Much Adoe abowte Nothinge, The Mayeds Tragedy, The Merye Dyvell of Edmonton, The Tempest, A Kinge and no Kinge, The Twins Tragedie, The Winters Tale, Sir John Falstaffe, The Moore of Venice, The Nobleman, Caesars Tragedye, And one other called Love lyes a bleedinge, All which Playes weare played with-in the tyme of this Accompte, viz: paid the some of iiij^{xx} xiij^{li} vj^s viij^d.

Item paid to the said John Heminges vppon the lyke warrant, dated att Whitehall xx° die Maij 1613, for presentinge sixe severall playes, viz: one playe called A badd begininge makes a good endinge, One other called the Capteyne, One other the Alcumist, One other Cardenno, One other The Hotspur, And one other called Benedicte and Betteris, All played within the tyme of this Accompte viz: paid Fortie powndes, And by waye of his Majesties rewarde twentie powndes, In all lx^{li}.

1613. London.

[1613, June 29. Globe. From *Letter* (2 July) of Sir Henry Wotton to Sir Edmund Bacon.]

Now, to let matters of state sleep, I will entertain you at the present with what has happened this week at the Bank's side. The King's players had a new play, called *All is True*, representing some principal pieces of the reign of Henry VIII, which was set forth with many extraordinary circumstances of pomp and majesty, even to the matting of the stage; the Knights of the Order with their Georges and garters, the Guards with their embroidered coats, and the like: sufficient in truth within a while to make greatness very familiar, if not ridiculous. Now, King Henry making a masque at the Cardinal Wolsey's house, and certain chambers being shot off at his entry, some of the paper, or other stuff, wherewith one of them was stopped, did light on the thatch, where being thought at first but an idle smoke, and their eyes more attentive to the show, it kindled inwardly, and ran round like a train, consuming within less than an hour the whole house to the very grounds. This was the fatal period of that virtuous fabric, wherein yet nothing did perish but wood and straw, and a few forsaken cloaks; only one man had his breeches set on fire, that would perhaps have broiled him, if he had not by the benefit of a provident wit put it out with bottle ale.

APPENDIX II

CONTEMPORARY ALLUSIONS

1592–1623

1. THOMAS NASHE (1592)

[From *Pierce Penilesse his Supplication to the Diuell*.]

How would it have ioyed braue *Talbot* (the terror of the French) to thinke that after he had lyne two hundred yeares in his Tombe, hee should triumphe againe on the Stage, and haue his bones newe embalmed with the teares of ten thousand spectators at least, (at seuerall times) who, in the Tragedian that represents his person, imagine they behold him fresh bleeding?

2. ROBERT GREENE (1592)

[From *Greenes Groats-worth of Wit*.]

To those Gentlemen his Quondam acquaintance, that spend their wits in making plaies, R. G. wisheth a better exercise, and wisdome to preuent his extremities....

Base minded men all three of you, if by my miserie you be not warnd: for vnto none of you (like mee) sought those burres to cleaue: those Puppets (I meane) that spake from our mouths, those Anticks garnisht in our colours. Is it not strange, that I, to whom they all haue beene beholding: is it not like that you, to whome they all haue beene beholding, shall (were yee in that case as I am now) bee both at once of them forsaken? Yes trust them not: for there is an vpstart Crow, beautified with our feathers, that with his *Tygers hart wrapt in a Players hyde*, supposes he is as well able to bombast out a blanke verse as the best of you: and beeing an absolute *Iohannes fac totum*, is in his owne conceit the onely Shake-scene in a countrey. O that I might intreat your rare wits to be imploied in more profitable courses: & let those Apes imitate your past excellence, and neuer more acquaint them with your admired inuentions. I knowe the best husband of you all will neuer proue an Usurer, and the kindest of them all will neuer proue a kind nurse: yet, whilest you may, seeke you better Maisters; for it is pittie men of such rare wits, should be subiect to the pleasure of such rude groomes.

In this I might insert two more, that both haue writ against these buckram Gentlemen: but lette their owne workes serue to witnesse against their owne wickednesse, if they perseuere to maintaine any more such peasants. For other new-commers, I leaue them to the mercie of these painted monsters, who (I doubt not) will driue the best minded to despise them: for the rest, it skils not though they make a ieast at them.

3. HENRY CHETTLE (1592, 1603)

(a) [From *Epistle* to *Kind-Harts Dreame* (n.d., S.R. 8 Dec. 1592).]

About three moneths since died M. *Robert Greene*, leauing many papers in sundry Booke sellers hands, among other his Groatsworth of wit, in which a letter written to diuers play-makers, is offensiuely by one or two of them taken; and because on the dead they cannot be auenged, they wilfully forge in their conceites a liuing Author: and after tossing it to and fro, no remedy, but it must light on me. How I haue all the time of my conuersing in printing hindered the bitter inueying against schollers, it hath been very well knowne; and how in that I dealt, I can sufficiently prooue. With neither of them that take offence was I acquainted, and with one of them I care not if I neuer be: The other, whome at that time I did not so much spare, as since I wish I had, for that as I haue moderated the heate of liuing writers, and might have vsde my owne discretion (especially in such a case) the Author beeing dead, that I did not, I am as sory as if the originall fault had beene my fault, because my selfe haue seene his demeanor no lesse ciuill than he exelent in the qualitie he professes: Besides, diuers of worship haue reported his uprightnes of dealing, which argues his honesty, and his facetious grace in writting, that aprooues his Art.

(b) [From *Englandes Mourning Garment* (n.d., S.R. 25 Apr. 1603).]

    Nor doth the siluer tonged *Melicert*,
    Drop from his honied muse one sable teare
    To mourne her death that graced his desert,
    And to his laies opend her Royall eare.
      Shepheard, remember our *Elizabeth*,
    And sing her Rape, done by that *Tarquin*, Death.

4. R. B. (1594)

[From *Greenes Funeralls*. By R. B. Gent. (1594, S.R. 1 Feb.), Sonn. ix (ed. R. B. McKerrow, 81). The identity of the author is uncertain.]

    Greene, is the pleasing Obiect of an eie:
    Greene, pleasde the eies of all that lookt vppon him.
    Greene, is the ground of euerie Painters die:
    Greene, gaue the ground, to all that wrote vpon him.
    Nay more the men, that so Eclipst his fame:
    Purloynde his Plumes, can they deny the same?

5. W. HAR (1594)

[From *Epicedium. A funeral Song, upon . . . the Lady Helen Branch*. This seems to be the first allusion to *Lucrece*. One might guess at William Harvey as the author, who later married Mary, Countess of Southampton.]

> You that haue writ of chaste Lucretia,
> Whose death was witnesse of her spotlesse life:
> Or pen'd the praise of sad Cornelia,
> Whose blamelesse name hath made her fame so rife,
> As noble Pompey's most renoumed wife:
>> Hither vnto your home direct your eies,
>> Whereas, vnthought on, much more matter lies.

6. HENRY WILLOBIE (1594)

[From *Willobie his Avisa* (1594, S.R. 3 Sept.), c. xliv.]

Henrico Willobego. Italo-Hispalensis.

H. W. being sodenly infected with the contagion of a fantasticall fit, at the first sight of *A*, pyneth a while in secret griefe, at length not able any longer to indure the burning heate of so feruent a humour, bewrayeth the secresy of his disease vnto his familiar frend W. S. who not long before had tryed the curtesy of the like passion, and was now newly recouered of the like infection; yet finding his frend let bloud in the same vaine, he took pleasure for a tyme to see him bleed, & in steed of stopping the issue, he inlargeth the wound, with the sharpe rasor of a willing conceit, perswading him that he thought it a matter very easy to be compassed, & no doubt with payne, diligence & some cost in time to be obtayned. Thus this miserable comforter comforting his frend with an im-possibilitie, eyther for that he now would secretly laugh at his frends folly, that had giuen occasion not long before vnto others to laugh at his owne, or because he would see whether an other could play his part better then himselfe, & in vewing a far off the course of this louing Comedy, he determined to see whether it would sort to a happier end for this new actor, then it did for the old player. But at length this Comedy was like to haue growen to a Tragedy, by the weake & feeble estate that H. W. was brought vnto, by a desperate vewe of an impossibility of obtaining his purpose, til Time & Necessity, being his best Phisitions brought him a plaster, if not to heale, yet in part to ease his maladye. In all which discourse is liuely represented the vnrewly rage of unbrydeled fancy, hauing the raines to roue at liberty, with the dyuers & sundry changes of affections & temptations, which Will, set loose from Reason, can deuise. &c.

7. ANON (1594)

[From commendatory verses to *Willobie his Avisa* (cf. no. 6), signed 'Contraria Contrarijs: Vigilantius: Dormitanus', in apparent allusion to St. Jerome's *Contra Vigilantium*, in which he calls his opponent Dormitantius.]

Though Collatine *haue deerely bought,*
To high renowne, a lasting life,
And found, that most in vaine haue sought,
To haue a Faire, *and* Constant *wife,*
  Yet Tarquyne *pluckt his glistering grape,*
  And Shake-speare, *paints poor Lucrece rape.*

8. FRANCIS MERES (1598)

[From *Palladis Tamia: Wits Treasury* (S.R. 7 Sept. 1598). Meres (1565–1647) was of Lincolnshire and Pembroke, Cambridge. He was living in London in 1597 and 1598, and seems to have been in touch with literary men. From 1602 he was rector and schoolmaster at Wing, Rutland.]

A comparatiue discourse of our English Poets
  with the *Greeke, Latine, and Italian Poets.*

. . . The English tongue is mightily enriched, and gorgeouslie inuested in rare ornaments and resplendent abiliments by sir *Philip Sidney, Spencer, Daniel, Drayton, Warner, Shakespeare, Marlow* and *Chapman*. . . .

As the soule of *Euphorbus* was thought to liue in *Pythagoras:* so the sweete wittie soule of *Ouid* liues in mellifluous & hony-tongued *Shakespeare,* witnes his *Venus* and *Adonis,* his *Lucrece,* his sugred Sonnets among his priuate friends, &c.

As *Plautus* and *Seneca* are accounted the best for Comedy and Tragedy among the Latines: so *Shakespeare* among the English is the most excellent in both kinds for the stage; for Comedy, witnes his *Gentlemen of Verona* his *Errors,* his *Loue labors lost,* his *Loue labours wonne,* his *Midsummers night dreame,* & his *Merchant of Venice:* for Tragedy his *Richard the 2. Richard* the *3. Henry the 4. King Iohn, Titus Andronicus* and his *Romeo* and *Iuliet.*

As *Epius Stolo* said, that the Muses would speake with *Plautus* tongue, if they would speak Latin: so I say that the Muses would speak with *Shakespeares* fine filed phrase, if they would speake English. . . .

As *Ouid* saith of his worke . . . as *Horace* saith of his . . . so say I seuerally of sir *Philip Sidneys, Spencers, Daniels, Draytons, Shakespeares,* and *Warners workes;*
  Non Iouis ira, imbres, Mars, ferrum, flamma, senectus,
  Hoc opus vnda, lues, turbo, venena ruent. . . .

As *Pindarus, Anacreon* and *Callimachus* among the Greekes; and *Horace* and *Catullus* among the Latines are the best Lyrick Poets: so in this faculty the best among our Poets are *Spencer* (who excelleth in all kinds) *Daniel, Drayton, Shakespeare, Bretton.* . . .

These are our best for Tragedie, the Lorde *Buckhurst,* Doctor *Leg* of Cambridge, Doctor *Edes* of Oxforde, maister *Edward Ferris,* the Author of the *Mirrour for Magistrates, Marlow, Peele, Watson, Kid, Shakespeare, Drayton, Chapman, Decker,* and *Beniamin Johnson.* . . .

FRANCIS MERES

The best for Comedy amongst us bee, *Edward* Earle of Oxforde, Doctor *Gager* of Oxforde, Maister *Rowley* once a rare Scholler of learned Pembrooke Hall in Cambridge, Maister *Edwardes* one of her Maiesties Chappell, eloquent and wittie *John Lilly*, *Lodge*, *Gascoyne*, *Greene*, *Shakespeare*, *Thomas Nash*, *Thomas Heywood*, *Anthony Mundye* our best plotter, *Chapman*, *Porter*, *Wilson*, *Hathway*, and *Henry Chettle*. . . .

These are the most passionate among us to bewaile and bemoane the perplexities of Loue, *Henrie Howard* Earle of Surrey, sir *Thomas Wyat* the elder, sir *Francis Brian*, sir *Philip Sidney*, sir *Walter Rawley*, sir *Edward Dyer*, *Spencer*, *Daniel*, *Drayton*, *Shakespeare*, *Whetstone*, *Gascoyne*, *Samuell Page* sometimes fellowe of *Corpus Christi* Colledge in Oxford, *Churchyard*, *Bretton*.

9. JOHN MARSTON (1598)

[From *The Scourge of Villanie*, Sat. x.]

Luscus, what's playd to day? faith now I know
I set thy lips abroach, from whence doth flow
Naught but pure *Iuliat* and *Romio*.
Say, who acts best? *Drusus* or *Roscio*?
Now I have him, that nere of ought did speake
But when of playes or Plaiers he did treate.
H'ath made a common-place booke out of plaies,
And speakes in print: at least what ere he sayes
Is warranted by Curtaine plaudeties.

10. GABRIEL HARVEY (1598⟨⟩1601)

[From MS. note in copy of Speght's *Chaucer* (1598), pr. with facs. in G. C. Moore Smith, *Gabriel Harvey's Marginalia*, 232. The date of the note remains uncertain; 'gabriel haruey. 1598' on the t.p. can only be taken as that of acquisition.]

The younger sort takes much delight in Shakespeares

Venus, & Adonis: but his Lucrece, & his tragedie of Hamlet, Prince of Denmarke, haue it in them, to please the wiser sort. Or such poets: or better: or none.

   Vilia miretur vulgus: mihi flavus Apollo
    Pocula Castaliae plena ministret aquae:
quoth Sir Edward Dier, betwene iest, & earnest. Whose written deuises farr excell most of the sonets, and cantos in print. His Amaryllis, & Sir Walter Raleighs Cynthia, how fine & sweet inuentions? Excellent matter of emulation for Spencer, Constable, France, Watson, Daniel, Warner, Chapman, Siluester, Shakespeare, & the rest of owr florishing metricians.

11. ELIZABETH WRIOTHESLEY, COUNTESS OF SOUTHAMPTON (1599)

[From *Letter* to the Earl of Southampton. Lady Southampton's gossip is probably of some acquaintance whom she nicknames Falstaff, rather than of Sh. One would guess at Henry Lord Cobham, but he appears to have had no children.]

Al the nues I can send you that I thinke wil make you mery is that I reade in a letter from London that Sir John Falstaf is by his Mrs Dame Pintpot made father of a godly milers thum, a boye thats all heade and veri litel body; but this is a secrit.

12. JOHN WEEVER (1599)

(*a*) [From *Epigrammes in the oldest Cut, and newest Fashion*, iv. 22 (ed. R. B. McKerrow, 75). Weever (1576–1632) was a Lancashire man, a student of Queens', Cambridge, and an antiquary.]

   Ad Gulielmum Shakespeare.

Honie-tong'd *Shakespeare* when I saw thine issue
 I swore *Apollo* got them and none other,

JOHN WEEVER

Their rosie-tainted features cloth'd in tissue,
Some heauen born goddesse said to be their mother:
Rose-checkt *Adonis* with his amber tresses,
Faire fire-hot *Venus* charming him to loue her,
Chaste *Lucretia* virgine-like her dresses,
Prowd lust-stung *Tarquine* seeking still to proue her:
Romea Richard; more whose names I know not,
Their sugred tongues, and power attractiue beuty
Say they are Saints althogh that Sts they shew not
For thousands vowes to them subiectiue dutie:
They burn in loue thy children *Shakespear* het them,
Go, wo thy Muse more Nymphish brood beget them.

(*b*) [From *The Mirror of Martyrs, or The Life and Death of Sir John Oldcastle* (1601), St. 4. The dedication says that the book 'some two yeares agoe was made fit for the Print'.]

The many-headed multitude were drawne
By *Brutus* speach, that *Caesar* was ambitious,
When eloquent *Mark Antonie* had showne
His vertues, who but *Brutus* then was vicious?

13. ANON (1599?, 1601?)

[From *Parnassus*, ed. W. D. Macray (1886), a series of plays: (1) *The Pilgrimage to Parnassus*, (2) *The Returne from Parnassus*, Part I, (3) *The Returne from Parnassus*, Part II, performed at St. John's, Cambridge, probably at the Christmases of 1598–9, 1599–1600, and 1601–2. An early inscription suggests the authorship of J. D., for whom John Day is a very doubtful conjecture.]

(*a*) [From 2 *Parnassus* (1599?).]

[iii. 1. 1006–55.] *Gull⟨io⟩*. Pardon, faire lady, thoughe sicke-thoughted Gullio maks amaine unto thee, and like a bould-faced sutore 'gins to woo thee.

Ingen⟨ioso⟩. (We shall have nothinge but pure Shakspeare and shreds of poetrie that he hath gathered at the theators!)

Gull. Pardon mee, moy mittressa, ast am a gentleman, the moone in comparison of thy bright hue a meere slutt, Anthonio's Cleopatra a blacke browde milkmaide, Hellen a dowdie.

Ingen. (Marke, Romeo and Juliet! O monstrous theft! I thinke he will runn throughe a whole booke of Samuell Daniell's!)

Gull. Thrise fairier than myselfe (—thus I began—)
The gods faire riches, sweete above compare,
Staine to all nimphes, ⟨m⟩ore lovely the⟨n⟩ a man.
More white and red than doves and roses are!
Nature that made thee with herselfe had ⟨at⟩ strife,
Saith that the worlde hath ending with thy life.

Ingen. Sweete Mr. Shakspeare! . . .

Ingen. My pen is youre bounden vassall to commande. But what vayne woulde it please you to have them in?

Gull. Not in a vaine veine (prettie, i'faith!): make mee them in two or three divers vayns, in Chaucer's, Gower's and Spencer's and Mr. Shakspeare's. Marry, I thinke I shall entertaine those verses which run like these;
Even as the sunn with purple coloured face
Had tane his laste leave on the weeping morne, &c.
O sweet Mr. Shakespeare! I'le have his picture in my study at the courte.

[iv. 1. 1211–27.] *Gull*.—Let mee heare Mr. Shakspear's veyne.

Ingen. Faire Venus, queene of beutie and of love,
Thy red doth stayne the blushinge of the morne,
Thy snowie necke shameth the milkwhite dove,
Thy presence doth this naked worlde adorne;
Gazinge on thee all other nymphes I scorne.

When ere thou dyest slowe shine that Satterday,
Beutie and grace muste sleepe with thee for aye!
Gull. Noe more! I am one that can judge accordinge to the proverbe, *bovem ex unguibus*. Ey marry, Sir, these have some life in them! Let this duncified worlde esteeme of Spencer and Chaucer, I'le worshipp sweet Mr. Shakspeare, and to honoure him will lay his Venus and Adonis under my pillowe, as wee reade of one (I doe not well remember his name, but I am sure he was a kinge) slept with Homer under his bed's heade.

(b) [From *3 Parnassus* (1601?).]

[i. 2. 304.] *Ingenioso.* . . . *William Shakespeare.*
  Iudicio. Who loues not *Adons* loue, or *Lucrece* rape?
His sweeter verse contaynes hart trobbing line,
Could but a graver subiect him content,
Without loues foolish lazy languishment.
[iv. 3. 1806–79.] *Kempe.* Few of the vniuersity men pen plaies well, they smell too much of that writer *Ouid*, and that writer *Metamorphosis*, and talke too much of *Proserpina* & *Iuppiter*. Why heres our fellow *Shakespeare* puts them all downe, I and *Ben Ionson* too. O that *Ben Ionson* is a pestilent fellow, he brought vp *Horace* giuing the Poets a pill, but our fellow *Shakespeare* hath giuen him a purge that made him beray his credit:
  Burbage. Its a shrewd fellow indeed: I wonder these schollers stay so long, they appointed to be here presently that we might try them: oh, here they come. . . .
  Bur. I like your face, and the proportion of your body for *Richard* the 3. I pray, M. *Phil.* let me see you act a little of it.
  Philomusus. 'Now is the winter of our discontent,
Made glorious summer by the sonne of Yorke.'

14. BEN JONSON (1599–1637)

(*a*) 1599. [From *Every Man Out of His Humour*, as printed in Q 1 (1600), iii. 1. 2010–47. The date of representation is given in F 1 as 1599 (cf. *Eliz. Stage*, iii. 360). Sogliardo's motto seems to glance at Shakespeare's, although the coat does not resemble his, and obviously Sogliardo, described as 'an essential clowne', who 'comes vp euery Tearm to learn to take Tabacco & see new Motions', is not a 'portrait' of Shakespeare. A few lines earlier (1956) comes Jonson's quotation of *Jul. Caes.* iii. 2. 109; p. 106.]

Sog⟨liardo⟩. Nay I will haue him, I am resolute for that, by this Parchment Gentlemen, I haue ben so toil'd among the Harrots yonder, you will not beleeue, they doe speake i'the straungest language, and giue a man the hardest termes for his money, that euer you knew.

Carl⟨o⟩. But ha' you armes? ha' your armes?

Sog. Yfaith, I thanke God I can write my selfe Gentleman now, here's my Pattent, it cost me thirtie pound by this breath.

Punt⟨arvolo⟩. A very faire Coat, well charg'd and full of Armorie.

Sog. Nay, it has as much varietie of colours in it, as you haue seene a Coat haue, how like you the Crest Sir?

Punt. I vnderstand it not well, what is't?

Sog. Marry Sir, it is your Bore without a head Rampant.

Punt. A Bore without a head, that's very rare.

Carl. I, and Rampant too: troth I commend the Heralds wit, he has deciphered him well: A Swine without a head, without braine, wit, any thing indeed, Ramping to Gentilitie. You can blazon the rest signior? can you not?

Sog. O I, I haue it in writing here of purpose, it cost me two shillings the tricking.

Carl. Let's heare, Let's heare.

Punt. It is the most vile, foolish, absurd, palpable, and ridiculous Escutcheon that euer this eye survis'd. Saue you good Mounsieur *Fastidius.*
      They salute as they meete in the walke.
Carl. Silence good Knight: on, on.

Sog. GYRONY of eight peeces, AZVRE and GVLES, between three plates a CHEV'RON engrailed checkey, OR, VERT and ERMINES; on a cheefe ARGENT between two ANN'LETS, sables a Bores head PROPER.

Carl. How's that? on a cheefe ARGENT?

Sog. On a cheefe ARGENT, a Bores head PROPER between two ANN'LETS sables.

Carl. S'lud, it's a Hogs Cheeke and Puddings in a Peuter field this.

Sog. How like you them signior?

Punt. Let the word be, *Not without mustard,* your Crest is very rare sir.

Carl. A frying pan to the Crest had had no fellow.

(b) [From *To the Reader*, 128–39, added to F 1, and called by Jonson 'an apologeticall Dialogue: which was only once spoken vpon the stage'. Shakespeare may be one of the 'better natures'.]

Now for the Players, it is true, I tax'd 'hem,
And yet, but some; and those so sparingly,
As all the rest might haue sat still, vnquestion'd,
Had they but had the wit, or conscience,
To thinke well of themselues. But, impotent they
Thought each mans vice belong'd to their whole tribe:
And much good doo't 'hem. What th'haue done 'gainst me,
I am not mou'd with. If it gaue 'hem meat,
Or got 'hem clothes. 'Tis well. That was their end.
Onely amongst them, I am sorry for
Some better natures, by the rest so drawne,
To run in that vile line.

(c) 1605? [From *Prologue* to *Every Man In His Humour*, as printed in F 1 (1616).]

Though neede make many *Poets*, and some such
As art, and nature haue not betterd much;
Yet ours, for want, hath not so lou'd the stage,
As he dare serue th'ill customes of the age:
Or purchase your delight at such a rate,
As, for it, he himselfe must iustly hate.
To make a child, now swadled, to proceede
Man, and then shoote vp, in one beard, and weede,
Past threescore yeeres: or, with three rustie swords,
And helpe of some few foot-and-halfe-foote words,
Fight ouer *Yorke*, and *Lancasters* long iarres:
And in the tyring-house bring wounds, to scarres.
He rather prayes, you will be pleas'd to see
One such, to day, as other playes should be.
Where neither *Chorus* wafts you ore the seas;
Nor creaking throne comes downe, the boys to please;
Nor nimble squibbe is seene, to make afear'd
The gentlewomen; nor roul'd bullet heard
To say, it thunders; nor tempestuous drumme
Rumbles, to tell you when the storme doth come;
But deedes, and language, such as men doe vse;
And persons, such as *Comœdie* would chuse,
When she would show an Image of the times,
And sport with humane follies, not with crimes.

(d) 1614. [From *Induction* to *Bartholomew Fayre* (as printed in 1631).]

Hee that will sweare, *Ieronimo*, or *Andronicus* are the best playes, yet, shall passe vnexcepted at, heere, as a man whose Iudgement shewes it is constant, and hath stood still, these fiue and twentie, or thirtie yeeres....

If there bee neuer a *Seruant-monster* i' the Fayre; who can helpe it? he ⟨the Author⟩ sayes; nor a nest of *Antiques*?

Hee is loth to make Nature afraid in his *Playes*, like those that beget *Tales, Tempests*, and such like *Drolleries*, to mix his head with other mens heeles; let the concupisence of *Iigges* and *Dances*, raigne as strong as it will amongst you.

(*e*) 1619. [From *Conversations with William Drummond*, during a visit to Hawthornden of *c*. Dec. 1618 to Jan. 1619.]

[l. 17]   His Censure of the English Poets was this . . . That Shaksperr wanted Arte.

[l. 208]   Sheakspear in a play brought in a number of men saying they had suffered Shipwrack in Bohemia, wher ther is no Sea neer by some 100 Miles.

[l. 590]   His Epitaph by a companion written is
here Lyes Benjamin Johnson dead
and hath no more wit than ⟨a⟩ goose in his head,
that as he was wont, so doth he still
live by his wit, and evermore will.
Ane other
here lyes honest Ben
that had not a beard on his chen.

(*f*) 1623. [From first preliminary leaf to F 1, placed opposite the portrait t.p.]

To the Reader.

This Figure, that thou here seest put,
  It was for gentle Shakespeare cut;
Wherein the Grauer had a strife
  with Nature, to out-doo the life:
O, could he but haue drawne his wit
  As well in brasse, as he hath hit
His face; the Print would then surpasse
  All, that was euer writ in brasse.

> But, since he cannot, Reader, looke
> Not on his Picture, but his Booke.
>
> B. I.

(*g*) 1623. [From fifth preliminary leaf to F 1.]

To the memory of my beloued,
The AVTHOR
MR. WILLIAM SHAKESPEARE:
AND
what he hath left vs.

To draw no enuy (Shakespeare) *on thy name,*
  Am I thus ample to thy Booke, and Fame:
While I confesse thy writings to be such,
  As neither Man, *nor* Muse, *can praise too much.*
'Tis true, and all mens suffrage. But these wayes
  Were not the paths I meant vnto thy praise:
For seeliest Ignorance on these may light,
  Which, when it sounds at best, but eccho's right;
Or blinde Affection, which doth ne're aduance
  The truth, but gropes, and vrgeth all by chance;
Or crafty Malice, might pretend this praise,
  And thinke to ruine, where it seem'd to raise.
These are, as some infamous Baud, or Whore,
  Should praise a Matron. What could hurt her more?
But thou art proofe against them, and indeed
  Aboue th' ill fortune of them, or the need.
I, therefore will begin. Soule of the Age!
  The applause! delight! the wonder of our Stage!
My Shakespeare, *rise; I will not lodge thee by*
  Chaucer, *or* Spenser, *or bid* Beaumont *lye*
A little further, to make thee a roome:
  Thou art a Moniment, without a tombe,
And art aliue still, while thy Booke doth liue,
  And we haue wits to read, and praise to giue.

DROESHOUT ENGRAVING

This engraving forms part of the title-page to the First Folio; it exists in two states, of the first of which—sometimes called the proof and here reproduced—only four examples are known.

That I not mixe thee so, my braine excuses;
  I meane with great, but disproportion'd Muses:
For, if I thought my iudgement were of yeeres,
  I should commit theé surely with thy peeres,
And tell, how farre thou didstst our Lily *out-shine,*
  Or sporting Kid, *or* Marlowes *mighty line.*
And though thou hadst small Latine, *and lesse* Greeke,
  From thence to honour thee, I would not seeke
For names; but call forth thund'ring Æschilus,
  Euripides, *and* Sophocles *to vs,*
Paccuuius, Accius, *him of* Cordoua *dead,*
  To life againe, to heare thy Buskin tread,
And shake a Stage: Or, when thy Sockes were on,
  Leaue thee alone, for the comparison
Of all, that insolent Greece, *or haughtie* Rome
  sent forth, or since did from their ashes come.
Triümph, my Britaine, *thou hast one to showe,*
  To whom all Scenes of Europe *homage owe.*
He was not of an age, but for all time!
  And all the Muses *still were in their prime,*
When like Apollo *he came forth to warme*
  Our eares, or like a Mercury *to charme!*
Nature her selfe was proud of his designes,
  And ioy'd to weare the dressing of his lines!
Which were so richly spun, and wouen so fit,
  As, since, she will vouchsafe no other Wit.
The merry Greeke, *tart* Aristophanes,
  Neat Terence, *witty* Plautus, *now not please;*
But antiquated, and deserted lye
  As they were not of Natures family.
Yet must I not giue Nature all: Thy Art,
  My gentle Shakespeare, *must enjoy a part.*
For though the Poets *matter, Nature be,*
  His Art doth giue the fashion. And, that he,

Who casts to write a liuing line, must sweat,
  (such as thine are) and strike the second heat
Vpon the Muses *anuile: turne the same,*
  (And himselfe with it) that he thinkes to frame;
Or for the lawrell, he may gaine a scorne,
  For a good Poet's *made, as well as borne.*
And such wert thou. Looke how the fathers face
  Liues in his issue, even so, the race
Of Shakespeares *minde, and manners brightly shines*
  In his well torned, and true filed lines:
In each of which, he seemes to shake a Lance,
  As brandish't at the eyes of Ignorance.
Sweet Swan of Auon! *what a sight it were*
  To see thee in our waters yet appeare,
And make those flights vpon the bankes of Thames,
  That so did take Eliza, *and our* Iames!
But stay, I see thee in the Hemisphere
  Aduanc'd, and made a Constellation there!
Shine forth, thou Starre of Poets, *and with rage,*
  Or influence, chide, or cheere the drooping Stage;
Which, since thy flight from hence, hath mourn'd like night,
  And despaires day, but for thy Volumes light.

BEN: IONSON.

(h) c. 1629. [From *Ode to Himselfe*, written after the failure of *The New Inn* (1629) and printed in Q (1631).]

No doubt some mouldy tale,
  Like *Pericles;* and stale
As the Shrieues crusts, and nasty as his fish-
  scraps, out [of] euery dish,
Throwne forth, and rak't into the common tub,
  May keepe vp the *Play-club:*
There, sweepings doe as well
As the best order'd meale.

BEN JONSON

For, who the relish of these ghests will fit,
Needs set them, but, the almes-basket of wit.

(*i*) 1623⟨⟩37. [From *Timber: or, Discoveries; Made upon Men and Matter* (F 2 of 1641), 98. This appears to be a selection from note-books of Jonson, partly prepared for the press. His earlier note-books perished in a fire of 1623. Probably *Timber*, which contains references to events of 1626 and 1630, is all later.]

De Shakespeare nostrati. *I remember*, the Players have often mentioned it as an honour to *Shakespeare*, that in his writing, (whatsoever he penn'd) hee never blotted out line. My answer hath beene, would he had blotted a thousand. Which they thought a malevolent speech. I had not told posterity this, but for their ignorance, who choose that circumstance to commend their friend by, wherein he most faulted. And to justifie mine owne candor, (for I lov'd the man, and doe honour his memory (on this side Idolatry) as much as any.) Hee was (indeed) honest, and of an open, and free nature: had an excellent *Phantsie;* brave notions, and gentle expressions: wherein hee flow'd with that facility, that sometime it was necessary he should be stop'd: *Sufflaminandus erat;* as *Augustus* said of *Haterius*. His wit was in his owne power; would the rule of it had beene so too. Many times hee fell into those things, could not escape laughter: As when hee said in the person of *Cæsar*, one speaking to him; *Cæsar thou dost me wrong*. Hee replyed: *Cæsar did never wrong, but with just cause* and such like: which were ridiculous. But hee redeemed his vices, with his vertues. There was ever more in him to be praysed, then to be pardoned.

(*k*) 1637. [From *Life* in Rowe's *Works of Sh.* (1709).]

In a Conversation between Sir *John Suckling*, Sir William *D'Avenant, Endymion Porter*, Mr. *Hales of Eaton*, and *Ben*

Johnson; Sir *John Suckling*, who was a profess'd admirer of *Shakespear*, had undertaken his Defence against *Ben Johnson* with some warmth; Mr. *Hales*, who had sat still for some time, hearing *Ben* frequently reproaching him with the want of Learning, and Ignorance of the Antients, told him at last, That if Mr. *Shakespear* had not read the Antients, he had likewise not stollen any thing from 'em; (a Fault the other made no Conscience of) and that if he would produce any one Topick finely treated by any of them, he would undertake to shew something upon the same Subject at least as well written by *Shakespear*.

(*l*) 1637. [From John Dryden's *Essay on the Dramatique Poetry of the Last Age*, appended to *The Conquest of Granada*, Part II (1672). Dryden (1631–1700) cannot have known Jonson personally.]

In reading some bombast speeches of *Macbeth*, which are not to be understood, he ⟨Ben. Johnson⟩ used to say that it was horrour.

15. JOHN MANNINGHAM (1602)

[From *Diary*.]

13 March 1601 ⟨1602⟩ . . . Vpon a tyme when Burbidge played Rich. 3. there was a citizen greue soe farr in liking with him, that before shee went from the play shee appointed him to come that night vnto hir by the name of Ri: the 3. Shakespeare overhearing their conclusion went before, was intertained, and at his game ere Burbidge came. Then message being brought that Rich. the 3.^{d} was at the dore, Shakespeare caused returne to be made that William the Conquerour was before Rich. the 3. Shakespeare's name William. (*Mr. Curle.*)

16. JOHN DAVIES OF HEREFORD
(1603, 1605, 1610)

(a) [From *Microcosmos* (1603), 215.]

Players, I loue yee, and your *Qualitie*,
As ye are Men, that pass time not abus'd:
And some ⟨in margin, W. S. R. B.⟩ I love for *painting*, *poesie*,
And say fell *Fortune* cannot be excus'd,
That hath for better *vses* you refus'd:
Wit, Courage, good shape, good partes, and all *good*,
As long as all these *goods* are no *worse* vs'd,
And though the *stage* doth staine pure gentle *bloud*,
Yet generous yee are in *minde* and *moode*.

(b) [From *The Civile Warres of Death and Fortune* (1605), st. 76.]

Some followed her by acting ⟨in margin, Stage plaiers⟩ all mens parts,
These on a Stage she rais'd (in scorne) to fall:
And made them Mirrors, by their acting Arts,
Wherin men saw their faults, thogh ne'r so small:
Yet some she guerdond not, to their ⟨in margin, W. S. R. B.⟩ desarts;
But, othersome, were but ill-Action all:
Who while they acted ill, ill staid behinde,
(By custom of their maners) in their minde.

(c) [From *The Scourge of Folly* (n.d.; S.R. 8 Oct. 1610), Epig. 159. The bit about 'companion for a King' is cryptic; possibly (a) and (b) allude even more obscurely to the same matter. One could fancy there had been some talk of making Shakespeare, and perhaps Burbadge, Esquires of the Bath, like Drayton, at the coronation of James. But although there are Companions of the Bath now, they were only introduced into the Order in 1815, and do not represent the old Esquires, who were not so called.]

To our English Terence, Mr. Will.
Shake-speare.

Some say (good *Will*) which I, in sport, do sing,
Had'st thou not plaid some Kingly parts in sport,
Thou hadst bin a companion for a *King;*
And, beene a King among the meaner sort.
Some others raile; but, raile as they thinke fit,
Thou hast no rayling, but, a raigning Wit:
  And honesty *thou sow'st, which they do reape;*
  So, to increase their Stocke *which they do keepe.*

17. ANTHONY SCOLOKER (1604)

[From *Epistle* to *Daiphantus, or the Passions of Love*, sign. E 4ᵛ.]
It should be like the *Neuer-too-well read Arcadia*, where the *Prose* and *Verce* (*Matter* and *Words*) are like his *Mistresses* eyes, one still excelling another and without Coriuall: or to come home to the vulgars *Element*, like *Friendly Shakespeare's Tragedies*, where the *Commedian* rides, when the *Tragedian* stands on Tip-toe: Faith it should please all, like Prince *Hamlet*. But in sadnesse, then it were to be feared he would runne mad: Insooth I will not be moone-sicke, to please: nor out of my wits though I displeased all.

18. WILLIAM CAMDEN (1605)

[From *Remaines of a greater Worke concerning Britaine*, Poems 8.]
These may suffice for some Poeticall descriptions of our aunciant Poets, if I would come to our time, what a world could I present to you out of Sir *Philipp Sidney, Ed. Spencer, Samuel Daniel, Hugh Holland, Ben: Johnson, Th. Campion, Mich. Drayton, George Chapman, Iohn Marston, William Shakespeare*, & other most pregnant witts of these our times, whom succeeding ages may iustly admire.

19. ANON (1609)

[From Cancel (sign. ¶ 2) in second issue of *Troil. & Cres.*]

A neuer writer, to an euer
reader. Newes.

Eternall reader, you haue heere a new play, neuer stal'd with the Stage, neuer clapper-clawd with the palmes of the vulger, and yet passing full of the palme comicall; for it is a birth of your braine, that neuer under-tooke any thing commicall, vainely: And were but the vaine names of commedies changde for the titles of Commodities, or of Playes for Pleas; you should see all those grand censors, that now stile them such vanities, flock to them for the maine grace of their grauities: especially this authors Commedies, that are so fram'd to the life, that they serue for the most common Commentaries, of all the actions of our liues shewing such a dexteritie, and power of witte, that the most displeased with Playes, are pleasd with his Commedies. And all such dull and heauy-witted worldlings, as were neuer capable of the witte of a Commedie, comming by report of them to his representations, haue found that witte there, that they neuer found in them selues, and have parted better wittied then they came: feeling an edge of witte set vpon them, more then euer they dreamd they had braine to grinde it on. So much and such sauored salt of witte is in his Commedies, that they seeme (for their height of pleasure) to be borne in that sea that brought forth *Venus*. Amongst all there is none more witty then this: And had I time I would comment upon it, though I know it needs not, (for so much as will make you thinke your testerne well bestowd) but for so much worth, as euen poore I know to be stuft in it. It deserues such a labour, as well as the best Commedy in *Terence* or *Plautus*. And beleeue this, that when hee is gone, and his Commedies out of sale, you will scramble for them, and set vp a new English Inquisition. Take this for a warning, and at the perrill of your pleasures losse, and Iudgements, refuse not, nor like this the lesse, for not being sullied, with the smoaky breath of the multitude; but thanke fortune for the scape it hath made amongst you. Since by the grand possessors will I beleeue you should have prayd for them rather then beene prayd. And so I leaue all such to bee prayd for (for the states of their wits healths) that will not praise it. Vale.

20. JOHN WEBSTER (1612)

[From *Epistle* to *The White Devil* (1612).]

Detraction is the sworne friend to ignorance: For mine owne part I haue euer truly cherisht my good opinion of other mens worthy Labours, especially of that full and haightned stile of Maister *Chapman*: The labor'd and vnderstanding workes of Maister *Johnson*; The no lesse worthy composures of the both worthily excellent Maister *Beamont* & Maister *Fletcher*: And lastly (without wrong last to be named), the right happy and copious industry of M. *Shake-speare*, M. *Decker*, & M. *Heywood*, wishing what I write may be read by their light: Protesting, that, in the strength of mine owne iudgement, I know them so worthy, that though I rest silent in my owne worke, yet to most of theirs I dare (without flattery) fix that of *Martiall*.

—*non norunt, Hæc monumenta mori.*

21. THOMAS HEYWOOD (1612, 1635)

(*a*) [From *Epistle* to the printer after *An Apology for Actors* (1612). The reference is to the two poems from Heywood's *Troia Britannica* (1609), pr. in the 1612 ed. of *The Passionate Pilgrim*.]

Here likewise, I must necessarily insert a manifest injury

done me in that worke, by taking the two Epistles of *Paris* to *Helen*, and *Helen* to *Paris*, and printing them in a lesse volume, vnder the name of another, which may put the world in opinion I might steale them from him; and hee to doe himselfe right, hath since published them in his owne name: but as I must acknowledge my lines not worthy his patronage, vnder whom he hath publisht them, so the Author I know much offended with M. *Jaggard* that (altogether vnknowne to him) presumed to make so bold with his name.

(b) [From *The Hierarchie of the Blessed Angels* (1635), iv, p. 206.]

Our moderne Poets to that passe are driuen,
Those names are curtal'd which they first had giuen;
And, as we wisht to haue their memories drown'd,
We scarcely can afford them halfe their sound....
Mellifluous *Shake-speare*, whose inchanting Quill
Commanded Mirth or Passion, was but *Will*.

22. RICHARD CAREW (1614)

[From *Epistle* from R. C. of Anthony Esquire to W. C. on *The Excellencie of the English Tongue*, added to the 2nd ed. (1614) of Camden's *Remaines of a Greater Worke concerning Britaine*, 36. Carew (1555–1620) was a Ch. Ch. man and a Cornish antiquary.]

Adde hereunto, that whatsoeuer grace any other language carrieth in verse or Prose, in Tropes or Metaphors, in Ecchoes and Agnominations, they may all bee liuely and exactly represented in ours: will you haue *Platoes* veine? reade Sir *Thomas Smith*, the *Ionicke*? Sir *Thomas Moore*. *Ciceroes? Ascham, Varro? Chaucer, Demosthenes?* Sir *Iohn Cheeke* (who in his treatise to the Rebels, hath comprised all the figures of Rhetorick). Will you reade *Virgill*? take the Earle of Surrey. *Catullus?* Shakespeare and *Barlowes* ⟨*Marlows*⟩ fragment, *Ouid? Daniell. Lucan? Spencer,*

Martial? Sir *John Dauies* and others: will you have all in all for Prose and verse? take the miracle of our age, Sir *Philip Sidney*.

23. C. B. (1614)

[From *The Ghost of Richard the Third*, Part II, stt. 1, 2. The initials appended to the dedication have been generally taken as those of Christopher Brooke (ob. 1628).]

> To him that impt my fame with Clio's quill;
> Whose magick rais'd me from Obliuion's den;
> That writ my storie on the Muses hill;
> And with my actions dignifi'd his pen:
> He that from Helicon sends many a rill;
> Whose nectared veines, are drunke by thirstie men:
>   Crown'd be his stile with fame; his head, with bayes;
>   And none detract, but gratulate his praise.
>
> Yet if his scaenes haue not engrost all grace,
> The much fam'd action could extend on stage.

24. THOMAS FREEMAN (1614)

[From *Runne and a Great Cast* (the second part of *Rubbe, and a Great Cast*), Epig. 92. Freeman was of Magdalen, Oxford.]

        To Master W. Shakespeare.

Shakespeare, that nimble *Mercury* thy braine,
Lulls many hundred *Argus*-eyes asleepe,
So fit, for all thou fashionest thy vaine,
At th' *horse-foote* fountaine thou hast drunk full deepe,
Vertues or vices theame to thee all one is:
Who loues chaste life, there's *Lucrece* for a Teacher:
Who list read lust there's *Venus* and *Adonis*,
True modell of a most lasciuious leatcher.
Besides in plaies thy wit windes like *Meander*:
Whence needy new-composers borrow more

Then *Terence* doth from *Plautus* or *Menander*.
But to praise thee aright I want thy store:
   Then let thine owne works thine owne worth upraise,
   And help t' adorne thee with deserued Baies.

25. SIR WILLIAM DRUMMOND (*c*. 1614)

[From notes appended, without separate heading, to abstract of Drummond's conversations with Jonson in *Works* (1711), 226. The date is suggested by a citation of Drayton's *Polyolbion* (1613) as 'in this edition 1614'. It was in 1614 that Drummond made the acquaintance of Alexander to whose *Aurora* (1604) as well as Shakespeare's *Sonnets* (1609) he seems to refer.]

Mr *Drummond* gave the following Character of several Authors. The Authors (saith he) I have seen on the Subject of Love, are the Earl of *Surrey*, Sir *Thomas Wyat* (whom, because of their Antiquity, I will not match with our better Times) *Sidney, Daniel, Drayton*, and *Spencer*. He who writeth the Art of *English* Poesy praiseth much *Rawleigh* and *Dyer*; but their Works are so few that are come to my Hands, I cannot well say any thing of them. The last we have are Sir *William Alexander* and *Shakespear*, who have lately published their Works.

26. EDMUND HOWES (1615)

[From continuation to 1614 in ed. 5 of John Stow's *Annales*.]

Our moderne, and present excellent Poets which worthely florish in their owne workes, and all of them in my owne knowledge lived togeather in this Queenes raigne, according to their priorities as neere as I could, I have orderly set downe (viz) *George Gascoigne* Esquire, *Thomas Churchyard* Esquire, Sir *Edward Dyer* Knight, *Edmond Spencer* Esquire, Sir *Philip Sidney* Knight, Sir *John Harrington* Knight, Sir *Thomas Challoner* Knight, Sir *Frauncis Bacon* Knight, & Sir *John Davie* Knight, Master *Iohn Lillie* gentleman, Maister *George Chapman* gentleman, M. *W. Warner* gentleman, M. *Willi. Shakespeare* gentleman, *Samuell Daniell* Esquire, *Michaell Draiton* Esquire, of the bath, M. *Christopher Marlo* gen., M. *Benjamine Johnson* gentleman, *Iohn Marston* Esquier, M. *Abraham Frauncis* gen., master *Frauncis Meers* gentle., master *Josua Siluester* gentle., master *Thomas Deckers* gentleman, M. John Flecher gentle., M. *John Webster* gentleman, M. *Thomas Heywood* gentleman, M. *Thomas Middleton* gentleman, M. *George Withers*.

27. J. M. (*c*. 1615) (?GERVASE [JERVIS] MARKHAM)

[From *The New Metamorphosis* (*Addl. MSS.* 14824–26), vol. i, pt. ii, p. 96.]

who hath a lovinge wife & loves her not,
he is no better then a witlesse sotte
Let such have wives to recompense their merite,
even Menelaus forked face inherite.
Is love in wives good, not in husbands too?
why doe men sweare they love then, when they wooe?
it seemes 't is true that W. S. said,
when once he heard one courting of a Mayde,—
Beleve not thou Mens fayned flatteryes,
Lovers will tell a bushell-full of Lyes!

28. FRANCIS BEAUMONT (*c*. 1615)[1]

[There are some indications of date. Marston's *Fawn* was played *c*. 1604–6 and printed in 1606, Sharpham's *Fleir* played in 1606 and printed in 1607 (*Eliz. Stage*, iii. 432, 490). Beaumont died on 6 Mar. 1616. It is possible that 'the post of Douer' and the 'Carriers pist-ling ghost' (ll. 11–12) are allusions respectively

[1] For particulars concerning the MSS. of this poem see *William Shakespeare*, where it was printed in full for the first time.

to Anthony Nixon's *A Straunge Foot-Post* (1613) which has a woodcut of the Dover postman and was reissued in 1616 as *The Foot-Post of Dover*, and to G⟨ervase⟩ M⟨arkham's⟩ *Hobsons Horse-load of Letters: or A President of Epistles* (1613). Thomas Hobson was a well-known Cambridge carrier. He had not strictly a ghost, however, until 1631. There is no book by Nicholas Breton called *Common Talke*, although the description might serve for many of his compilations, including the *Wits Private Wealth*, of which a new edition appeared in 1613. Beaumont, who was a lawyer, which Jonson was not, might intelligibly refer here to the law-book ascribed to John Breton. It is an analysis of common pleas. But the title of the *c.* 1540 print is simply *Britton*, and *Common Talke* would be a very forced name to give it. If one may take 1613–16 as the limits, there were two Garter installations at Windsor (l. 27) during this period; for Frederick Count Palatine and Count Maurice of Nassau, afterwards Prince of Orange, on 7 Feb. 1613, and for Thomas Erskine, Viscount Fenton, and William Lord Knollys on 22 May 1515 (G. F. Beltz, *Memorials of the Garter*, clxxxv). It is uncertain whose the white and orange tawny liveries were. One would suppose them a compliment to Maurice of Nassau, but he was only installed by proxy, and presumably with no unusual splendour. John Chamberlain (Birch, *James*, i. 362) records the contention to make the best show between the knights of 1615. Fenton was to be followed by all the Bedchamber, and a hundred of the Guard, of which he was Captain, in 'new rich coats'. James Lord Hay was then a Gentleman of the Bedchamber, and he had tawny liveries on an embassy to France in 1616 (A. Wilson in W. Kennett, *Hist. of England*, ii. 704). He was rich in royal gifts, but extravagant and sometimes in debt. No doubt he had many needy followers. On the whole, 1615 is likely to have been the occasion which Beaumont had in mind.]

To M^r B: J:.

Neither to follow fashion nor to showe
my witte against the State, nor that I knowe
any thing now, with which I am with childe
till I haue tould, nor hopeinge to bee stilde

a good Epist'ler through the towne, with which
I might bee famous, nor with any ytch
like these, wrote I this Letter but to showe
the Loue I carrie and mee thinkes do owe
to you aboue the number, which ⟨can⟩ best
in something which I vse not, be exprest.
to write this I invoake none, but the post
of Douer, or some Carriers pist-ling ghost,
for if this equall but the stile, which men
send Cheese to towne with, and thankes downe agen,
tis all I seeke for: heere I would let slippe
(If I had any in mee) schollershippe,
And from all Learninge keepe these lies as ⟨cl⟩eere
as Shakespeares best are, which our heires shall heare
Preachers apte to their auditors to showe
how farr sometimes a mortall man may goe
by the dimme light of Nature, tis to mee
an helpe to write of nothing; and as free,
As hee, whose text was, god made all that is,
I meane to speake: what do you thinke of his
state, who hath now the last that hee could make
in white and Orrenge tawny on his backe
at Windsor? is not this mans miserie more
then a fallen sharers, that now keepes a doore,
hath not his state almost as wretched beene
as ⟨h⟩is, that is ordainde to write the ⟨grinne⟩
after the fawne, and fleere shall bee? as sure
some one there is allotted to endure
that Cross. there are some, I could wish to knowe
to loue, and keepe with, if they woulde not showe
their studdies to me; or I wish to see
their workes to laugh at, if they suffer mee
not to knowe them: And thus I would Commerse
with honest Poets that make scuruie verse.

by this time you perceiue you did a misse
to leaue your worthier studies to see this,
which is more tedious to you, then to walke
in a Jews Church, or Bretons Com̃on talke.
but know I write not these lines to the end
to please Ben. Johnson but to please my frend. ffinis. FB.

29. WILLIAM BASSE (1616◊1623)

[From *Lansdowne MS.* 777, f. 67ᵛ. Basse (*c.* 1583–*c.* 1653) was an Oxford student and a retainer of Lord Wenman of Thame.]

On Mr. Wm. Shakespeare
he dyed in Aprill 1616.

Renowned Spencer, lye a thought more nye
To learned Chaucer, and rare Beaumont lye
A little neerer Spenser to make roome
For Shakespeare in your threefold fowerfold Tombe.
To lodge all fowre in one bed make a shift
Vntill Doomesdaye, for hardly will a fift
Betwixt this day and that by Fate be slayne
For whom your Curtaines may be drawn againe.
If your precedency in death doth barre
A fourth place in your sacred sepulcher,
Vnder this carued marble of thine owne
Sleepe rare Tragœdian Shakespeare, sleep alone,
Thy vnmolested peace, vnshared Caue,
Possesse as Lord not Tenant of thy Graue,
    That vnto us and others it may be
    Honor hereafter to be layde by thee.

Wm. Basse.

30. JOHN TAYLOR (1620)

[From *The Praise of Hemp-seed*, 26.]

In paper, many a Poet now suruiues
Or else their lines had perish'd with their liues.

Old *Chaucer*, *Gower*, and Sir *Thomas More*,
Sir *Philip Sidney*, who the Lawrell wore,
Spencer, and *Shakespeare* did in Art excell,
Sir *Edward Dyer*, *Greene*, *Nash*, *Daniell*.
Siluester, *Beaumont*, Sir *John Harrington*,
Forgetfulnesse their workes would ouer run,
But that in paper they immortally
Doe liue in spight of death, and cannot die.

31. NICHOLAS RICHARDSON (1620)

[From *Bodl. MS. Eng. Misc.* d. 28, p. 359, col. 705. This is one of several passages from Shakespeare in a commonplace book formerly preserved in the Principal's lodgings at Brasenose, and possibly compiled by Principal Samuel Radcliffe (1614–48). Richardson became a Fellow of Magdalen in 1614.]

Tis' almost morning I would haue thee gone
And yet no farther then a wantons bird,
That lets it hop a little from his hand,
Like a poore prisoner, in his twisted gyues,
Then with a silken thread plucks it back againe
So iealous louing of his liberty. Tragedy of
Romeo and Juliet. 4°: pag. 84:
   Said by Juliet: pro eadem.
this Mr Richard^{son} Coll. Magd: inserted hence into his Sermon, preached it twice at St Maries 1620. 1621. applying it to gods loue to his Saints either hurt with sinne, or aduersity neuer forsaking thē.

32. JOHN HEMINGES AND HENRY CONDELL (1623)

(*a*) [*Epistle* to the Earls of Pembroke and Montgomery, on third preliminary leaf of F 1; cf. vol. i, p. 142.]

Right Honourable,
Whilst we studie to be thankful in our particular, for the many fauors we have receiued from your L. L we are falne

vpon the ill fortune, to mingle two the most diuerse things that can bee, feare, and rashnesse; rashnesse in the enterprize, and feare of the successe. For, when we valew the places your H. H. sustaine, we cannot but know their dignity greater, then to descend to the reading of these trifles: and, while we name them trifles, we haue depriu'd our selues of the defence of our Dedication. But since your L. L. haue beene pleas'd to thinke these trifles some-thing, heeretofore; and haue prosequuted both them, and their Authour liuing, with so much fauour: we hope, that (they out-liuing him, and he not hauing the fate, common with some, to be exequutor to his owne writings) you will vse the like indulgence toward them, you haue done vnto their parent. There is a great difference, whether any Booke choose his Patrones, or finde them: This hath done both. For, so much were your L L. likings of the seuerall parts, when they were acted, as before they were published, the Volume ask'd to be yours. We haue but collected them, and done an office to the dead, to procure his Orphanes, Guardians; without ambition either of selfe-profit, or fame: onely to keepe the memory of so worthy a Friend, & Fellow aliue, as was our SHAKESPEARE, by humble offer of his playes, to your most noble patronage. Wherein, as we haue iustly obserued, no man to come neere your L. L. but with a kind of religious addresse; it hath bin the height of our care, who are the Presenters, to make the present worthy of your H. H. by the perfection. But, there we must also craue our abilities to be considerd, my Lords. We cannot go beyond our owne powers. Country hands reach foorth milke, creame, fruites, or what they haue: and many Nations (we haue heard) that had not gummes & incense, obtained their requests with a leauened Cake. It was no fault to approch their Gods, by what meanes they could: And the most, though meanest, of things are made more precious, when they are dedicated to Temples. In that name therefore, we most humbly consecrate to your H. H. these remaines of your seruant *Shakespeare*; that what delight is in them, may be euer your L. L. the reputation his, & the faults ours, if any be committed, by a payre so carefull to shew their gratitude both to the liuing, and the dead, as is

> *Your Lordshippes most bounden*,
> IOHN HEMINGE.
> HENRY CONDELL.

(*b*) [*To the great Variety of Readers*, on fourth preliminary leaf of F 1.]

From the most able, to him that can but spell: There you are number'd. We had rather you were weighd. Especially, when the fate of all Bookes depends vpon your capacities: and not of your heads alone, but of your purses. Well! It is now publique, & you wil stand for your priuiledges wee know: to read, and censure. Do so, but buy it first. That doth best commend a Booke, the Stationer saies. Then, how odde soeuer your braines be, or your wisedomes, make your licence the same, and spare not. Judge your sixe-pen'orth, your shillings worth, your fiue shillings worth at a time, or higher, so you rise to the iust rates, and welcome. But, what euer you do, Buy. Censure will not driue a Trade, or make the Iacke go. And though you be a Magistrate of wit, and sit on the Stage at *Black-Friers*, or the *Cock-pit*, to arraigne Playes dailie, know, these Playes haue had their triall alreadie, and stood out all Appeales; and do now come forth quitted rather by a Decree of Court, then any purchas'd Letters of commendation.

It had bene a thing, we confesse, worthie to haue bene wished, that the Author himselfe had liu'd to haue set forth, and ouerseen his owne writings; But since it hath bin ordain'd otherwise, and he by death departed from that right, we pray you do not envie his Friends, the office of their care, and paine, to haue collected & publish'd them; and so to haue publish'd them, as where (before) you were abus'd with diuerse stolne, and surreptitious copies, maimed, and deformed by the frauds and stealthes of iniurious impostors, that expos'd them: euen those, are now offer'd to your view cur'd, and perfect of their limbes; and all the rest, absolute in their numbers, as he conceiued them. Who, as he was a happie imitator of Nature, was a most gentle expresser of it. His mind and hand went together: And what he thought, he vttered with that easinesse, that wee haue scarce receiued from him a blot in his papers. But it is not our prouince, who onely gather his works, and giue them you, to praise him. It is yours that reade him. And there we hope, to your diuers capacities, you will finde enough, both to draw, and hold you: for his wit can no more lie hid, then it could be lost. Reade him, therefore; and againe, and againe: And if then you doe not like him, surely you are in some manifest danger, not to vnderstand him. And so we leaue you to other of his Friends, whom if you need, can bee your guides: if you neede them not, you can leade your selues, and others. And such Readers we wish him.

IOHN HEMINGE.
HENRIE CONDELL.

APPENDIX III

TRADITION

(*from* 1625)

1. RICHARD JAMES (*c.* 1625)

[From *Epistle* to Sir Harry Bourchier, with a copy of Occleve's *Legend and Defence of Sir John Oldcastle*. James (1592–1638) was of C.C.C. Oxford and librarian to Sir Robert Cotton.]

A young Gentle Lady of your acquaintance, having read ye works of Shakespeare, made me this question. How Sr John Falstaffe, or Fastolf, as he is written in ye Statute book of Maudlin Colledge in Oxford, where everye day that society were bound to make memorie of his soul, could be dead in ye time of Harrie ye Fift and again live in ye time of Harrie ye Sixt to be banished for cowardice: Whereto I made answear that it was one of those humours and mistakes for which Plato banisht all poets out of his commonwealth. That Sr John Falstaffe was in those times a noble valiant souldier, as apeeres by a book in ye Heralds Office dedicated unto him by a Herald who had binne with him, if I well remember, for the space of 25 yeeres in ye French wars; that he seems also to have binne a man of learning, because, in a Library of Oxford, I find a book of dedicating Churches sent from him for a present unto Bishop Wainflete, and inscribed with his own hand. That in Shakespeares first shew of Harrie the fift, the person with which he undertook to playe a buffone was not Falstaffe, but Sir Jhon Oldcastle, and that offence beinge worthily taken by Personages descended from his title (as peradventure by many others allso whoe ought to have him in honourable memorie) the poet was putt to make an ignorant shifte of abusing Sir Jhon Falstophe, a man not inferior of Vertue, though not so famous in pietie as the other, who gave witnesse unto the truth of our reformation with a constant and resolute Martyrdom, unto which he was pursued by the Priests, Bishops, Moncks, and Friers of those days.

2. ANON (1632)

[From preliminary matter to F 2. The unknown author seems to claim personal knowledge of Shakespeare.]

Upon the Effigies of my worthy Friend, the Author Master William Shakespeare, and his Workes.

Spectator, this Life's Shaddow is; To see
The truer image and a livelier he
Turne Reader. But, observe his Comicke vaine,
Laugh, and proceed next to a Tragicke straine,
Then weepe; So when thou find'st two contraries,
Two different passions from thy rapt soule rise,
Say, (who alone effect such wonders could)
Rare *Shake-speare* to the life thou dost behold.

3. JOHN BENSON (1640)

[*Epistle* to *Poems: Written by Wil. Shake-speare. Gent.* (1640, John Benson).]

To the Reader.

I here presume (under favour) to present to your view, some excellent and sweetely composed Poems, of Master *William Shakespeare,* Which in themselves appeare of the same purity, the Authour himselfe then living avouched; they had not the fortune by reason of their Infancie in his death, to have the due accommodation of proportionable glory, with the rest of his everliving Workes, yet the lines of themselves will afford you a more authentick approbation than my assurance any way can, to invite your allowance, in your perusall you shall finde them

Seren, cleere and eligantly plaine, such gentle straines as shall recreate and not perplexe your braine, no intricate or cloudy stuffe to puzzell intellect, but perfect eloquence; such as will raise your admiration to his praise: this assurance I know will not differ from your acknowledgement. And certaine I am, my opinion will be seconded by the sufficiency of these ensuing Lines; I have beene some what solicitus to bring this forth to the perfect view of all men; and in so doing, glad to be serviceable for the continuance of glory to the deserved Author in these his Poems.   I. B.

4. SIR NICHOLAS L'ESTRANGE (1629–55)

[From *Merry Passages and Jeasts* (*Harl. MS.* 6395, f. 2), pr. W. J. Thoms, *Anecdotes and Traditions* (1839, C.S.). The MS. is anonymous, but can be safely ascribed to L'Estrange (ob. 1655), who was of Hunstanton, Norfolk, and as many items are initialed S. N. L. was presumably compiled after he became a baronet in 1629.]

Shake-speare was Godfather to one of *Ben: Johnsons* children, and after the christning being in a deepe study, Johnson came to cheere him vp, and askt him why he was so Melancholy? no faith *Ben:* (sayes he) not I, but I haue beene considering a great while what should be the fittest gift for me to bestow vpon my God-child, and I haue resolu'd at last; I pry'the what, sayes he? I faith *Ben:* I'le e'en giue him a douzen good Lattin Spoones, and thou shalt translate them.

5. THOMAS FULLER (1643–61)

[From *Worthies, Warwickshire*, 126. Fuller (1608–61) seems to have been collecting material for the *Worthies* as early as 1643. His passage on Shakespeare and Jonson reads like fancy, not tradition.]

WILLIAM SHAKSPEARE was born at *Stratford* on *Avon* in

this County, in whom three eminent Poets may seem in some sort to be compounded.

1. *Martial* in the *Warlike* sound of his Sur-name (whence some may conjecture him of a *Military extraction,*) *Hasti-vibrans*, or *Shake-speare*.

2. *Ovid*, the most *naturall* and *witty* of all Poets, and hence it was that Queen *Elizabeth*, coming into a Grammar-School, made this extemporary verse,

> '*Persius* a Crab-staffe, Bawdy *Martial*,
> *Ovid* a fine Wag.'

3. *Plautus*, who was an exact Comædian, yet never any Scholar, as our *Shake-speare* (if alive) would confess himself. Adde to all these, that though his Genius generally was *jocular*, and inclining him to *festivity*, yet he could (when so disposed) be *solemn* and *serious*, as appears by his Tragedies, so that *Heraclitus* himself (I mean if secret and unseen) might afford to smile at his Comedies, they were so *merry*, and *Democritus* scarce forbear to sigh at his Tragedies they were so *mournfull*.

He was an eminent instance of the truth of that Rule, *Poeta not fit, sed nascitur*, one is not *made*, but *born* a Poet. Indeed his Learning was very little, so that as *Cornish diamonds* are not polished by any Lapidary, but are pointed and smoothed even as they are taken out of the Earth, so *nature* it self was all the *art* which was used upon him.

Many were the *wit-combates* betwixt him and *Ben Johnson*, which two I behold like a *Spanish great Gallion* and an *English man of War*; Master *Johnson* (like the former) was built far higher in Learning; *Solid*, but *Slow* in his performances. *Shake-spear*, with the *English-man of War*, lesser in *bulk*, but lighter in *sailing*, could turn with all tides, tack about and take advantage of all winds, by the quickness of his Wit and Invention. He died *Anno*

Domini 16 . ., and was buried at *Stratford* upon *Avon*, the Town of his Nativity.

6. ANON (*c.* 1650)

[From *Bodl. Ashm. MS.* 38, a collection of verses, many of them Caroline, in the hand of Nicholas Burgh, a Poor Knight of Windsor, who was alive in 1661.]

(*a*) [p. 180.]

On John Combe A Coueteous rich man m^r Wm. Shakspear wright this att his request while hee was yett Liueing for his Epitaphe

Who Lies In this Tombe
Hough; Quoth the Deuill, Tis my Sonn John A Combe.
            finis

but being dead, and making the poore his heiers hee after wrightes this for his Epitaph

How ere he liued Judge not
John Combe shall neuer be forgott
While poor, hath Memmorye, for hee did gather
To make the poore his Issue; hee their father
As record of his tilth and seede
Did Crowne him In his Latter deede.
          Finis W: Shak.

(*b*) [p. 181.]

m^r Ben: Johnson and m^r W^m: Shake-speare Being Merrye att a Tauern, m^r Jonson haueing begune this for his Epitaph

  Here lies Ben Johnson that was once one

he giues ytt to m^r Shakspear to make vpp who presently wrightes

  Who while hee liu'de was a sloe thinge
  and now being dead is Nothinge.
      finis

(c) [p. 186.]

Another on hym [Sir John Spenser].

Ten In the hundred lies vnder this stone
yttes a hundred to ten to the deuill he's gone.

7. THOMAS PLUME (c. 1657)

[From *Plume MS.* 25 in library at Maldon, Essex, founded by Plume (1630–74), Archdeacon of Rochester. Plume was compiling MS. 25 at various dates from 1657 to 1680, but these notes, or at least those of the first pagination, seem to be in his hand of *c.* 1657. The only Sir John Mennis known was born in Kent on 1 Mar. 1599, and could not have remembered John Shakespeare who died in Sept. 1601. His brother Sir Matthew Mennis, born about 1593, might have. Possibly Plume confused the two.]

[f. 161.]

He was a glovers son—S*ir* John Mennis saw once his old F*athe*r in h*is* shop—a merry Cheekd old man—*that* s*ai*d—Will was a g*oo*d Hon*est* Fellow, but he durst h*ave* crackt a jeast w*i*th him at any time.

8. JOHN WARD (1661–3)

[From his *Diary*. Ward (1629–81) was vicar of Stratford 1662–81.]

Shakespear had but 2 daughters, one whereof M. Hall, ye physitian, married, and by her had one daughter, to wit, ye Lady Bernard of Abbingdon....

I have heard y^t M^r. Shakespeare was a natural wit, without any art at all; hee frequented ye plays all his younger time, but in his elder days lived at Stratford: and supplied ye stage with 2 plays every year, and for y^t had an allowance so large, y^t hee spent att ye Rate of a 1,000*l.* a year, as I have heard.

Remember to peruse Shakespears plays, and bee versd in *them*, y^t I may not bee ignorant in y^t matter. ...

Shakespear, Drayton, and Ben Jhonson, had a merry meeting, and itt seems drank too hard, for Shakespear died of a feavour there contracted. ...

9. DAVID LLOYD (1665)

[From *Statesmen and Favourites of England since the Reformation* (1665), 504. The historical accuracy of Lloyd (1635–92) is discredited by Anthony Wood (*Athenae*, iv. 352), who calls him an 'impudent plagiary' and a 'false writer and meer scribbler'. There seems no particular reason for falsity here. But it is impossible to say what the statement about Shakespeare and Jonson rests on.]

One great argument for his ⟨Fulke Greville, Lord Brooke's⟩ worth, was his respect of the worth of others, desiring to be known to posterity under no other notions than of *Shakespear's* and *Ben Johnson's* Master, Chancellor *Egerton's* Patron, Bishop *Overal's* Lord, and Sir *Philip Sidney's* friend.

10. JOHN DRYDEN (1672, 1684)

[From *Essay on the Dramatique Poetry of the Last Age*, appended to *The Conquest of Granada*, Part ii (1672). For a passage reporting a criticism by Jonson, cf. p. 206.]

Shakespear show'd the best of his skill in his *Mercutio*, and he said himself, that he was forc'd to kill him in the third Act, to prevent being kill'd by him. But, for my part, I cannot find he was so dangerous a person: I see nothing in him but what was so exceeding harmless, that he might have liv'd to the end of the Play, and dy'd in his bed, without offence to any man.

11. JOHN AUBREY (1681)

[Aubrey (1626–97) collected his *Brief Lives* as material for the *Athenae Oxonienses* of Anthony Wood (cf. no. 14) from Bodleian MSS. William Beeston was a Caroline and Restoration actor, and the son of Christopher Beeston, a Chamberlain's man in 1598.]

(a)

the more to be admired q⟨uia⟩ he was not a company keeper
lived in Shoreditch, wouldnt be debauched, & if invited to writ; he was in paine.

    W. Shakespeare.

              Lacy
q⟨uaere⟩ Mr Beeston who knows most of him fr⟨om⟩ M^r;
he lives in Shore-ditch at Hoglane.
within 6 dores—Norton—folgate.
q⟨uaere⟩ etiam for B. Jonson.

(b)

M^r. William Shakespear. [*bay-wreath in margin*] was borne at Stratford vpon Avon, in the County of Warwick; his father was a Butcher, & I have been told heretofore by some of the neighbours, that when he was a boy he exercised his father's Trade, but when he kill'd a Calfe, he would doe it in a *high style*, & make a Speech. There was at that time another Butcher's son in this Towne, that was held not at all inferior to him for a naturall witt, his acquaintance & coetanean, but dyed young. This Wm. being inclined naturally to Poetry and acting, came to London I guesse about 18. and was an Actor at one of the Play-houses and did act exceedingly well: now B. Johnson was never a good Actor, but an excellent Instructor. He began early to make essayes at Dramatique Poetry, which at that time was very lowe; and his Playes tooke well: He was a handsome well shap't man: very good company, and of a very readie and pleasant smooth Witt. The Humour of . . . the Constable in a Midsomersnight's Dreame, he happened to take at Grendon [*In margin*, 'I thinke it was Midsomer night that he happened to lye there'.] in Bucks which is the roade from London to Stratford, and there was living that Constable about 1642 when I first came to Oxon. M^r. Jos. Howe is of that parish and knew him. Ben Johnson and he did gather Humours of men dayly where every they came. One time as he was at the Tavern at Stratford super Avon, one Combes an old rich Usurer was to be buryed, he makes there this extemporary Epitaph

> Ten in the Hundred the Devill allowes
> But *Combes* will have twelve, he sweares & vowes:
> If any one askes who lies in this Tombe:
> Hoh! quoth the Devill, 'Tis my John o' Combe.

He was wont to goe to his native Country once a yeare. I thinke I have been told that he left 2 or 300 ^{li} per annum there and thereabout: to a sister. [*In margin*, 'V. his Epitaph in Dugdales Warwickshire'.] I have heard S^r Wm. Davenant and M^r. Thomas Shadwell (who is counted the best Comœdian we have now) say, that he had a most prodigious Witt, and did admire his naturall parts beyond all other Dramaticall writers. He was wont to say, That he never blotted out a line in his life: sayd Ben: Johnson, I wish he had blotted out a thousand. [*In margin*, 'B. Johnsons Underwoods'.] His Comœdies will remaine witt, as long as the English tongue is understood; for that he handles mores hominum; now our present writers reflect so much upon particular persons, and coxcombeities, that 20 yeares hence, they will not be understood. Though as Ben: Johnson sayes of him, that he had but little Latine and lesse Greek, He understood Latine pretty well: for he had been in his younger yeares a Schoolmaster in the Countrey. [*In margin*, 'from M^r—— Beeston'.]

(*c*) [The passages in square brackets are scored out, perhaps by Anthony Wood.]

Sr William Davenant Knight Poet Laureate was borne in —— street in the City of Oxford, at the Crowne Taverne (*In margin*, 'V. A. W. Antiq: Oxon:'). His father was John Davenant a Vintner there, a very grave and discreet Citizen: his mother was a very beautifull woman, & of a very good witt and of conversation extremely agreable. ... Mr William Shakespeare was wont to goe into Warwickshire once a yeare, and did commonly in his journey lye at this house in Oxon: where he was exceedingly respected. [I have heard parson Robert D⟨avenant⟩ say that Mr W. Shakespeare here gave him a hundred kisses.] Now Sr. W^m would sometimes when he was pleasant over a glasse of wine with his most intimate friends e.g. Sam: Butler (author of Hudibras) &c. say, that it seemed to him that he writt with the very spirit that Shakespeare, and seemed contentended enough to be thought his Son: he would tell them the story as above. [in which way his mother had a very light report, whereby she was called a whore.]

12. EDWARD RAVENSCROFT (1687)

[From *Address* to *Titus Andronicus, or the Rape of Lavinia*, adapted from *Tit. Andr.* by Ravenscroft, and produced, according to the *Address*, 'at the beginning of the pretended Popish Plot', in 1678.]

I think it a greater theft to Rob the dead of their Praise then the Living of their Money. That I may not appear

Guilty of such a Crime, 'tis necessary I should acquaint you, that there is a Play in M^r. *Shakespears* Volume under the name of *Titus Andronicus*, from whence I drew part of this. I have been told by some anciently conversant with the Stage, that it was not Originally his, but brought by a private Authour to be Acted, and he only gave some Master-touches to one or two of the Principal Parts or Characters; this I am apt to believe, because 'tis the most incorrect and indigested piece in all his Works; It seems rather a heap of Rubbish then a Structure.

13. RICHARD DAVIES (1688–1708)

[From *MS.* in the library of C.C.C. Oxford. Davies became rector of Sapperton, Gloucestershire, on 5 Mar. 1695 and Archdeacon of Coventry in the diocese of Lichfield on 26 July 1703. He was buried at Sapperton on 19 June 1708.]

William Shakespeare.

William Shakespeare was born at Stratford upon Avon in Warwickshire about 1563·4.

much given to all unluckinesse in stealing venison & Rabbits particularly from S^r   Lucy who had him oft whipt & sometimes Imprisoned & at last made Him fly his Native Country to his great Advancem^t. but His reveng was so great that he is his Justice Clodpate and calls him a great man & y^t in allusion to his name bore three lowses rampant for his Arms

From an Actor of Playes, he became a Composer
Ætat. 53.

He dyed Apr. 23. 1616. probably at Stratford, for there he is buryed, and hath a Monument on w^c He lays a Heavy curse vpon any one who shal remoove his bones He dyed a papist.

Dugd., p. 520.

14. ANTHONY WOOD (1692)

[From *Athenae Oxonienses*, 292. Wood (1632–95) may have taken this from Aubrey (cf. no. xiii), but was himself a life-long Oxford resident.]

WILLIAM D'AVENANT. . . . His father John Davenant was a sufficient vintner, kept the tavern now known by the name of the Crown (wherein our poet was born) and was mayor of the said city in the year 1621. His mother was a very beautiful woman, of a good wit and conversation, in which she was imitated by none of her children but by this William. The father, who was a very grave and discreet citizen (yet an admirer and lover of plays and play-makers, especially Shakespeare, who frequented his house in his journies between Warwickshire and London) was of a melancholic disposition, and was seldom or never seen to laugh, in which he was imitated by none of his children but by Robert his eldest son, afterwards fellow of St. John's College and a venerable doct. of div.

15. MR. DOWDALL (1693)

[1693, Apr. 10. From *Letter* written at Butler's Marston, Warwickshire, signed 'John at Stiles', addressed to 'Mʳ Southwell' who is the writer's 'cousin', and endorsed 'From Mʳ Dowdall'.]

the clarke that shew'd me this Church [at Stratford] is aboue 80 yʳˢ old; he says that this *Shakespear* was formerly in this Towne bound apprentice to a butcher; but that he Run from his master to London, and there was Recᵈ Into the playhouse as a serviture, and by this meanes had an oppertunity to be wᵗ he afterwards prov'd. he was the best of his family but the male Line is extinguished; not one for feare of the Curse abouesᵈ Dare Touch his Grave Stone, tho his wife and Daughters Did Earnestly Desire to be Layd in the same Graue wᵗʰ him.

16. WILLIAM HALL (1694)

[From *Letter* of W. Hall to Edward Thwaites. Hall was son of a G⟨ul?⟩ Hall, innkeeper of Lichfield, took his B.A. from Queen's, 1694, and became rector of Acton, Middlesex, and prebendary of St. Paul's (Foster, *Alumni*; Elton 340).]

Dear Neddy,

I very greedily embraced this occasion of acquainting you with something which I found at Stratford upon Avon. That place I came unto on Thursday night, and ye next day went to visit ye ashes of the Great Shakespear which lye interr'd in that Church. The verses which in his life-time he ordered to be cut upon his tomb-stone (for his Monument have others) are these which follow;

> Reader, for Jesus's Sake forbear
> To dig the dust enclosed here:
> Blessed be he that Spares these Stones,
> And cursed be he that moves my bones.

The little learning these verses contain, would be a very strong argument of ye want of it in the Author; did not they carry something in them which stands in need of a comment. There is in this Church a place which they call the bone-house, a repository for all bones they dig up; which are so many that they would load a great number of waggons. The Poet being willing to preserve his bones unmoved, lays a curse upon him that moves them; and haveing to do with Clarks and Sextons, for ye most part a very ⟨i⟩gnorant sort of people, he descends to ye meanest of their capacitys; and disrobes himself of that art, which none of his Co-temporaryes wore in greater perfection. Nor has the design mist of its effect; for lest they should not onely draw this curse upon themselvs, but also entail it upon their posterity, they have laid him full seventeen foot deep, deep enough to secure him. And so much for Stratford. . . .

Direct your letter for
W^m. Hall Junr. at y^e
White-hart in Lichfield.

Your friend and Servant
W^m. Hall.

17. CHARLES GILDON (1694–1710)

[Gildon (1665–1724) was a dramatist and booksellers' hack, pilloried by Pope in the *Dunciad*.]

(*a*) [From *Reflections on Rymer's Short View of Tragedy* in *Miscellaneous Letters and Essays, on several Subjects. By several Gentlemen and Ladies* (1694), 88.]

I'm assur'd from very good hands, that the Person that Acted Jago was in much esteem for a Comoedian, which made *Shakespear* put several words, and expressions into his part (perhaps not so agreeable to his Character) to make the Audience laugh, who had not yet learnt to endure to be serious a whole Play.

(*b*) [From *The Lives and Characters of the English Dramatick Poets. First begun by Mr Langbain, improv'd and continued down to this Time, by a Careful Hand* (n.d.), 126.]

William Shakespear.

. . . I have been told that he writ the scene of the Ghost in *Hamlet*, at his House which bordered on the Charnel-House and Church-Yard. . . .

(*c*) [From *Remarks on the Plays of Shakespear* in *The Works of Mr William Shakespear. Volume the Seventh* (1710).]
[p. 291.]

The *Fairys* in the fifth Act ⟨of *Merry Wives of W.*⟩ makes a Handsome Complement to the Queen, in her Palace of *Windsor*, who had oblig'd him to write a Play of *Sir John*

Falstaff in Love, and which I am very well assured he perform'd in a Fortnight; a prodigious Thing, when all is so well contriv'd, and carry'd on without the least Confusion.

[p. 404.]

The former Scene ⟨*Ham.* i. 4⟩, which as I have been assur'd he wrote in a Charnel House in the midst of the Night.

18. JAMES WRIGHT? (1699)

[From *Historia Histrionica . . . In a Dialogue of Plays and Players*, anonymous, but usually ascribed to Wright (1643–1713), an antiquary and play-collector.]

Lovewit. Pray Sir, what Master Parts can you remember the Old *Black-friers* men to Act, in *Johnson*, *Shakespear*, and *Fletcher's* Plays?

Truman. What I can at present recollect I'll tell you; *Shakespear* (who, as I have heard, was a much better Poet, than Player) *Burbadge*, *Hemmings*, and others of the Older sort, were Dead before I knew the Town.

19. JOHN DENNIS (1702–4)

[Dennis (1657–1734) of Caius and Trinity Hall, Cambridge, was an unsuccessful dramatist, an enemy of Pope, and a critic of some merit.]

(*a*) [From *Epistle* to *The Comicall Gallant* (1702), based on *Merry Wives of W.*]

That this Comedy was not despicable, I guess'd for several Reasons: First, I knew very well, that it had pleas'd one of the greatest Queens that ever was in the World, great not only for her Wisdom in the Arts of Government, but for her knowledge of Polite Learning, and her nice taste of the Drama, for such a taste we may be sure she had, by the relish which she had of the

JOHN DENNIS

Ancients. This Comedy was written at her Command, and by her direction, and she was so eager to see it Acted, that she commanded it to be finished in fourteen days; and was afterwards, as Tradition tells us, very well pleas'd at the Representation.

20. JOHN DOWNES (1708)

[From *Roscius Anglicanus, or, an Historical Review of the Stage*, 21. Downes was a prompter in London theatres from 1662 to 1706. He gives a list of plays acted at Lincoln's Inn Fields during 1662–5. Shakespeare may have instructed Lowin, but hardly Taylor, who joined the King's in 1619.]

The Tragedy of *Hamlet*; *Hamlet* being Perform'd by M^r. *Betterton*, Sir *William* ⟨Davenant⟩ (having seen M^r. *Taylor* of the *Black-Fryars* Company Act it, who being Instructed by the Author Mr *Shaksepeur*) taught Mr *Betterton* in every Particle of it. . . .

King *Henry* the *8th*. . . . The part of the King was so right and justly done by Mr *Betterton*, he being instructed in it by Sir *William*, who had it from Old Mr *Lowen*, that had his Instructions from Mr *Shakespear* himself, that I dare and will aver, none can, or will come near him in this Age, in the performance of that part.

21. NICHOLAS ROWE (1709)

[Extracts from *Life* in *Works of Shakespeare* (1709), i. 1.]

. . . His Father, who was a considerable Dealer in Wool, had so large a Family, ten Children in all, that tho' he was his eldest Son, he could give him no better Education than his own Employment. He had bred him, 'tis true, for some time at a Free-School, where 'tis probable he acquir'd that little *Latin* he was Master of: But the narrowness of his Circumstances, and the want of his assistance at Home, forc'd his Father to withdraw him from thence, and unhappily prevented his further Proficiency in that Language.... Upon his leaving School, he seems to have given intirely into that way of Living which his Father propos'd to him; and in order to settle in the World after a Family manner, he thought fit to marry while he was yet very Young. His Wife was the Daughter of one *Hathaway*, said to have been a substantial Yeoman in the Neighbourhood of *Stratford*. In this kind of Settlement he continu'd for some time, 'till an Extravagance that he was guilty of, forc'd him both out of his Country and that way of Living which he had taken up; and tho' it seem'd at first to be a Blemish upon his good Manners, and a Misfortune to him, yet it afterwards happily prov'd the occasion of exerting one of the greatest *Genius*'s that ever was known in Dramatick Poetry. He had, by a Misfortune common enough to young Fellows, fallen into ill Company; and amongst them, some that made a frequent practice of Deer-stealing, engag'd him with them more than once in robbing a Park that belong'd to Sir *Thomas Lucy* of *Cherlecot*, near *Stratford*. For this he was prosecuted by that Gentleman, as he thought, somewhat too severely; and in order to revenge that ill Usage, he made a Ballad upon him. And tho' this, probably the first Essay of his Poetry, be lost, yet it is said to have been so very bitter, that it redoubled the Prosecution against him to that degree, that he was oblig'd to leave his Business and Family in *Warwickshire*, for some time, and shelter himself in *London*.

It is at this Time, and upon this Accident, that he is said to have made his first Acquaintance in the Play-house. He was receiv'd into the Company then in being, at first in a very mean Rank; but his admirable Wit, and the natural Turn of it to the Stage, soon distinguish'd him, if not as an extraordinary Actor, yet as an excellent Writer. His Name is Printed, as the Custom was in those Times, amongst those of the other Players, before some old Plays, but without any particular Account of what sort of Parts he us'd to play; and tho' I have inquir'd, I could never meet with any further Account of him this way, than that the top of his Performance was the Ghost in his own *Hamlet*. . . . Besides the advantages of his Wit, he was in himself a good-natur'd Man, of great sweetness in his Manners, and a most agreeable Companion; so that it is no wonder if with so many good Qualities he made himself acquainted with the best Conversations of those Times. Queen *Elizabeth* had several of his Plays Acted before her, and without doubt gave him many gracious Marks of her Favour: . . . She was so well pleas'd with that admirable Character of *Falstaff*, in the two Parts of *Henry* the Fourth, that she commanded him to continue it for one Play more, and to shew him in Love. This is said to be the Occasion of his Writing *The Merry Wives* of Windsor. How well she was obey'd, the Play it self is an admirable Proof. . . . What Grace soever the Queen confer'd upon him, it was not to her only he ow'd the Fortune which the Reputation of his Wit made. He had the Honour to meet with many great and uncommon Marks of Favour and Friendship from the Earl of *Southampton*, famous in the Histories of that Time for his Friendship to the unfortunate Earl of *Essex*. It was to that Noble Lord that he Dedicated his *Venus* and *Adonis*, the only Piece of his Poetry which he ever publish'd himself, tho' many of his Plays were surrepticiously and lamely Printed in his Life-time. There is one instance so singular in the Magnificence of this Patron of *Shakespear's*, that if I had not been assur'd that the Story was handed down by Sir *William D'Avenant*, who was probably very well acquainted with his Affairs,

I should not have ventur'd to have inserted, that my Lord *Southampton*, at one time, gave him a thousand Pounds, to enable him to go through with a Purchase which he heard he had a mind to.

What particular Habitude or Friendships he contracted with private Men, I have not been able to learn, more than that every one who had a true Taste of Merit, and could distinguish Men, had generally a just Value and Esteem for him. His exceeding Candor and good Nature must certainly have inclin'd all the gentler Part of the World to love him, as the power of his Wit oblig'd the Men of the most delicate Knowledge and polite Learning to admire him. . . . His Acquaintance with *Ben Johnson* began with a remarkable piece of Humanity and good Nature; Mr *Johnson*, who was at that Time altogether unknown to the World, had offer'd one of his Plays to the Players, in order to have it Acted; and the Persons into whose Hands it was put, after having turn'd it carelessly and superciliously over, were just upon returning it to him with an ill-natur'd Answer, that it would be of no service to their Company, when *Shakespear* luckily cast his Eye upon it, and found something so well in it as to engage him first to read it through, and afterwards to recommend Mr *Johnson* and his Writings to the Publick. After this they were profess'd Friends; tho' I don't know whether the other ever made him an equal return of Gentleness and Sincerity. . . . .

Falstaff is allow'd by everybody to be a Master-piece; . . . Amongst other Extravagances, in *The Merry Wives of Windsor*, he has made him a Dear-stealer, that he might at the same time remember his *Warwickshire* Prosecutor, under the Name of Justice *Shallow*; he has given him very near the same Coat of Arms which *Dugdale*, in his Antiquities of that County, describes for a Family there, and makes the *Welsh* Parson descant very pleasantly upon 'em....

... I cannot leave *Hamlet*, without taking notice of the Advantage with which we have seen this Master-piece of *Shakespear* distinguish it self upon the Stage, by Mr *Betterton's* fine Performance of that Part. A Man who tho' he had no other good Qualities, as he has a great many, must have made his way into the Esteem of all Men of Letters, by this only Excellency.... I must own a particular Obligation to him, for the most considerable part of the Passages relating to his Life, which I have here transmitted to the Publick; his Veneration for the Memory of *Shakespear* having engaged him to make a Journey into *Warwickshire*, on purpose to gather up what Remains he could of a Name for which he had so great a Value....

... The latter Part of his Life was spent, as all Men of good Sense will wish theirs may be, in Ease, Retirement, and the Conversation of his Friends. He had the good Fortune to gather an Estate equal to his Occasion, and, in that, to his Wish; and is said to have spent some Years before his Death at his native *Stratford*. His pleasurable Wit, and good Nature, engag'd him in the Acquaintance, and entitled him to the Friendship of the Gentlemen of the Neighbourhood....

22. THOMAS HEARNE (1709)

[From notes at end of diary for June–July 1709. Hearne (1678–1735) was a lifelong student of antiquities in Oxford.]

'Twas reported by Tradition in Oxford that Shakespear as he us'd to pass from London to Stratford upon Avon, where he liv'd & now lies buried, always spent some time in ye Crown Tavern in Oxford, which was kept by one Davenant who had a handsome Wife, & lov'd witty

Company, tho' himself a reserv'd and melancholly Man. He had born to him a Son who was afterwards Christen'd by ye Name of W^m. who prov'd a very Eminent Poët, and was knighted (by ye name of S^r. William Davenant) and ye said M^r. Shakespear was his God-father & gave him his name. (In all probability he got him.) 'Tis further said that one day going from school a grave Doctor in Divinity met him, and ask'd him, *Child whither art thou going in such hast?* to wch the child reply'd, *O Sir my Godfather is come to Town, & I am going to ask his blessing.* To wch the D^r. said, *Hold Child, you must not take the name of God in vaine.*

23. ANON (*c.* 1709)

[From *Advertisement* on A 2^v of *A Collection of Poems* . . . By M^r. William Shakespeare, London.]

I cannot omit inserting a Passage of Mr *Shakespeare's* Life, very much to his Honour, and very remarkable, which was either unknown, or forgotten by the Writer of it.

That most learn'd Prince, and great Patron of Learning, King *James* the First, was pleas'd with his own Hand to write an amicable Letter to Mr *Shakespeare*; which Letter, tho now lost, remain'd long in the Hands of Sir *William D'avenant*, as a credible Person now living can testify.

24. ANON (1728)

[From *Essay against too much Reading* (1728), 14.]

I will give you a short Account of Mr *Shakespear's* Proceeding; and that I had from one of his intimate Acquaintance. His being imperfect in some Things, was owing to his not being a Scholar, which obliged him to have one of those chuckle-pated Historians for his particular Associate, that could scarce speak a Word but upon

that Subject; and he maintain'd him, or he might have
starv'd upon his History. And when he wanted anything
in his Way, as his plays were all Historical, he sent to him,
and took down the Heads of what was for his Purpose in
Characters, which were thirty times as quick as running
to the Books to read for it: Then with his natural flowing
Wit, he work'd it into all Shapes and Forms, as his beautiful Thoughts directed. The other put it into Grammar;
and instead of Reading, he stuck close to Writing and
Study without Book. How do you think, Reading could
have assisted him in such great Thoughts? It would only
have lost Time. When he found his Thoughts grow on
him so fast, he could have writ for ever, had he liv'd so
long.

25. JOSEPH SPENCE (1728–30)

[From *Anecdotes, Observations and Characters, of Books and
Men. Collected from the Conversation of Mr Pope, and other
eminent Persons of his Time.*]

(*a*) [p. 5.] It was a general opinion, that Ben Jonson and
Shakspeare lived in enmity against one another. Betterton
has assured me often, that there was nothing in it: and
that such a supposition was founded only on the two
parties, which in their lifetime listed under one, and
endeavoured to lessen the character of the other mutually.
—Dryden used to think that the verses Jonson made
on Shakspeare's death, had something of satire at the
bottom; for my part, I can't discover any thing like it in
them.—*P[ope]*.

(*b*) [*p.* 23.] That notion of Sir William Davenant being
more than a poetical child only of Shakspeare, was common
in town; and Sir William himself seemed fond of having it
taken for truth.—*P[ope]*.

26. WILLIAM OLDYS (c. 1743-61)

[Oldys was the illegitimate son of William Oldys, chancellor of Lincoln. Born in 1696, he became an antiquarian at an early age. In 1724 he left London for Yorkshire and housed mainly at Wentworth Woodhouse with Thomas Lord Malton, afterwards 1st Marquis of Rockingham. In 1730 he returned to London, sold his literary collections to Edward Harley, Earl of Oxford, and studied in the Harleian Library. In 1738 Oxford made him his literary secretary, and he thus became known to Pope and other literary men. Oxford died in 1741, and his library was sold to Thomas Osborne the bookseller, who employed Oldys with Samuel Johnson in compiling the *Harleian Miscellany* (1744-6). During 1747-60 he contributed several lives, including one of Edward Alleyn (1747) and a revised one of Fastolf (1750), to the *Biographia Britannica* (1747-66). He was appointed Norroy King-at-Arms in 1755. He lived at the Heralds' College until his death on 15 Apr. 1761.]

(a) [From G. Steevens, *World of Sh.* (1778) i. 202.]

Mr Oldys had covered several quires of paper with laborious collections for a regular life of our author. From these I [George Steevens] have made the following extracts, which (however trivial) contain the only circumstances that wear the least appearance of novelty or information.

(1) One of Shakespeare's younger brothers, who lived to a good old age, even some years, as I compute, after the restoration of *K. Charles II.* would in his younger days come to London to visit his brother *Will*, as he called him, and be a spectator of him as an actor in some of his own plays. This custom, as his brother's fame enlarged, and his dramatic entertainments grew the greatest support of our principal, if not of all our theatres, he continued it seems so long after his brother's death, as even to the latter end of his own life. The curiosity at this time of the most noted actors to learn something from him of his brother, &c. they justly held him in the highest veneration.

And it may well be believed, as there was besides a kinsman and descendant of the family, who was then a celebrated actor among them, this opportunity made them greedily inquisitive into every little circumstance, more especially in his dramatick character, which his brother could relate of him. But he, it seems, was so stricken in years, and possibly his memory so weakened with infirmities (which might make him the easier pass for a man of weak intellects) that he could give them but little light into their enquiries; and all that could be recollected from him of his brother *Will*, in that station was, the faint, general, and almost lost ideas he had of having once seen him act a part in one of his own comedies, wherein being to personate a decrepit old man, he wore a long beard, and appeared so weak and drooping and unable to walk, that he was forced to be supported and carried by another person to a table, at which he was seated among some company, who were eating, and one of them sung a song.

(2) 'Verses by Ben Jonson and Shakespeare, occasioned by the motto to the Globe Theatre—*Totus mundus agit histrionem.*

Jonson.

If, but *stage actors*, all the world displays,
Where shall we find *spectators* of their plays?

Shakespeare.

Little, or much, of what we see, we do;
We're all both *actors* and *spectators* too.

(3) Old Mr Bowman the player reported from Sir William Bishop, that some part of Sir John Falstaff's character was drawn from a townsman of Stratford, who either faithlessly broke a contract, or spitefully refused to part

with some land for a valuable consideration, adjoining to Shakespeare's, in or near that town.

(4) There was a very aged gentleman living in the neighbourhood of Stratford, (where he died fifty years since,) who had not only heard, from several old people in that town, of Shakespeare's transgression, but could remember the first stanza of that bitter ballad, which, repeating to one of his acquaintance, he preserved it in writing; and here it is, neither better nor worse, but faithfully transcribed from the copy which his relation very curteously communicated to me.

> A parliemente member, a justice of peace,
> At home a poor scare-crowe, at London an asse,
> If lowsie is Lucy, as some volke miscalle it,
> Then Lucy is lowsie whatever befall it:
> > He thinks himselfe greate,
> > Yet an asse in his state,
> We allowe by his ears but with asses to mate.
> > If Lucy is lowsie, as some volke miscalle it,
> > Sing lowsie Lucy, whatever befall it.

Contemptible as this performance must now appear, at the time when it was written it might have sufficient power to irritate a vain, weak, and vindictive magistrate; especially as it was affixed to several of his park-gates, and consequently published among his neighbours.—It may be remarked likewise, that the jingle on which it turns, occurs in the first scene of *The Merry Wives of Windsor*.

(*b*) [From Malone, *Supplementary Observations* (1780), i. 44.]

Oldys, in one of his manuscripts, says that Shakspeare received but *five pounds* for his *Hamlet*; whether from the players who first acted it, or the printer or bookseller who first published it, is not distinguished.

27. ANON (1748)

[From 'a manuscript note preserved in the University Library, Edinburgh, written about the year 1748'.]

Sir William Davenant, who has been call'd a natural son of our author, us'd to tell the following whimsical story of him;—Shakespear, when he first came from the country to the play-house, was not admitted to act; but as it was then the custom for all the people of fashion to come on horseback to entertainments of all kinds, it was Shakespear's employment for a time, with several other poor boys belonging to the company, to hold the horses and take care of them during the representation;—by his dexterity and care he soon got a good deal of business in this way, and was personally known to most of the quality that frequented the house, insomuch that, being obliged, before he was taken into a higher and more honorable employment within doors, to train up boys to assist him, it became long afterwards a usual way among them to recommend themselves by saying that they were Shakespear's boys.

28. EDWARD CAPELL (1774)

[Capell (1713–81) was of Catharine Hall, Cambridge, and inspector of plays under the Lord Chamberlain.]

[*Note* on *As You Like It*, ii. 6, from *Notes* (1774), i. 60.]

A traditional story was current some years ago about Stratford,—that a very old man of that place,—of weak intellects, but yet related to Shakespeare,—being ask'd by some of his neighbours, what he remember'd about him; answer'd,—that he saw him once brought on the stage upon another man's back; which answer was apply'd by the hearers, to his having seen him perform in this scene the part of Adam: That he should have done so, is made not unlikely by another constant tradition,—that he was no extraordinary actor, and therefore took no parts upon him but such as this: for which he might also be peculiarly fitted by an accidental lameness, which,— as he himself tells us twice in his '*Sonnets*', v. 37, and 89, —befell him in some part of life; without saying how, or when, of what sort, or in what degree; but his expressions seem to indicate—latterly.

29. GEORGE STEEVENS (1780)

[From note in Malone's *Supplement* (1780), ii. 369. West (*c.* 1704–72) was a Secretary to the Treasury (1741–62), and President of the Royal Society (1768–72). He was from Prior's Marston, Warwickshire, and had a house at Alscot in Gloucestershire, three miles from Stratford.]

The late Mr James West, of the Treasury, assured me, that at his house in Warwickshire he had a wooden bench, once the favourite accommodation of Shakespeare, together with an earthen half-pint mug, out of which he was accustomed to take his draughts of ale at a certain publick house in the neighbourhood of Stratford, every Saturday afternoon.

30. EDMUND MALONE (1780)

[From *Supplement*, i. 67; 1790, i. 1. 107 (with the added words here bracketed).]

There is a stage tradition that his first office in the theatre was that of [*Call-boy*, or] prompter's attendant; whose employment it is to give the performers notice to be ready to enter, as often as the business of the play requires their appearance on the stage.

31. JAMES DAVENPORT (1790)

[From Malone (1790), i. 1. 118. Davenport was vicar of Stratford from 1787 to 1841. Malone (*Var.* i. 252) acknowledges his help. The planting was ascribed to Shakespeare at the time of the destruction in 1758. Modern speculation has decided that Shakespeare planted his mulberry in 1609 when James I issued *Instructions* to encourage the growth of them and the breeding of silkworms.]

The Rev. Mr Davenport informs me, that Mr Hugh Taylor, (the father of his clerk,) who is now eighty-five years old, and an alderman of Warwick, where he at present resides, says, he lived when a boy at the next house to New-Place; that his family had inhabited the house for almost three hundred years; that it was transmitted from father to son during the last and the present century, that this tree (of the fruit of which he had often eaten in his younger days, some of its branches hanging over his father's garden,) was planted by Shakspeare; and that till this was planted, there was no mulberry-tree in that neighbourhood. Mr Taylor adds, that he was frequently, when a boy, at New-Place, and that this tradition was preserved in the Clopton family, as well as in his own.

32. THOMAS SHARP (1799)

[From 'a declaration made upon oath shortly before his death in 1799'. Sharp had been making and selling as relics articles of mulberry wood since the destruction of the New Place tree in 1758.]

I have often heard the said Sir Hugh Clopton solemnly declare that the mulberry-tree which growed in his garden was planted by Shakespear, and he took pride in shewing it to and entertaining persons of distinction whose curiosity excited them to visit the spot known to be the last residence of the immortal bard.

33. SIR RICHARD PHILLIPS (1818)

[From *The Monthly Magazine; or British Register*, xlv. 1. Phillips (1767–1840), a publisher and sheriff of London, who edited the periodical, found descendants of Joan Hart in poverty at Tewkesbury, and was led to pay a visit to Stratford. Mary Hornby was caretaker in Henley St. from 1793 to 1820 (*B.P. Cat.* 1).]

Mrs Hornby shows a very small deep cupboard, in a dark corner of the room in which Shakspeare was born; and relates that a letter was found in it some years since, which had been addressed by Shakspeare from the playhouse in London to his wife. She asserts that this letter was in her possession, and that she used to show it to visitors; that one morning, a few years since, she exhibited it to a company, who went from her house to the church; but presently sent a message to beg that she would send the letter for further inspection at the tomb,—a request with which she complied. She saw nothing further, however, of her letter; but the parties, on leaving Stratford, sent her a shilling, and their thanks! Persons in Stratford doubt the truth of this relation; but the woman persists.

34. RICHARD RYAN (1825)

[From *Dramatic Table Talk*, ii. 156, anonymous but ascribed (*D.N.B.*) to the editorship of Richard Ryan (1796–1849), a bookseller.]

It is well known that Queen Elizabeth was a great admirer of the immortal Shakspeare, and used frequently (as was the custom of persons of great rank in those days) to appear upon the stage before the audience, or to sit delighted behind the scenes, when the plays of our bard were performed. One evening, when Shakespeare himself was personating the part of a King, the audience knew of her Majesty being in the house. She crossed the stage when he was performing, and, on receiving the accustomed greeting from the audience, moved politely to the poet, but he did not notice it! When behind the scenes, she caught his eye, and moved again, but still he would not throw off his character, to notice her: this made her Majesty think of some means by which she might know, whether he would depart, or not, from the dignity of his character while on the stage.—Accordingly, as he was about to make his exit, she stepped before him, dropped her glove, and re-crossed the stage, which Shakespeare noticing, took up, with these words, immediately after finishing his speech, and so aptly were they delivered, that they seemed to belong to it:

'And though now bent on this high embassy,
Yet *stoop* we to take up our *Cousin's* glove!'

He then walked off the stage, and presented the glove to the Queen, who was greatly pleased with his behaviour, and complimented him upon the propriety of it.

NOTE

Since the publication of *William Shakespeare*, Dr. Leslie Hotson, in his *Shakespeare versus Shallow* (1931), has shown that in Michaelmas Term 1596, one William Wayte applied to the Court of Queen's Bench for security against a breach of the peace by Shakespeare, Francis Langley, who was the owner of the Swan Theatre, and others. Shortly before, Langley had brought a similar action against Wayte and his step-father, William Gardiner, a prominent Justice of Peace in Surrey, and Gardiner had sued Langley for slander. There is nothing to show how Shakespeare came into the dispute.

INDEX

Actor-lists, 144–6.
Addenbroke, John, 59.
Admiral's men, 30–8, 43–4, 86, 90, 105 n.
Alchemist, 186.
Alleyn company, 37, 39–41, 43.
Alleyn, Edward, 34–7, 244.
Alleyn, John, 31–2.
Apologetical Dialogue, 50.
Arden family, 11.
Arden, Robert, 10–11, 139–40.
Arden of Faversham, 37.
Arraignment of London, 87.
Arraignment of Paris, 114.
Asbies, 11, 13.
Aspley, William, 70.
Aston Cantlow, 2, 10.
Aubrey, John, 10, 15–16, 21, 58, 60, 65–6, 229–31, 233.
Audley, John, 130.

Bancroft, Richard, Bishop of London, 30.
Barnes, Joshua, 19.
Basse, William, 217.
Beaumont, Francis, 49, 87, 93, 108, 202, 210, 214–17, 218.
Beeston, William, 21, 60, 66, 229, 231.
Belott-Mountjoy suit, 148, 149–54.
Benfield, Robert, 142, 145.
Benson, John, 122, 223–4.
Berkeley, Sir Thomas, 47, 130.
Bernard, Sir John, 66, 138.
Betterton, Thomas, 15, 237, 241, 243.
Biographia Britannica, 19.
Bishopsgate, 54, 146–8.
Bishop's Hampton, 2, 10.
Bishopstown, 2, 158, 165.
Blackfriars theatre, 29, 56–8, 142–3, 177, 220, 236–7.
Blount, Edward, 71, 73–4.
Bonian, Richard, 71.
Boy players, 29–30, 44, 56, 106, 115, 143.

Brayne, Mrs., 31–2.
Bridgetown, 2.
Brooke, Christopher, 212.
Bryan, George, 34, 36, 145.
Buckingham, 41.
Burbadge, Cuthbert, 56, 58, 142–3.
Burbadge, James, 31–2, 51, 56.
Burbadge, Richard, 31, 36, 56, 58, 62, 64, 142–5, 161, 165, 172, 179, 206–7, 236.
Burbadge, William, 142–3.
Burby, Cuthbert, 69–70.
Burgh, Nicholas, 226.
Busby, John, 69, 71.
Butter, Nathaniel, 71–2.

Camden, William, 208, 211.
Capell, Edward, 18, 247–8.
Carew, Richard, 211–12.
Carey, later Berkeley, Elizabeth, 47, 130.
Carey, Sir George, *see* Hunsdon.
Cecil, Sir Robert, 104, 173, 179.
Censorship of plays, 44–6, 56, 99.
Chamberlain's men, 36, 42–5, 50–1, 55, 86–7, 90, 99, 105 n., 125, 130.
Chapman, George, 92–3, 103, 131, 192–4, 208, 210.
Charlecote, 2, 17–19, 238.
Chettle, Henry, 39, 59, 90, 193.
Clayton, John, 42–3.
Clopton, hamlet of, 2.
Clopton, Sir Hugh, 5, 9, 53, 249.
Cobham, Lord, 105 n.
Collins, Francis, 164, 166–7, 169.
Combe family, 63–5, 160, 161, 164, 169, 226, 230.
Condell, Henry, 47, 58, 64, 73, 75–6, 79, 81, 84, 90, 143–5, 165, 218–21.
Contention of York and Lancaster, 69, 72, 75, 91, 118.
Copyright, 67–9, 72–3.
Cross Keys theatre, 31, 36.

INDEX

Curtain theatre, 28, 32, 40, 54, 56.
Cuts, 95–6, 98, 105 *n.*

Daborne, Robert, 87.
Daniel, Samuel, 130–1, 192–4, 196, 208, 211, 213–14, 218.
Danter, John, 51, 69–70.
Davenant family, 60, 66.
Davenant, Sir William, 40, 42, 55, 60, 205, 230–1, 233, 237, 239–42, 243, 247.
Davenport, James, 249.
Davies, John, of Hereford, 59, 207–8.
Davies, Richard, 17, 19, 61, 232.
Davison, Francis, 104 *n.*
Deer-stealing; see Shakespeare.
Dekker, Thomas, 50–1, 87–8, 90, 192, 210, 214.
Dennis, John, 236–7.
Derby's men, 25, 29, 34–6, 43.
Dido, 37, 86.
Dowdall, 15, 20, 40, 136, 171, 233.
Downes, John, 237.
Drayton, Michael, 64, 93, 130–1, 136, 192–3, 207–8, 213–14, 228.
Droeshout engraving, 65, 74, 201–2.
Drummond, William, 48, 122, 201, 213.
Dryden, John, 206, 228, 243.
Dursley, 23.

Edward I, 59.
Edward II, 37.
Edward III, 44, 97.
Elizabeth, Queen, 25–6, 37, 45–6, 51, 54, 56, 124, 126–7, 130, 176–7, 177, 179, 189, 204, 225, 235–7, 239, 250–1.
Essex, Robert Devereux, 2nd Earl of, 45–7, 102, 105, 127–8, 155, 239.
Every Man in his Humour, 59, 143, 178, 200.
Every Man out of his Humour, 49, 101, 106 and *n.*, 178, 198–9.

Farmer, Richard, 21.
Field, Richard, 22.
Fisher, Thomas, 70.
Fitton, Mary, 128–9.
Fletcher, John, 87, 210, 214, 236.
Folio, First, 39, 47–8, 65, 71–7, 79–85, 99, 130, 218–21.
Folios, later, 74, 84.
Forman, Simon, 107–8, 180–5.
Freeman, Thomas, 212–13.
Fulbrook, 19.
Fuller, Thomas, 224–6.

Gardiner, William, 252.
Gild of Holy Cross, 4–6.
Gildon, Charles, 99 *n.*, 235–6.
Globe theatre, 54, 56, 58, 101, 142–3, 174–5, 180, 183, 186, 245.
Gorboduc, 86.
Gosson, Henry, 71.
Gray's Inn, 103, 172.
Greene, Robert, 20, 38–40, 86, 91–2, 95, 102, 114, 187–8, 193, 218.
Greene, Thomas, 62–3, 159.
Greenes Groats-worth of Wit, 39, 187–8.

Hales, John, 49, 170–1, 205.
Hall, Elizabeth, 62, 65–6, 135–6, 138, 163–4, 166, 168.
Hall, John, 62–3, 65, 134–7, 166–8, 170–1, 227.
Hall, William, 128–9, 234–5.
Hall, William, of Acton, 134–5.
Hamlet, Katharine, 24, 134.
Hart family, 62, 66, 134–7, 164, 250.
Harvey, Gabriel, 83, 106, 193–4.
Harvey, Sir William, 128, 189–90.
Hathaway, Anne, *see* Shakespeare, Anne.
Hathaway family, 16, 142.
Hathaway, Richard, 16, 238.
Hearne, Thomas, 241–2.
Heminges, John, 34, 36, 47, 58, 64, 73, 75–7, 79, 81, 84, 90, 143–5, 165, 185, 218–21, 236.
Henslowe, Philip, 33–6, 41, 43, 86, 101, 103.

INDEX

Herbert, family of, 47.
Hertford's men, 33.
Hewland, 16.
Heyes, Thomas, 70.
Heywood, Thomas, 210–11, 214.
Higford, Henry, 12.
Hoby, Sir Edward, 104, 173.
Holinshed, Raphael, 92.
Home, Sir George, 144.
Hornby, Mary, 250.
Horneby, Thomas, 59.
Howard, Charles, 36.
Howes, Edmund, 213–14.
Hunsdon, George Carey, 2nd Lord, 47, 130, 145.
Hunsdon, Henry Carey, 1st Lord, 45, 47.
Hunsdon's men, 25, 29, 36.

Isle of Dogs, 44.

Jaggard, Isaac, 73–4, 84, 211.
Jaggard, William, 73.
James I, 51, 54–7, 99, 107 and *n.*, 126, 131, 161, 177–8, 204, 207, 242, 249.
James IV, 114.
James, Richard, 222–3.
Janssen, Gheerart, 65.
Jocasta, 86.
Johnson, Arthur, 69, 72.
Jones, Robert, 106.
Jones, Thomas, 19.
Jonson, Ben, 21, 45, 48–50, 55, 64, 66, 83, 86–8, 90, 93, 97–8, 101, 106 and *n.*, 143–4, 178, 186, 192, 197–8, 206, 208 210, 213–17, 224–6, 228–30, 236, 240, 243, 245.
Jordan, John, 19.

Keeling, William, 179–80.
Keep the Widow Waking, 87.
Kempe, William, 34, 36, 50–1, 58, 144–5, 172, 197.
Kind-Harts Dreame, 39, 188–9.
King's men, 43, 55–7, 62, 73, 99, 144–5, 170, 178–9, 185, 237.
Kyd, Thomas, 37, 83, 92, 95, 114, 192, 203.

Lambert, Edmund, 13.
Lambert, John, 13, 20.
Lane, John, 137–8.
Langley, Francis, 252.
Law, Matthew, 70, 72.
Leicester's men, 25–6, 29, 40.
Leir, 92, 107.
L'Estrange, Sir Nicholas, 224.
Ling, Nicholas, 70–2.
Lloyd, David, 228.
Locrine, 74, 84, 86.
Lodge, Thomas, 38, 86, 95, 114, 193.
London Prodigal, 74, 84.
Looking Glass, 86, 114.
Lopez, Roderigo, 101, 104 and *n.*
Love Labours Won, 83, 100, 118–19, 192.
Lucy, family of, 2, 17
Lucy, Sir Thomas, 17–19, 24, 232, 238, 246.
Luddington, 2, 16.
Lyly, John, 29, 38, 193, 203, 213.

Maid's Metamorphosis, 115.
Malone, Edmund, 40, 60, 123, 246, 248–9.
Manningham, John, 66, 177, 206.
Markham, Gervase, 131, 214–15.
Marlowe, Christopher, 37–9, 48, 83, 86, 92–3, 95, 114, 130, 192, 203, 211, 214.
Marston, John, 49–50, 193, 208, 214.
Martin Marprelate, 30.
Master of the Revels, 25–8, 30, 68.
Mennis, Sir John, 227.
Meres, Francis, 51, 83, 85, 100, 104–8, 118–20, 122, 191–3, 214.
Meyricke, Sir Gelly, 174–6.
Milcote, 2, 5.
Millington, Thomas, 69.
Mirror of Martyrs, 106, 195.
Misfortunes of Arthur, 86.
Mountjoy-Belott suit, 60, 62, 148, 149–54.
Mulberries, 63, 249.
Munday, Anthony, 86, 193.

Nash, Thomas, 66, 135–6, 137–8, 170.
Nashe, Thomas, 38–9, 83, 86, 95, 103, 131, 187, 193, 218.
New Place, 20, 53–4, 61–2, 136, 161, 249.
Newington Butts theatre, 33, 36, 43.

Old Stratford, 2, 7, 54, 135–6, 142, 158, 165.
Oldys, William, 18, 54, 59, 244–6.
'Originals' of plays, 74–5, 78–81.
Orlando Furioso, 38.
Oxford's men, 25, 29.

Palladis Tamia, 51, 83, 85, 100, 104–8, 118–20, 122, 191–3.
Parnassus, 50–1, 195–7.
Paul's boys, 29–30.
Pavier, Thomas, 69, 72–3.
Peele, George, 29, 38–9, 59, 92, 95, 114, 192.
Pembroke, Mary Herbert, formerly Sidney, Countess of, 55, 131, 177.
Pembroke, William Lord Herbert, 3rd Earl of, 47, 52, 85, 127–31, 218–20.
Pembroke's men, 34–5, 41, 47.
Phillips, Augustine, 34, 36, 58, 143–5, 175–6.
Phillips, Sir Richard, 250.
Pierce Penilesse, 103, 187.
Plague, 33–6, 38, 41, 44, 56–7, 116.
Platter, Thomas, 106, 173.
Plume, Thomas, 227.
Plutarch, 92.
Poetaster, 48–50, 88, 106 and *n*.
Poetomachia, 49.
Pope, Thomas, 34, 36, 58, 144–5.
Porter, Henry, 38.
Puritan, 74, 84.

Quartos, 'bad', 69–73, 75–9, 81, 83, 95, 99 and *n*., 105 *n*., 239.
Quartos, 'good', 69–71, 77–81, 83.
Queen's men, 25, 28–30, 33, 36–8, 46.
Queen's Revels, 58.
Quiney, Adrian, 12, 157.

Quiney, Richard, 12, 54, 136, 155–8.
Quiney, Thomas, 64, 135–6, 168.

Rainsford, Anne, Lady, 64.
Rainsford, Sir Henry, 64.
Ravenscroft, Edward, 84, 90, 231–2.
Replingham, William, 158–60.
Revels Accounts, 83, 178–9, 185.
Richardson, Nicholas, 218.
Roberts, James, 70–2.
Robin Goodfellow, 118.
Rogers, Phillip, 59.
Rowe, Nicholas, 10, 15–20, 40, 42, 48, 58, 62, 65–6, 205–6, 237–41.
Rowington, 54, 163, 168–9.
Russell, Thomas, 164, 166.
Rutland, Francis Manners, 6th Earl of, 62, 161.
Ryan, Richard, 250–1.

Sadler, Hamnet, 17, 134, 164, 166.
Sadler, Judith, 17.
Salisbury, Sir John, 51.
Satiromastix, 50–1.
Scoloker, Anthony, 208.
Sejanus, 48, 59, 87, 97, 144.
Selimus, 114.
Shadow of Night, 103 and *n*., 131.
Shakespeare, the name, spelling of, 12.
Shakespeare, formerly Hathaway, Anne (wife), 16–17, 20, 65–6, 124, 136, 140–2, 166, 169, 171, 233, 238.
Shakespeare, Anne (sister), 133.
Shakespeare, Edmund (brother), 62, 133.
Shakespeare, Gilbert (brother), 62, 133, 135.
Shakespeare, Hamnet (son), 17, 20, 52, 134.
Shakespeare, Henry (uncle), 13.
Shakespeare, Joan, i (sister), 11, 133.
Shakespeare, Joan, ii, later Hart (sister), 62, 65, 133–4, 136–7, 163–4, 168, 250.

INDEX

Shakespeare, John (father), 9–15, 24, 53–4, 133–4, 139–40, 227, 237.
Shakespeare, John, corvizer, 11.
Shakespeare, John, of Clifford Chambers, 10.
Shakespeare, later Quiney, Judith (daughter), 17, 53, 62, 64–6, 134–6, 138, 162–4, 166–8, 170, 227, 233.
Shakespeare, Margaret (sister), 133.
Shakespeare, formerly Arden, Mary (mother), 11, 13, 53, 62, 135, 139–40.
Shakespeare, Richard (grandfather), 9–10.
Shakespeare, Richard (brother), 62, 133, 135.
Shakespeare, later Hall, Susanna (daughter), 17, 52, 62, 64–6, 133–4, 137–8, 163, 165–8, 170–1, 227, 233.
Shakespeare, William, ancestry, 1–15, 139–40; birth and christening, 1, 11, 133, 232; interest in Wilmcote property, 13, 20, 53; Henley St. houses, 15, 53, 65, 165, 238, 250; schooling, 15, 21, 237–8; alleged apprenticeship to a butcher, 15–16, 16 n., 229, 233; marriage, 16–17, 20, 66, 140–2, 169, 250; alleged deer-stealing, 17–20, 232, 238, 240, 246; alleged drinking exploits, 20, 64, 228, 248; early sojourn in London, 20; as actor, 20, 58–9, 229, 232, 236, 239, 244–5, 247–8, 250–1; hiatus in early history, 21, 24; alleged schoolmastering, 21, 231; knowledge of Latin and Greek, 21, 49, 203, 224, 231, 237–8, 242–3; library, 21–2, 170; forged signatures, 21–2; conjectured occupations, 15–16, 22; conjectured residence in Worcestershire, 23; Warwickshire names in plays, 23–4; theatrical beginnings, 20, 38–40, 233, 238, 247–8; attacked by Greene as 'Shake-scene', 38–9, 91, 184–8; praised by Chettle, 39, 188–9; alleged work for Leicester's men at Stratford, 40; alleged call-boy, 40, 233, 238, 248; alleged horsekeeper, 40, 247; conjectured travels, 41; unsuccessful love affair, 42, 190–1; relations with Earl of Southampton, 41–2, 47, 52; acquisition of property, 42, 53–4, 63, 65, 163, 168; acquires share in Lord Chamberlain's company, 42, 143; relations with Elizabeth, 45; with James I, 54–5; with contemporary authors, 48–50, 224, 226, 231; armorial bearings, 53, 65, 138–40; as maltster, 154–5; and the Welcombe enclosure, 63–4, 158–61; acquisition of New Place, 53–4, 61–2; of tithes, 60, 63; residence in Bishopsgate, 54, 146–8; in Clink on Bankside, 54, 60, 148; in Cripplegate, 60, 153; in Shoreditch, 60, 229; in King's company, 55; financial position, 59, 227, 230, 240, 241; visits to Stratford, 59–60; lawsuits, 59, 62, 148–54; entertains a preacher, 63, 161; religion, 61, 232; migration to Stratford, 62; collaboration with Fletcher, 62; visits to London, 62; last days, 63, 241; mulberries, 63, 249; death, 64–5, 135, 226, 228, 232; will, 58, 63–6, 134–5, 162–70; doggerel curse, 65, 136, 171, 232–4; epitaph, 171; monument, 53, 65, 136, 171, 232, 234; portraits and busts, 65, 74, 201–2, 223; personal appearance and character, 64–5, 233, 240, 248; publication of the plays, 68–82; doubtful plays, 72, 83–5, 94, 97; 'originals' as basis of texts, 74–5, 78–81; chronology of plays, 61, 100–21; collaboration and revision, 48, 62, 84–94, 97–100, 124, 232;

258 INDEX

Shakespeare—*continued.*
　characteristic styles, 94–5, 109–16; songs, 99; 'metrical tests,' 113–15; rhyme proportion, 114–15; William Wayte and, 252.
　Works, actual and attributed:
　All's Well that Ends Well, 71, 74, 81, 92, 96 and *n.*, 97, 108, 111, 117, 119, 120 *n.*
　Antony & Cleopatra, 61, 71, 74, 107, 109, 110 *n.*, 118, 196.
　As You Like It, 48 *n.*, 50, 55, 59, 71, 74, 81, 98, 106, 109, 117, 119, 177, 247–8.
　Comedy of Errors, 41, 71, 74, 83, 92, 100, 103, 116, 119, 172, 177–8, 192.
　Coriolanus, 74, 108, 111, 118.
　Cymbeline, 74, 81, 98, 108–9, 118, 182.
　Edward III, 44, 97.
　Hamlet, 24, 43, 45, 47, 52, 58–9, 61, 70–2, 75, 77–80, 82–3, 96 and *n.*, 98–9, 106, 109, 117, 120, 180, 194, 208, 235–7, 239, 241, 246.
　Henry IV, 20, 44, 70–2, 78–80, 83–4, 96 *n.*, 99–100, 105, 109, 117–9, 174–5, 192, 239.
　Henry V, 44–6, 49–50, 69, 71–3, 75, 83, 92, 99, 101, 105, 109, 117, 178, 222.
　1 Henry VI, 39–40, 81, 83, 85, 98, 100, 103, 109, 114, 116, 132, 187, 200, 222.
　2, 3 Henry VI, 39–41, 69, 71–5, 81, 83, 91, 98, 100, 102, 116, 118, 200.
　Henry VIII., 74, 85, 97, 101, 108–9, 118–19, 186, 237.
　John, 52, 71, 74, 84, 100, 104, 109, 111, 117, 192.
　Julius Caesar, 48–9, 71, 74, 83, 92–3, 98, 101, 106, 109–10, 117, 173, 195, 205.
　Lear, 61, 71–2, 77, 80, 82–3, 96 *n.*, 98–9, 102, 107, 109, 117, 120–1.
　Locrine, 74, 84, 86.
　London Prodigal, 74, 84.
　Lover's Complaint, 51.

　Love's Labour's Lost, 48, 70–1, 77–8, 80, 83, 98, 100, 103, 109, 114, 116, 119, 178–9, 192.
　Macbeth, 49, 55, 74, 81–2, 96, 98, 101, 107, 109, 117, 120, 180–2, 206.
　Measure for Measure, 74, 81, 83, 92, 97, 107, 111, 117, 178.
　Merchant of Venice, 23, 44, 70–2, 78, 80, 83, 98–9, 100, 101, 104, 111, 117, 179, 192.
　Merry Wives of Windsor, 1, 17–20, 44, 50, 69, 71–3, 75, 83, 99, 106, 109, 117, 120, 178, 235–7, 239–40, 246.
　Midsummer Night's Dream, 47, 70–2, 78–80, 89 *n.*, 98, 100, 102, 104, 109, 114, 117, 119, 130, 155, 192, 230.
　Much Ado about Nothing, 70–1, 78, 80, 97, 99, 105, 109, 111, 117, 119–20, 185–6.
　Othello, 72, 77–80, 83, 96 *n.*, 99 and *n.*, 107, 109, 117, 178, 185, 235.
　Passionate Pilgrim, 51, 122, 210–11.
　Pericles, 49, 61, 71–4, 83–4, 94, 97, 108, 111, 118, 204.
　Phoenix and Turtle, 51.
　Puritan, 74, 84.
　Rape of Lucrece, 41–2, 122, 127–8, 132, 189–92, 194–5, 197, 212.
　Richard II, 44–5, 70–2, 78, 80, 82–3, 92, 96 *n.*, 99–100, 104, 109, 117, 175–7, 180, 192.
　Richard III, 41, 59, 70–2, 77, 80, 83, 92, 96 *n.*, 100, 103, 116, 132, 173, 192, 197, 206.
　Romeo and Juliet, 69–72, 75, 77–8, 80, 82–3, 92, 98, 100, 103, 109, 116, 192–3, 196, 218, 228.
　Sir John Oldcastle, 72, 74, 84, 105 *n.*, 119, 174.
　Sir Thomas More, 78, 88.
　Sonnets, 47–8, 51–2, 59, 66, 122–32, 192, 213, 248.

INDEX 259

Shakespeare (Works) *continued.*
  Taming of the Shrew, 23, 43, 71, 74, 81, 83, 85, 96–8, 108, 116, 118–20, 120 n.
  Tempest, 49, 74, 81, 96 and n., 98, 108–9, 118–19, 185, 201.
  Thomas Lord Cromwell, 74, 84.
  Timon of Athens, 61, 74, 81, 98, 108, 111, 118, 120–1.
  Titus Andronicus, 41, 43, 69, 71, 78, 80, 83–5, 90, 96 n., 97, 100, 103, 109, 116, 132, 192, 200, 231–2.
  Troilus and Cressida, 50–1, 61, 71, 77–80, 92, 98–9, 106, 109, 117, 209.
  Twelfth Night, 71, 74, 106, 109, 117–19, 177.
  Two Gentlemen of Verona, 71, 74, 92, 100, 103, 109, 111, 116, 120 n., 192.
  Two Noble Kinsmen, 83, 97, 108, 118.
  Venus and Adonis, 41–2, 122, 127–8, 192, 194–7, 209, 212, 239.
  Winter's Tale, 49, 74, 81, 83, 108–9, 118, 184–5.
  Yorkshire Tragedy, 72, 74, 84.
Shottery, 2, 16, 141–2, 156.
Sidney, Sir Philip, 208, 212, 213, 218.
Simmes, Valentine, 70.
Sir John Oldcastle, 72, 74, 84, 105 n., 119, 174.
Sir Thomas More, 78, 88.
Sly, William, 58, 144–5.
Smethwick, John, 70, 72.
Snitterfield, 2, 9–11, 13.
Southampton, Elizabeth Wriothesley, countess of, 47, 128, 194.
Southampton, Henry Wriothesley, 3rd earl of, 41–2, 47, 52, 102, 127–31, 179, 194, 239–40.
Spanish Tragedy, 37–8, 85, 114.
Spence, Joseph, 243.
Spenser, Edmund, 21, 38, 95, 130–1, 192–4, 196–7, 208, 211, 213, 217–18.
Stationers' Company, 67–9, 71, 73.
Stationers' Register, 67–8, 101, 106.
Strange's men, 30–7.
Stratford-on-Avon, 1–2, 4–20, 118; manor, 2, 5–7, 15, 63, 158; charters, 6–7; gild, 4–7, 53; corporation, 6, 9, 13, 15, 63–4, 135; college, 6, 60; grammar school, 4, 6, 8–9, 21; decay, 7; almshouse, 6–7; church, 65, 136–7, 171, 233–4, 250; Leicester's men at, 40; New Place, 20, 53–4, 61–2, 136, 161, 249.
Sturley, Abraham, 155–8.
Sussex's men, 25, 29, 33, 35–6, 41.
Sydney, Sir Robert, 129–30.
Swallow, Clement, 24.

Tamburlaine, 37, 85.
Tancred and Gismund, 86.
Tarlton, Richard, 29, 38.
Taylor, John, 217–18.
Temple Grafton, 16, 140.
Theatre, the, 28, 31–2, 40, 54–6, 142.
Thomas Lord Cromwell, 74, 84.
Thorpe, Thomas, 122, 128–9.
Tilney, Edmund, 25, 31.
Timber, 48, 205.
Tourneur, Cyril, 87.
Troublesome Reign of John, 84, 92.
True Tragedy of Richard Duke of York, 69.
Trundell, John, 70.
Tunstall, James, 32.
Two Noble Kinsmen, 83, 97, 108, 118.
Tyler, Thomas, 129.

Underhill, family of, 53.

Vere, Lady Bridget, 129.

Walkley, Thomas, 72.
Walley, Henry, 71.
Walsingham, Sir Francis, 25.
Ward, John, 64, 116, 227–8.
Watson, Thomas, 95, 194.
Wayte, William, 252.
Webster, John, 210, 214.

Weever, John, 83, 106, 194–5.
Welcombe, 2, 63, 158–61, 165.
Whatcott, Robert, 137–8, 166.
White, Edward, 69.
Whitefriars theatre, 57.
Whittington, Thomas, 141–2.
Whyte, Rowland, 129–30, 173.
Wilkins, George, 108.
Willobie his Avisa, 42, 66, 131–2, 190–1.

Wilmcote, 10, 13, 20, 53, 139.
Wise, Andrew, 70.
Wood, Anthony, 228–9, 231, 233.
Worcester, bishop of, 16, 140–1.
Worcester's men, 86.
Worrall, Thomas, 73.
Wright, James, 236.
Wyat, Sir Thomas, 213.

Yorkshire Tragedy, 72, 74, 84.

www.ingramcontent.com/pod-product-compliance
Lightning Source LLC
Chambersburg PA
CBHW020834160426
43192CB00007B/640